GOD
and the
VICTIM

the responsibilities of civic duty and carrying out the simple tasks of caring for their neighbors.

This is less and less the case in our country today. We have experienced an extraordinary cultural transformation in the last fifty years. A recent Gallup poll asked, "Do you trust your neighbor?" and two-thirds of the respondents answered no. Compare that with a 1964 Gallup survey in which 54 percent said that, yes, they *did* trust their neighbors. A radical change! Thus, we now have a Christian organization called Neighbors Who Care — as if a caring neighbor were some sort of a phenomenon.

This is due in large part to our deteriorating sense of community. In 1997 the Harvard School of Public Health and the University of Chicago released research from a study of 343 Chicago neighborhoods of great racial, ethnic, economic, and social diversity. They discovered — or confirmed — that there is no correlation between the rate of violent crime and the economic or ethnic status of the community. They found no single predicting factor of violent crime in a community other than what they call "collective efficacy." They describe "collective efficacy" in terms of what was classically called a "neighborhood": a place where there is a sense of trust, common values, and cohesion. The more cohesion — the more people who are neighbors to neighbors — the less crime. Because there is trust. There is a sense of people caring for one another.[1]

Robert Samson, professor of sociology at the University of Chicago and co-author of the study, said that "cohesion is the product of a shared vision." It involves "effusion of a shared willingness of residents to intervene, a sense of engagement and ownership of public space." What a beautiful description in secular terms of the Christian view of community!

As Christians, we have a responsibility, a cultural mandate, to care about and for our neighbors and communities. When I first founded Prison Fellowship, evangelicals would ask me if ministry to prisoners was the "social gospel" — that being a negative phrase. This goes back

1. Felton Earls, R. J. Sampson, and S. W. Raudenbush, *Project on Human Development in Chicago Neighborhoods* (University of Chicago: Harvard School of Public Health, 1995).

to the split in the Church in the early part of the twentieth century. The conservatives were saying, "We are just going to preach to the lost"; the liberals were saying, "We are going to care for the poor." This was an unfortunate historical break, based on false theology.

Which is exactly why grounding Neighbors Who Care and ministry to victims in solid theology and a biblical understanding is *so* important. The confusion comes when we make no distinction between what the Reformers understood and knew as "saving grace" and "common grace."

Through saving grace, our sovereign God reaches down with a convicting power of His Word and transforms the hardest heart and brings the lost to Himself with His redeeming love. Through common grace, God reaches down and restrains the consequences of sin and evil. Through this common grace, God provides some semblance of order within His creation.

So we are to be instruments of saving grace as we proclaim the Gospel. We are witnesses to the fact that the Word of God cuts like a two-edged sword and goes right to the heart. But we also are to be instruments of common grace — that is, we are to influence our society so that we are the embodiment of that common grace which holds back the consequences of the Fall.

In starting Neighbors Who Care after founding Prison Fellowship, we realized that if we were to attack the problem of crime, it was not enough to preach the Gospel in prisons. We couldn't stop there. We saw how important it is that we care about the full cycle of restoration: We care about the victim's restoration, the offender's restoration to the community, and the peace of the community.

We care about restoring what has been broken by crime. This is what we at Prison Fellowship now call the "full-circle vision": to reach out with the Good News to the men and women who are lost; to minister in practical ways to all those impacted by crime; to reach out for justice in the criminal-justice structures; to reach out to bring God's healing grace into our communities.

When Prison Fellowship first asked questions about launching a ministry to victims, some of us thought narrowly in terms of what I might call "crime cleanup" — spiritually, emotionally, and physically restoring the order destroyed by the chaos of crime.

But now I see ministry to victims as being redemptively double-edged. As we reach out to victims and rebuild community trust, we can reduce crime — so we have fewer criminal offenders in prison.

What could be a more dramatic witness than modeling to the world what it means to restore *shalom* — what the Jews understood as the peace and harmony of the community as God had created it?

It is time for the Church to rise up and reach out. To do that, we should take advantage of every opportunity to equip ourselves for effective ministry. And that is what this book does by laying out foundational theological, cultural, historical, and practical aspects of key issues in victim ministry and community healing.

I commend these pages to you as you seek to broaden and deepen your understanding of the need for the restorative work of victim ministry.

CHARLES W. COLSON
Chairman
Prison Fellowship Ministries

Introduction

In October 1997, Neighbors Who Care, the crime-victim ministry of Prison Fellowship Ministries, hosted a theological forum on crime victims and the church. We believed that if crime — at its root and in its effects — is primarily a spiritual issue, then the Bible must have something significant to say about it. We believed that since the examples of victimization recorded in Scripture are similar to modern-day victimization, then a study of Scripture should shed light on how better to understand and reach out to victims today. And we believed that to reach out to those who suffer with the same compassion and commitment as Christ, we must have a solid biblical foundation to guide us.

The forum focused on four key topics: evil, victimization, justice, and forgiveness. We probed and examined these issues not only to come up with some succinct theological analysis but also to translate theology into *practical application,* to personalize the Word of God and bring it into the lives of needy people — as Jesus did.

This book is a product of the papers presented at the forum and the discussions that followed the presentations. Chapters 1 and 11 through 13 were added after the forum to provide further insight and information for study. Each chapter begins with a summary paragraph that functions as an introduction to its topic. In addition, each chapter features sidebars highlighting comments from the paper's author or other forum participants. Many of the chapters contain the stories of victims whose names have been changed to respect their privacy.

The theological positions and scriptural interpretations of the participants do not necessarily represent the theological perspective of Prison Fellowship Ministries or Neighbors Who Care. Neighbors Who Care intentionally brought together a diverse group of scholars, practitioners, pastors, and victims to study and discuss the topics and to see what would result. The essays are presented to further theological exploration and discussion and to promote a deeper understanding of the topics of evil, victimization, justice, and forgiveness.

Throughout the book, readers will note that the word *church* is sometimes capitalized and sometimes not. Church is used to refer to the body of Christ, all those whom God has called to Himself and has regenerated, the community of saints from the beginning of time to the end. The Church includes denominations, congregations, parachurch organizations, small groups, and individuals. The church is used to refer to a local church congregation within a given community, which is the visible expression of the body of Christ in the church particular.

As you read the following essays, I pray that they will give you a greater awareness of the spiritual significance of crime and suffering — and also remind you how intimately Jesus ministers to us at our deepest level of pain. May they give you a deeper understanding of what victims experience, what they need, and how you and your church can wisely and sensitively address those needs.

May these essays also help equip us all to think more biblically about crime and those who suffer, so that when we come upon a victim, *we* won't respond like the evasive priest and the Levite of Jesus' parable. Rather, we can respond as the good Samaritan did — and, ultimately, like Jesus — by coming alongside and even helping to carry the hurting one.

I want to thank each of the authors who contributed their expertise and time to the essays and the discussion. I also want to thank the thirty participants who attended the forum and enriched the process with their thoughtful comments and discussion of the topics, often sharing their personal experiences of victimization and crisis in their own lives. Forum participants included victim-assistance professionals, law-enforcement officers, pastors, seminary professors, theologians, think-tank representatives, and Christian media representatives.

My thanks also go to Eerdmans Publishing Company for its support of the forum and this book. I want to extend particular thanks to Jon Pott, editor-in-chief. His counsel on topics and speakers significantly helped shape the content of both the forum and the book.

Thanks also go to Ann Weinheimer for her skilled work in editing the essays in preparation for publication, to Gregory Strong, Ph.D., for preparing a thoughtful, easy-to-use study guide to accompany the book, and to T. M. Moore for his work in providing a theological review of the book.

Finally, my deepest appreciation to the Neighbors Who Care staff, who worked tirelessly to see the forum come to fruition. Particular thanks to Michelle Shattuck for her efforts in coordinating all aspects of the forum and overseeing and contributing to the development of the book.

LISA BARNES LAMPMAN
President
Neighbors Who Care

CHAPTER ONE

Finding God in the Wake of Crime: Answers to Hard Questions

LISA BARNES LAMPMAN AND MICHELLE D. SHATTUCK

Crime leaves many victims in its wake. Surely the victimized and their loved ones suffer. The pain and anguish of many victims border on the unbearable. And in a different way, those of us who are witnesses to crime suffer, also. We want to feel safe. We want to believe that we will not fall prey to the harm that has engulfed the other. Crime leaves everyone with hard questions — questions that can shake our very confidence in God. But when Christians are willing to put aside their vulnerability and help victims address their needs — including spiritual needs — then both can find the anchors of faith holding firmly. It is only as we come to understand the heart of God that we are able to cope — victims and helpers alike.

I t was Memorial Day weekend in 1993. A young couple in Memphis had been looking forward to a quiet holiday with family and church friends. Late that Friday evening, drug dealers, apparently enraged to discover that they had broken into the wrong apartment, killed both husband and wife, leaving their three-year-old daughter alone with the bodies.

The couple's church, Abundant Grace Fellowship, mobilized quickly to support and minister to the child as well as to the young wife's parents, who were also members of the church. Immediately the church set up a fund to pay for the child's future education and counseling needs. As a result of publicity efforts, the family received an outpouring of love and contributions from people across the city.

But addressing the family's tormenting grief proved more difficult. The parents of the young woman who was murdered began to attend a support group for those who had lost loved ones in homicides. It soon became evident, however, that the group did not begin to deal with the spiritual questions and needs of the family. "There was nothing with a Christian focus," the father explained. "Nothing that dealt with the spiritual issues and brought in faith as a foundation for healing."

The family turned to Pastor Dwayne Hunt for help — they needed to know that there was hope in the midst of their grief. In response, Pastor Hunt asked Dr. Katherine Lawson, associate pastor of counseling, to develop a faith-based support group for this family and other families in Memphis who had lost loved ones to homicide. Now an ongoing ministry of Abundant Grace Fellowship, Victims to Victory provides opportunities for victims to voice their anger, pain, and questions to one another — and to God. It offers victims a spiritual balm for their wounds.

*   *   *

As much as our secular society and culture might suggest otherwise, we are, fundamentally, spiritual beings. When a crisis or a tragedy disrupts the cycle of daily living, it revives our recognition of the spiritual aspect of life. It brings into focus the fact that God has created us with a body, mind, soul, and spirit, that there is more to life than meets the eye, and that we are not as in control of things as we would like to be.

When crime strikes, it causes a crisis and leaves a trail of wounded victims. These victims have needs — physical, financial, emotional, *and* spiritual. In order for victims to experience healing and restoration, their spiritual needs must be acknowledged and addressed. This is just as important as bandaging a wound, repairing a kicked-in door, or replacing stolen goods.

Whether prepared or not, the local church is often the place that individuals turn to in a time of crisis. Some victims discover their spiritual roots in the search for comfort for and answers to their pain. But sadly, many who crave the help that the larger church community could give them never receive that support.

In 1982, when President Ronald Reagan convened a presidential task force on victims of crime, victims specifically listed the *clergy and church* as vital sources of support. The final report of the task force stated,

> In hearing after hearing across the country, victims identified the religious community as a vital and largely untapped source of support for crime victims. The Government may compensate for economic loss; the state may punish; doctors may physically heal; but the lasting scars to spirit and faith are not so easily treated. Many victims question the faith they thought secure, or have no faith on which to rely. Frequently, ministers and their congregations can be a source of solace that no other sector of society can provide.[1]

Although this government report recognized — almost two decades ago — that victims have spiritual needs, Christians and the church as a whole have been slow to respond. We have not recognized the needs of the *millions* of crime victims as a call to ministry.

---

1. President's Task Force on Victims of Crime, Final Report, December 1982, p. 95.

WHY WE FIND IT HARD TO RESPOND

We read the headlines in the paper; we see the shocked and tear-stained faces of the victims on the evening news; we sometimes even hear their names. But the reality doesn't quite sink in. Crime strikes someone else, somewhere else. As members of the church community, we can easily find ourselves watching as detached observers.

We rarely consider the needs of victims as a call to minister to members of our congregation and our communities — although statistics tell us that 99 percent of Americans will become victims of crime at least once in their lifetime.[2] Ministries to prisoners — in the form of visits, Bible studies, and ongoing assistance for those released from jail or prison — are well established; in fact, they've existed since the days of Paul and Silas. But ministry to victims of crime? "Well, it never occurred to me before," commented one pastor of an inner-city church located in a high-crime area.

And while we need to deal with our own difficult questions regarding crime in the world, far too often we cope by separating ourselves from the victims, leaving them hurt, angry, and alone. It is not until crime touches us, our family, our friends, or our congregation that we are forced to think about spiritual needs in the face of crime.

This detached observance of the victimization of others is an understandable, even normal response — it is how we cope with something that seems threatening. But it is a response worth examining, because it reveals both our personal fears as well as the fears of the larger church community and provides a window onto the questions and issues that crime victims face.

WHY WE DETACH OURSELVES

The story of Job in the Old Testament illustrates the way we often respond to someone else's victimization. We can easily become like

2. U.S. Department of Justice Bureau of Statistics, 1988.

Job's friends, who first come to "sympathize with him and comfort him" (2:11)[3] but soon turn on him with harsh accusations.

In the beginning of the book, the reader steps into a cosmic conversation that God and Satan are having about Job. God praises Job, a well-to-do landowner who is a servant of God, as "blameless and upright, a man who fears God and shuns evil" (1:8). But Satan brashly responds by declaring Job a charlatan, his righteousness solely dependent on God's blessings. Once those blessings are taken away, Satan proposes, Job will abandon God and fall into the abyss of sin and unrighteousness.

In response, God allows Satan to test Job with trials, although within limits. Soon Job experiences disaster after disaster. Every seeming blessing of God is removed from his life. Job is devastated; he has no wealth, no livelihood, no children, no foreseeable future.

Job's wife and his friends respond to his painful situation by telling him that he has brought it on himself. Look at the comments of Job's friend Eliphaz: "Consider now: Who, being innocent, has ever perished? Where were the upright ever destroyed? As I have observed, those who plow evil and those who sow trouble reap it" (4:7-8).

Job's friends respond as many of us do — by trying to figure out what Job has done to bring disaster on himself. While we may not question someone's righteousness or directly accuse him or her of sin (as Job's friends do), we try, nevertheless, to figure out what the person could have done to prevent the crisis.

For example, when we hear of a person who was robbed or physically attacked in some way, our first reaction may be to blame the person who was harmed. We do this by asking questions such as "Did she lock her doors?" and "Did he park in a safe place?" and "Why was she walking alone in that area at night?" Without intending to, our questions imply that the victim took unnecessary risks and could have prevented the victimization.

We do this because it somehow makes us feel safer. Crime victimization makes us uncomfortable and fearful. If other people could have prevented their own victimization, then we, too, can prevent

---

3. Unless otherwise indicated, all Scripture quotations are taken from the New International Version.

ours. We can make sure that what has happened to them never happens to us. And so we try to convince ourselves that we live in a world that is predictable and — if you follow the rules — safe.

We do not want to acknowledge that even if we lock our doors and walk only in safe areas and take all the precautions we can, we still are not totally safe from harm. We might still become a victim of crime — even violence. This opens the door to many unsettling questions — questions about God's sovereignty, God's goodness, the presence of evil in the world, and how we as Christians live with the uncertainty that God may not always protect us from earthly harm. These are hard, uncomfortable, faith-stretching questions.

We respond similarly if a crime strikes someone close to us — a friend or a family member. We don't know how to respond. We are uncomfortable with the coarse, unedited feelings that spew from deep inside the one who has been victimized — the pain, anger, despair, grief, and desire for revenge. These raw, resounding emotions are hard to hear. The questions are even harder to hear: "Why me?" "How could God let this happen?" "Why didn't God protect me, my home, my child?" We don't know how to answer those questions; we don't even know how to begin. A victim's pain and questions too easily remind us of our own vulnerability, our own fears, and our own unanswered questions. We might offer condolences or a hug, but our own fear and desire for safety keep us from reaching out fully to embrace another's pain.

Yet as Christians we cannot ignore victims' pleas for help. We cannot turn our backs on their needs. We cannot close our ears to the spiritual questions and issues that arise from their pain — which means we have to face our own questions and the disturbing emotions they invoke.

WHY WE *CAN'T* DETACH OURSELVES

We cannot remain detached, first of all, because we as Christians are representatives of Jesus Christ — and *He* is not detached. Jesus comes alongside to walk with and at times carry the troubled and brokenhearted across the rough terrain of life and faith.

Jesus uses this very idea to define "a neighbor" in the Parable of the Good Samaritan in Luke 10. In the parable, a crime victim lies dying on the side of the road while two of the religious leaders of the day walk hurriedly by. Only a Samaritan, the outcast of Jewish society, stops, bandages the victim's wounds, and carries him on a donkey to a safe place for help and healing. At the end of the parable, Jesus asks His listener, "Which of these three do you think was a neighbor to the man who fell into the hands of robbers?" The listener replies, "The one who had mercy on him." Jesus responds, "Go and do likewise" (vv. 36-37). As Christ's disciples, we must follow His call to "go" and care for our neighbors.

And we cannot remain detached because Christ has called us as Christians to live in a world where "He causes his sun to rise on the evil and the good, and sends rain on the righteous and unrighteous" (Matt. 5:45). This can mean not only that those who are "evil" receive the benefit of God's blessings, but also that those who are "righteous" are not fully protected from harm. There are numerous examples of this uncomfortable truth, but here are particularly poignant ones: In 1977 in a high school in Paducah, Kentucky, three girls were killed by a fellow student just as they finished a prayer session. In Littleton, Colorado, in 1999, two teenage boys went on a shooting rampage at their school. When they asked a fellow student if she believed in God, she answered "yes" — and they shot her to death.

God may choose to protect us, but He does not always guarantee our safety. Instead, Christ pursues us, loves us, and invites us to wrestle with Him and get to know Him even through the difficult times. To choose detachment or avoid the hard questions because they make us uncomfortable is to pass up an opportunity to grow in faith and get to know our Lord better.

Resisting detachment is important for another reason: when a victim's spiritual needs, as well as other needs, are not acknowledged and addressed, the result can be a devastating revictimization. This lack of compassionate caring can set back the process of restoration and recovery indefinitely.

This is illustrated in the Old Testament story of the rape of Tamar, King David's daughter and Absalom's sister (2 Sam. 13). Because this instance of victimization was not addressed appropriately, it yielded grave consequences for all involved.

Amnon, David's oldest son, had an insatiable sexual desire for his half-sister Tamar, the virgin princess. One day, pretending to be ill, Amnon lured Tamar into his bedchamber, where he sexually assaulted her. Having quenched his lustful thirst, Amnon then despised the young woman and sent her away — sentencing her to a life of rejection and condemnation.

Observing Tamar's intense distress, Absalom attempted to calm his sister but did not acknowledge the crime's impact on her life. Absalom told Tamar, "Be quiet now, my sister; he is your brother. Don't take this thing to heart" (v. 20).

David, although furious, did no better. There is no record of his taking any action against Amnon on his daughter's behalf. He neither addressed Tamar's disgrace personally nor, as king of Israel, responded as judge and ruler of the people with appropriate punishment. Thus, by not acknowledging or acting on the crime and its impact, David abdicated his responsibility as both father and king.

In the face of this inaction, Absalom responded by plotting and carrying out his own revenge against his half-brother Amnon: he had Amnon murdered. In addition, Absalom later took revenge against his father by attempting to overthrow David's reign.

The last thing we hear about Tamar in the Scriptures is that she "lived in her brother Absalom's house, a desolate woman" (v. 20). Like Tamar, too many other victims live lives of desolation and quiet desperation because their needs, particularly their spiritual needs, have not been acknowledged or addressed.

Finally, we cannot remain detached because, as members of Christ's Body, we are called to provide for and assist those who are hurt and wounded because of crime — both those in the church and those in our communities. We not only have an obligation; we have a mandate:

> You are the salt of the earth. But if the salt loses its saltiness, how can it be made salty again? It is no longer good for anything, except to be thrown out and trampled by men. You are the light of the world. A city on a hill cannot be hidden. Neither do people

light a lamp and put it under a bowl. Instead they put it on its stand, and it gives light to everyone in the house. In the same way, let your light shine before men, that they may see your good deeds and praise your Father in heaven. (Matt. 5:13-16)

As Jesus had compassion on those in need around Him (Matt. 14:14; 15:32), so we are to have compassion on those in need around us. We can manifest that compassion by reaching out and serving victims of crime in practical ways — repairing a broken door, window, or lock; providing emergency food and clothing; offering transportation to a doctor's office or to court. We can also offer emotional and spiritual support: by listening with compassion, by offering to pray with or for the person, by offering Scripture verses for comfort and encouragement, by inviting the person to church or a church activity when appropriate, and by sharing the gospel.

THE VICTIM'S COPING RESPONSE: THE SEARCH FOR FAITH

We have the choice of whether or not to reach out to help victims recover. We can bury the hard questions or face them and carry forth the ministry of Christ. Victims, of course, have little choice but to face the devastation of crime. Escape from the pain is rarely achievable. But they can choose how they will cope. Those who address their spiritual needs find that it helps their healing enormously.

Faith that Heals

Some victims discover that their faith provides the strength and hope they need to face the crisis of crime and go on. In fact, some victims find their faith deepened and strengthened as a result of the crisis.

Cynthia was driving home from the store with four-year-old

Scott and her mother in the back seat. Suddenly a drunk driver ran a stop sign and barreled into Cynthia's side of the minivan. Crushed by the steel around her, Cynthia was unconscious until she awoke in the hospital hours later.

"When I woke up," she remembers, "my first thought was — thank you, God, I'm alive. After I found out that Scott and Mom were okay, too, I just had this peace that truly passed all understanding. And that peace sustained me through three surgeries on my left leg. It's God who has given me the strength to go through this. I couldn't do it without Him."

Richard, a tall, dignified-looking man whose sister was murdered only a few years ago, recalls the tragedy vividly:

> I remember it clearly — the date, the time, the place. I was in my car and the car phone rang. It was my wife crying and trying to tell me that Susan had been killed. It was two girls — only nineteen years old — who had tried to car-jack my sister's car. I've never been in such grief and pain.
>
> The only person I could truly turn to, to let go of all that anger and rage, was God. Believe it or not, this whole tragic situation has made me more dependent on God and stronger in my faith.

Faith that Questions

For many people, suffering puts their faith to a severe test. As one victim remembers, "I found myself questioning some of the deep, basic beliefs that I had grown up with. At one time they had comforted me."

Again, the story of Job illustrates the spiritual questions that many crime victims wrestle with — questions steeped in pain, anger, and fear.

> Where are you, God? Do you hear me? Do you care?
> *Even if I summoned Him and He responded, I do not believe He would give me a hearing. (Job 9:16)*

Why did you do this to me, God?
If I have sinned, what have I done to you, O watcher of men? Why have you made me your target? (Job 7:20)

Where is justice?
Though I cry, "I've been wronged!" I get no response; though I call for help, there is no justice. (Job 19:7)

Sharon, another victim, also shared Job's questions. She described how difficult her marriage had been. It was the second marriage for her, the first for her husband, Jack. They had always followed strict religious regimens — daily prayer, daily Bible study — but Jack didn't allow their practices to extend beyond the family. They didn't attend church. They didn't have friends. Jack didn't want to get involved. He wanted to be the husband, the father, the pastor, the friend — everything.

Jack's emotional abuse of Sharon never stopped. Nothing she did was quite right — at least in Jack's opinion. She couldn't fry an egg. She was a horrible housekeeper — and a worse mother. And Sharon had suffered the effects of physical abuse for years — pulled hair, bruised arms and legs. She had gotten used to it; she didn't know things could be any different.

One morning as they finished their mandatory family prayer, Jack turned to Sharon with a knife in his hand. With an unforeseen fury, he stabbed her in the neck. Somehow Sharon escaped, ran to a nearby house, and pleaded with her neighbors to call the police. Jack was arrested and later sentenced to prison for attempted murder.

But that didn't end the torment for Sharon. She didn't have a job; she couldn't drive; she had no one to turn to and no one to depend on. Sharon explained it this way: "No one can understand the pain a victim goes through unless they've been there. I was attacked in my home, which should have been a safe place for me. I was attacked by my husband, who was supposed to love me."

What was worse was that she felt God had abandoned her: "How could He allow this to happen? Where was He?" Her pain echoed in a desperate cry: "My God, my God, why hast Thou forsaken me?"

11

The pain and the questions were too intense for Sharon. Although she felt hopeless, she somehow found the strength to check herself into a mental hospital for help. Eventually Sharon found people — caring Christians — who helped her regain a sense of stability and grapple with her difficult questions about faith.

There are many other victims like Sharon who tremble under the weight of such challenges to their spirit and their faith. In some cases, the victims struggle alone, afraid to ask questions openly or even acknowledge their existence. In other situations, victims may risk voicing their concerns and questions, only to be cut short by their listeners. Well-meaning but unaware family members, friends, and even pastors sometimes dispense quick answers or prod the victims to "get over it and get on with your life."

Faith that Seeks

For some victims, crime touches a spiritual chord that has long been silent or has never been played. The crisis compels them to ask questions of faith and sends them on a spiritual search.

Arthur, an elderly gentleman, was knocked down and robbed by gang members on a busy Denver street. He had been carrying all the money he had — ninety dollars. Volunteers from Neighbors Who Care, the crime-victim assistance ministry of Prison Fellowship Ministries, were called to help Arthur when he was discharged from the hospital.

Alone and vulnerable, Arthur gladly responded to the offer of food, transportation, and support from two church volunteers, Arlene and Michael. The next day, they came back again to offer transportation and support as Arthur wended his way through the social-service maze. As they drove in Arlene's Oldsmobile, Arthur began to talk openly about his questions and concerns. He was not a man of faith, but the crime and the hospital stay made him wonder what would happen to him when he died. He began to ask Arlene about God, faith, and life and death. There in Arlene's car, Arthur prayed to God for help and invited Christ into his life.

Because Arthur was able to address the spiritual questions that surfaced as a result of becoming a crime victim, he found the source of strength he needed to grapple with his victimization. And, gradually, he was able to let God pour His peace into his heart.

THE COSMIC STORY:
PUTTING THE STRUGGLE INTO PERSPECTIVE

Let us return to the book of Job and the dialogue between Job and his friends, which occupies the majority of this scriptural text. Job argues his case before his friends and God. He complains loudly. Job questions God and accuses Him of alienation and estrangement from an obedient and faithful servant. Job's friends are appalled. They attempt to quell his questions and complaints with their own theological "insights."

Then, "out of the storm," God responds (chapters 38–41). He does not reply to Job's challenges but instead turns the tables and asks questions of Job. God does not provide a direct explanation for Job's suffering but instead refocuses Job's attention on His incomparable majesty and power.

God lists the works of His hands and describes the wisdom of His heart. This quiets Job's questions, and he responds with awe: "Surely I spoke of things I did not understand, things too wonderful for me to know. . . . My ears had heard of you but now my eyes have seen you. Therefore I despise myself and repent in dust and ashes" (42:3, 5).

Why does God respond with a laundry list of His miraculous works and wisdom? Why doesn't God instead directly answer Job's questions and laments? A clue may be found earlier in the book when one of his friends, Elihu, takes those present to task for questioning God. Elihu says, "But I tell you, in this you are not right, for God is greater than man. Why do you complain to Him that He answers none of man's words? For God does speak — now one way, now another — though man may not perceive it" (33:12-14).

Could it be that God's revelation of His mighty power and majesty is meant to invite Job — and us — to look beyond the circumstances of our individual lives? Are we to ask what God is doing on a cosmic scale and how the tragedy and joy of our individual lives fit in?

In their book *The Sacred Romance,* Brent Curtis and John Eldredge take a look at the larger cosmic story in which each of us plays a role. The book begins by asking some of the same questions that Job and many of us ask:

> He [God] can spin the earth, change the weather, topple govern-
> ments, obliterate armies and resurrect the dead. Is it too much
> to ask that He intervene in our story? . . . Would it be any worse if
> there were no God? . . . Sometimes the way God treats us feels
> like betrayal. We find ourselves in a dangerous world, unable to
> arrange for the water our thirsty souls so desperately need.[4]

And so, when faced with a crisis of evil, whether triggered by being a crime victim or the victim of multiple disasters like Job, we can ask questions like these and wonder how we are to trust or love a God who could let these things happen to us. We may recognize God as powerful and knowledgeable in ways beyond our comprehension. But, like Job, what we all really want to know is what is in the heart of God — is He really good?

To begin to address these questions, we must look back to the very beginning and ask what God's purpose was in creating us and what He is trying to accomplish in the world and in our lives. The first chapter of Ephesians tells us that God created us to be the object of His affection: "Long before He laid down earth's foundations, He had us in mind, had settled on us as the focus of His love, to be made whole and holy by His love. Long, long ago He decided to adopt us into His family through Jesus Christ. . . . He wanted us to enter into the celebration of His lavish gift-giving by the hand of His beloved Son" (vv. 3-6, The Message).

Unfortunately, even Adam and Eve, living in a perfect world before the Fall, with no sin or sorrow or disaster to mar them or their environment, questioned whether God's heart was really good. Just

---

4. Brent Curtis and John Eldredge, *The Sacred Romance: Drawing Closer to the Heart of God* (Nashville: Thomas Nelson Publishers, 1997), p. 69.

like our first parents, Adam and Eve, we need little coaxing to begin to doubt God's goodness (whether or not we have been victimized) and to let that doubt grow into full-fledged rebellion against our creator.

Does God give up? He did not give up on Adam and Eve. He did not give up on Job. He does not give up on the victim who questions. He does not give up on us. In His amazing and unpredictable love, He continues pursuing us, determining that He will not abandon us to our doubts, sin, and rebellion but will bring us back to Him. The Bible is the story that reveals God's plan for winning us back through His son, Jesus Christ.

Curtis and Eldredge tell Kierkegaard's version of the biblical story to illustrate God's plan for rescuing us:

> Suppose there was a king who loved a humble maiden. The king was like no other king. Every statesman trembled before his power. No one dared breathe a word against him, for he had the strength to crush all opponents. And yet this mighty king was melted by love for a humble maiden. How could he declare his love for her? In an odd sort of way, his kingliness tied his hands. If he brought her to the palace and crowned her head with jewels and clothed her body in royal robes, she would surely not resist — no one dared resist him. But would she love him?
>
> She would say she loved him, of course, but would she truly? Or would she live with him in fear, nursing a private grief for the life she had left behind? Would she be happy at his side? How could he know? If he rode to her forest cottage in his royal carriage, with an armed escort waving bright banners, that too would overwhelm her. He did not want a cringing subject. He wanted a lover, an equal. He wanted her to forget that he was a king and she a humble maiden and to let shared love cross the gulf between them. For it is only in love that the unequal can be made equal.[5]

---

5. Quoted from *Disappointment with God* by Philip Yancey, in Curtis and Eldredge, p. 80.

In order to win the maiden's love, the king renounces his throne and clothes himself as a beggar.

The Gospel is the true story. It is the final Word. The Incarnation, the life and death of Jesus, answers once and for all the questions "What is God's heart toward me? Is He really good? Does He truly care for me?" The good that God accomplished through sending His Son to die on the cross for our sins and raising Him to life again on the third day is more powerful than any evil or crisis of crime that we can experience.

Without this perspective on what God is actively doing in the world and what His purposes are, it becomes difficult to look at the specific spiritual issues and needs of crime victims. We need the larger picture and the larger story. It may not always satisfy our questions about why a specific thing happened or how to deal with it. But it does provide us with the final Word on God's heart: He is good, He does love us, and His goal is to bring us into intimate relationship with Him.

To assist a victim on the road to healing and restoration, we as members of the Body of Christ — family, friends, and professionals — must recognize how crime and suffering can assault, awaken, or deepen spirituality. We must understand the vital role of *faith* in a victim's recovery. We must be willing to confront our own and other's deepest questions related to good and evil and God's power, compassion, justice, and goodness. And we must be ready to reach out and help.

To delve into these issues takes courage. We fear that, like Job, we won't get all our questions answered. Or that looking too deeply will uncover a crack in the foundation of our own faith, a tremor in our sense of security. But only by facing these questions will we be able to discover the true answer to our deepest questions: God is far more than we think He is. He is good, and we can trust Him in the hardest circumstances of life.

CHAPTER TWO

Original Crime, Primal Care

MIROSLAV VOLF

Crime against one's brother. This tragic picture has roots in earliest time, for it is in the story of Cain and Abel — Adam and Eve's two sons of inequality — that we see evil spreading into human history. This story is vital for an examination of some crucial questions about the origins of crime: How have our views been shaped by not wanting to face the question of morality? What about the influence of our environment? And what does the Christian faith teach about the origin of evil and its remedy?

Although I will not be delving into personal experience in this chapter, I want to open by mentioning the war in former Yugoslavia and how the crimes perpetrated there, along with my personal experiences of victimization, shaped my theological thinking over the past years.

I was a Croat in that war, and clearly, from my perspective, Croats were the victims. One-third of Croatian territory was captured, cities were destroyed — I could go down the line naming crimes against that group of people. And yet, I found myself — all of us, really — to be a lousy kind of victim. By that I mean that we were not the kind of victims that I expected us to be. In responding to Soviet aggression, we ourselves were shaped by infighting into the image of our enemy. And, what is more, I have to face the fact that this was not an isolated occurrence of dark behavior by Croatians. I look back into Croatian history and recognize there, too, the same ugly features.

So I bear within myself a history of victimhood but also of perpetration. This shapes my understanding of violence and retribution, a study that we now turn to. Blame? Moral order? Personal versus divine retribution? All questions and answers are framed for us in a familiar story from the Bible. This is the story of the original crime. This is the story of Cain and Abel. ·

The events surrounding these two brothers, described in the fourth chapter of the book of Genesis, and the puzzling disparity of the sacrifices they offered to God have intrigued ardent scholars and lay readers alike. Why did God accept Abel's offering and reject Cain's? What fueled Cain's murderous rage? Further, we wonder: How shall laws of moral order guide us? And what does our interpretation of this story tell us about our own view of evil in the world?

In a recent book entitled *The Curse of Cain*, Regina M. Schwartz places the story of Cain and Abel at the center of an attempt to explain the mystery of pervasive violence in Western societies. Because her interpretation of this pivotal historic event is novel — even subversive — it offers us a good starting point for the original crime. She writes,

> Why did God condemn Cain's sacrifice? What would have happened if He had accepted both Cain's and Abel's offerings instead

18

of choosing one, and had thereby promoted cooperation between the sower and the shepherd instead of their competition and violence? What kind of God is this who chooses one sacrifice over the other? This God who excludes some and prefers others, who casts some out, is a monotheistic God — monotheistic not only because He demands allegiance to Himself alone but also because He confers His favor on one alone. While the biblical God certainly does not always govern His universe in this way, the rule presupposed and reinforced here, in the story of Cain and Abel, is that there can be no multiple allegiances, neither directed toward the deity nor, apparently, emanating from Him. Cain kills in the rage of his exclusion. And the circle is vicious: because Cain is outcast, Abel is murdered and Cain is cast out. We are the descendants of Cain because we too live in a world where some are cast out, a world in which whatever law of scarcity made that ancient story describe only one sacrifice as acceptable — a scarcity of goods, land, labor, or whatever — still prevails to dictate the terms of a ferocious and fatal competition.[1]

Notice three features of Schwartz's interpretation of the story of Cain and Abel. The first is noncontroversial; the second and the third are bound to be hotly disputed. First, she argues that the story discloses the origins of violence. Although we do not kill one another *because* Cain killed, we do kill "for similar reasons."[2] Second, in her view Cain is not so much the first criminal as the first victim. Before Cain killed, he suffered exclusion, and he killed *because* he suffered exclusion. Third, Schwartz concludes that the God of the Bible, the one who demands exclusive allegiance, is the original criminal. God favors some and excludes others, thereby igniting the fire and fanning the flames of deadly rivalries. From Schwartz's perspective, then, the "curse of Cain" is a consequence of belief in one God, not of a transgression against the will of the one God. Monotheism's legacy is inescapably violent.

1. Regina M. Schwartz, *The Curse of Cain: The Violent Legacy of Monotheism* (Chicago: University of Chicago Press, 1997), pp. 3-4.
2. Schwartz, *The Curse of Cain*, p. 2.

The important point here for our discussion of evil is that Schwartz's interpretation, although radical at first glance, actually conforms to widespread contemporary sensibilities about the origins and dynamics of evil. Two culturally pervasive convictions correspond reasonably well with Schwartz's two controversial assertions.

First, she argues that Cain is not to blame; something made him do it. Similarly, our culture hesitates to ascribe personal blame. We tend to seek causal explanations for evil acts behind the persons who committed them.

Second, Schwartz postulates that the God who favors one and rejects the other, and thereby arbitrarily establishes "good" and "evil" as opposites, is the instigator of violence. Similarly, many of our contemporaries tend to follow the philosopher Friedrich Nietzsche[3] — or rather, tend to follow a flat reading of Nietzsche[4] — and see a moral code organized around binary opposites as a source of violence rather than an instrument of peace.

These two interrelated convictions — a conviction about the absence of true blame and a conviction about the inherently oppressive nature of moral codes — combine to render our moral tongue mute. They explain partly why, as Andrew Delbanco has pointed out in *The Death of Satan,* "a gulf has opened up in our culture between the visibility of evil and the intellectual resources available for coping with it."[5]

Not everyone ascribes to these convictions, obviously. A patient, sick to death, was pronounced healthy, and the only medicine capable of curing her was declared poisonous. This is how the two above convictions about the origins and dynamics of evil strike the more conservative thinkers in contemporary culture. In response to the reckless mindlessness exhibited in the claim that moral codes are inherently oppressive and in the reluctance to ascribe blame, they tend

3. Friedrich Nietzsche, *"The Birth of Tragedy" and "The Genealogy of Morals,"* trans. Francis Golffing (Garden City, N.Y.: Doubleday, 1956).

4. Peter Berkowitz, *Nietzsche: The Ethics of an Immoralist* (Cambridge: Harvard University Press, 1995).

5. Andrew Delbanco, *The Death of Satan: How Americans Have Lost the Sense of Evil* (New York: Farrar, Straus & Giroux, 1995), p. 3.

simply to reassert that the patient is ill and the medicine is good. They insist on the clear ascription of blame and the full responsibility of each person for his or her behavior. If they are Christians, they advocate belief in the Christian God as the only adequate resource to sustain a strict moral code that tells people what is right and what is wrong, and what the appropriate rewards and punishments are.

Recognizing the oversimplification, we can put things as follows: A contemporary "liberal" agenda is countered with its mirror image, a traditional "conservative" agenda. The former blames the Bible and its God for underwriting a system of exclusion with a violent legacy; the latter celebrates the Bible and its God for providing moral absolutes necessary to bring order into a world of violence. I will argue here that both "liberal" and "conservative" agendas, which, like all good enemies, feed upon each other, misconstrue what Christian faith teaches about both the origin of evil and its remedy. On the assumption that the story of Cain and Abel embodies profound lessons about the "original crime" and God's "primal care," I will use the story to show that the mystery of evil is deeper and the remedy more complex than either of these admittedly stereotypical positions acknowledges. Let's begin with a theological reading of the story and then revisit the problem of responsibility and moral order.

CAIN'S VIOLENCE AND GOD'S CARE[6]

On the surface the story of Cain and Abel is a narrative about one brother killing the other. But Cain can also be taken to allude to the Kenites, the descendants of Cain and southern neighbors of the Israelites, represented by Abel. The story of Cain and Abel becomes, then, not only an example of rivalry between two brothers but also a narrative of an encounter between "us" and "them" — between Israel

---

6. The following section is reproduced (with a few modifications) from Miroslav Volf's book entitled *Exclusion and Embrace: A Theological Exploration of Identity, Otherness, and Reconciliation* (Nashville: Abingdon Press, 1996), pp. 92-98.

and the Kenites, who were unwilling to accept the special grace that the Israelites received from God, as manifested in the blessings of King David's rule.[7]

If, as seems likely, "Cain" alludes to the Kenites, the story could easily function as a self-congratulating narrative of proud neighbors at the height of their glory seeking to incriminate others: the difficult nomadic life of the Kenites in the deep south of Palestine stood as a sign of God's judgment for wrongs they had committed against innocent Israel. Yet, as Walter Dietrich explains, the point of the story is precisely to undermine self-congratulation.[8]

This is not a free-floating parable that "we" can tell about our relationship to "them" and thereby portray ourselves as "Abel" and cast "them" into the image of Cain. The story is located within primal history. As Claus Westermann has argued, the intention of primal history is to underscore that *every human being* is potentially Cain *and* Abel, just as every human being is Adam and Eve.[9] Cain's envy and murder do not prefigure how "they" (the Kenites) behave in distinction to "us" (Israel), but how *all human beings* tend to behave toward others.

In *Things Hidden since the Foundation of the World*, René Girard suggests that the full significance of the story emerges when we recognize that, unlike the typical mythological texts, which take the perspective of perpetrators in order to legitimize their deeds, the story of Cain and Abel takes the perspective of the victim and condemns the perpetrator.[10] Girard is right, though his way of putting things misses one of the most important dimensions of the story. For

7. Thomas Willi, "Der Ort von Genesis 4:1-16 innerhalb der althebräischen Geschichtschreibung," in *Isac Leo Seeligmann Volume: Essays on the Bible and the Ancient World*, ed. Alexander Rofé and Yair Zakovitch, vol. 3 (Jerusalem: E. Rubenstein's Publishing House, 1983), pp. 99-113.

8. Walter Dietrich, "'Wo ist dein Bruder?' Zu Tradition und Intention von Genesis 4," in *Beiträge zur Alttestamentlichen Theologie: Festschrift für Walter Zimmerli zum 70. Geburtstag*, ed. Herbert Donner et al. (Göttingen: Vandenhoeck & Ruprecht, 1977), pp. 94-111.

9. Claus Westermann, *Genesis 1–11: A Commentary* (Minneapolis: Augsburg Publishing House, 1984), p. 318.

10. René Girard, *Things Hidden since the Foundation of the World*, trans. S. Bann and M. Metteer (Stanford: Stanford University Press, 1987), pp. 146-47.

> The development of conscience or a sense of social interest, very intriguingly, is the capacity to hear one's own pain and be able to speak to the pain that you have caused another. So I need to hear your story. I need to hear the pain within your story. I need to hear the damage I have done to you in order for me to grow in conscience.
>
> Dan B. Allender

within primal history, the story about a murderous "them" is a story about a murderous "us." Cain is "them" *and* Cain is "us"; Cain is all the sons and daughters of Adam and Eve in relation to their brothers and sisters.

The story takes the perspective of the victim not only to condemn the perpetrator, as Girard claims, but at the same time to counter the tendency of the victim to turn into a perpetrator. Its greatness lies precisely in that it combines a clear judgment against the perpetrator with the commitment to protect him from the rage of the victim. God both relentlessly questions and condemns Cain (Gen. 4:6-12) and graciously places a protective mark upon him (v. 15).

Unequal Equals

Formally, Cain and Abel are equals. They are two brothers, born of the same parents; they engage in two equally respectable and complementary vocations, one a keeper of sheep and the other a tiller of the ground; they offer two equally appropriate sacrifices to God, animal offering and fruit offering. The equality of the brothers is underscored even more by a literary device: in verses one through five of Genesis 4, the names of the two alternate in the text four times: Cain, Abel, Abel, Cain, Cain, Abel, Abel, Cain. The effect is that neither takes center stage.[11]

11. Ellen Van Wolde, "The Story of Cain and Abel: A Narrative Study," *Journal for the Study of the Old Testament* 52 (1991): 29.

Yet the formal equality of the two conceals as well as heightens an inequality that defines their relation from the outset. Their mother greets the birth of the first son with a proud and joyous exclamation: "I have produced a man with the help of the Lord" (Gen. 4:1).[12] She expresses her exuberance in the name of her firstborn: Cain, a name of honor that means "to produce," "to bring forth." The birth of her second son seems more a matter of course. He receives a name whose meaning marks him as inferior: Abel, meaning "breath," "vapor," "sheer transience," "worthlessness," "nothingness."

The occupations of both are equally respectable, but — it has been postulated, supporting the theme of their inequality — Cain is a rich farmer, a big landowner, whereas Abel is a poor man with just enough infertile land to keep a small flock.[13] Each brings an equally acceptable form of offering to God, but the "great" Cain offers simply "the fruit of the ground" (v. 3), whereas poor Abel (keenly aware of his dependence on God?) brings the best parts — "fat portions" of the best animals, the "firstlings" (v. 4).[14] Appropriately, God notes

12. Scripture references are taken from The New Revised Standard Version of the Bible.

13. So posits Professor Hartmut Gese of the University of Tübingen in an unpublished transcript of his lectures on Genesis.

14. Together with many contemporary scholars (Pinchas Lapide, *Von Kain bis Judas: Ungewohnte Einsichten zu Sünde und Schuld*, GTB 1439 [Gütersloh: Gütersloher Verlagshaus, 1994], p. 12; Gordon J. Wenham, *Genesis 1–15*, WBC 1 [Waco: Word Books, 1987], p. 103; Willi, "Der Ort von Genesis 4:1-16 innerhalb der althebräischen Geschichtschreibung," p. 101), I follow the older commentators, both Jewish and Christian (see Heb. 11:4; 1 John 3:12), who consider the mention of "firstlings" and "fat portions" in Abel's offering significant (V. Aptowitzer, *Kain und Abel in der Agada, den Apokryphen, der hellenistischen, christlichen und muhammedanischen Literatur*, Veröffentlichungen der Alexander Kohut Memorial Foundation 1 [Wien: R. Löwit Verlag, 1922], pp. 37ff.). The difference in the kind of relation to God suggested by Abel's offering of the best of his flock explains the otherwise inexplicable behavior of God, who, as the righteous judge, cannot simply capriciously have regard for Abel and his offering but not for Cain and his offering (vv. 4-5). To trace the inequality between Cain and Abel in the "inexplicable" action of God toward them (Westermann, *Genesis 1–11*, p. 297) rightly underscores the "inexplicability" of inequality — this is the way life simply is — but locates the inexplicability wrongly in the choice of God.

the difference, and has regard for Abel's offering but not for Cain's (vv. 4-5).

Before God, both offerings could easily have been received as equal (divine regard for the one in no way excludes regard for the other). Yet it is precisely here that the most profound inequality between Cain and Abel emerges. God's recognition of *this* inequality inverts the order of inequalities between Cain and Abel that Eve (through her blessing) and Cain (through his wealth) have established: *Abel* (not just his offering) was regarded by God; Cain was not (vv. 4-5). Cain's reaction to this divine inversion makes up the heart of the story.

The initial problem of the story is the formal equality and common belonging (brothers with complementary vocations) in relation to the inescapable difference of being first and second, rich and poor, honored and despised, regarded and disregarded. From the outset, all human relations are fraught with the tension between equality and difference; it is in this context that relation between the self and the other has to be negotiated.

Outside the Garden of God, rivalry sets in, which drives the protagonists even further "east of Eden" (Gen. 3:24; 4:16). Since human work is threatened with failure, since value tags are inescapably placed on differences, and since recognition can be given or withheld by the ultimate Judge, the self will struggle to maintain its identity and will attempt to assert itself at the expense of the other. This tendency opens the gate to the land of exclusion, a place in which exclusion is perpetrated and the excluding ones themselves live "banished"* from "the presence" though never from the continued care of God.

*J. J. Rabinowitz, "The Susa Tablets, the Bible, and the Aramaic Papyri," *Vestus Testamentum* II (1961): 56.

The Act of Exclusion

First comes Cain's envy that Abel, who is clearly "nobody," should be regarded, and that he, Cain, who is clearly "somebody," should be disregarded — and that by God, whose judgment is incontrovertible. Then comes anger, that "passionate againstness,"[15] directed at both God and Abel. It is against God not because God dealt unfairly with Cain,[16] but precisely because it was *justice* that slighted Cain's greatness. It is against Abel not because Abel is to be faulted — though there is a non-innocent way of being innocent, as Joaquín Monegro of Miguel de Unamuno's "Abel Sanchez" points out[17] — but because Abel's offering was truly acceptable, whereas Cain's was not.

Cain is confronted with God's measure of what truly matters and what is truly great. Since he cannot change the standard of measure and refuses to change himself, he excludes both God and Abel from his life. Anger is the first link in a chain of exclusions: Instead of looking up toward God, "his countenance fell" in a breach of communion with God (v. 5); instead of listening to God, he turned a deaf ear to God's warning (vv. 6-7); by proposing to Abel that they "go out to the field," he banished the community from exercising judgment over his act (v. 8). Finally, he performed the ultimate act of exclusion: he "rose up against his brother Abel" and murdered him (v. 8).

Cain's murder has been described as "meaningless."[18] It is not; murders rarely are. It is governed by a faultless logic, provided Cain's premises are right:

> *Premise 1:* "If Abel is who God declared him to be, then I am not who I understand myself to be."

15. Cornelius Plantinga, *Not the Way It's Supposed to Be: A Breviary of Sin* (Grand Rapids: William B. Eerdmans, 1995), p. 165.

16. Westermann, *Genesis 1–11*, p. 297.

17. Miguel de Unamuno, *"Abel Sanchez" and Other Stories,* trans. Anthony Kerrigan (Chicago: Henry Regnery Company, 1956), pp. 58-59.

18. Erich Zenger, "'Das Blut deines Bruders schreit zu mir' (Gen. 4:10): Gestalt und Aussageabsicht der Erzählung von Kain und Abel," in *Kain und Abel — Rivalität und Brudermord in der Geschichte des Menschen,* ed. Dietmar Bader (Munich: Verlag Schnell & Steiner, 1983), p. 17.

Premise 2: "I am who I understand myself to be."
Premise 3: "I cannot change God's declaration about Abel."
Conclusion: "Therefore Abel cannot continue to be."

Since Cain's identity was constructed from the start in relation to Abel — he was great in relation to Abel's nothingness — God's pronouncement that Abel is "better" left Cain with two alternatives: either to radically readjust his identity or to eliminate Abel.

The act of exclusion has its own good reasons. The power of sin rests less on the insuppressible urge than on the persuasive reasoning generated by a perverted self in order to maintain its own false identity. Of course, these reasons are persuasive only to the self. God would not have been convinced, which is why Cain keeps silent when God asks, "Why are you angry?" (v. 6). To God, Cain would have had to give the answer that contains no reasons, the same answer that the evil protagonist of Thomas Harris's *The Silence of the Lambs* tries to persuade Officer Starling to accept as the explanation of his own horrible crimes: I am angry "because I am evil."[19]

Cain is impervious to God's warning against giving in to anger. The logic of sin proves stronger than the injunction to do good. This is exactly what we should expect, for the logic of sin was originally designed for the very purpose of overcoming the obligation to do good. The knowledge of sin is impotent in the face of sin. Like a dangerous animal, sin is "lurking," "prowling," "desiring" to attack and destroy;[20] to protect oneself, one must not simply be aware of the animal but set out to "master" it (v. 7), as Cain's failure to do so suggests.

Hence, even the knowledge that the knowledge of sin cannot overcome sin does not suffice. As a lawgiver and counselor only, God is impotent. Sin is not so much a failure of knowledge as a misdirection of will, which generates its own counter-knowledge. In an important sense, Cain alone is capable of overcoming his sin. And yet it is a mistake to think that he freely chose to sin, unconstrained

---

19. Thomas Harris, *The Silence of the Lambs* (New York: St. Martin's, 1988), p. 21.
20. Victor Hamilton, *The Book of Genesis: Chapters 1-17,* New International Commentary on the Old Testament (Grand Rapids: William B. Eerdmans, 1990), p. 227.

> When powerlessness, a natural response, is experienced, rage or violence results. But people can begin to learn to channel that sense of powerlessness into a new and effective direction. They can also learn what it means to wait. This not only gives people the potential to have an effect on their individual lives and on the larger corporate community life, but also implicitly teaches them to hope. Biblical hope always involves a heart that is willing to wait, that is willing to suffer in the waiting. And with that comes a sense of power.
>
> Dan B. Allender

by anything but the freedom of his own will. To commit sin is not simply to make a wrong choice but to succumb to an evil power. Before the crime, Cain is both a potential prey and a potential master of a predator called sin; Cain murdered because he fell prey to what he refused to master.

The Will to Sin

The will to sin provides not only "good reasons" for the act but also creates the conditions under which the act could remain undetected, and, if detected, the blame could be evaded. First, there is the *geography* of sin. The crime scene is "the field" outside the public sphere (v. 8) where no help can be procured, no witnesses are available, and no communal judgment can be passed. It may be that "the face facing a face" is "shot through with a moment of commitment," as Arne Vetlesen argues, echoing Emmanuel Lévinas.[21] But in a deserted place, a face facing the face that has wronged it is shot through with the ultimate temptation: "Now is your chance" eclipses "Thou shalt

---

21. Arne Vetlesen, *Perception, Empathy, and Judgment: An Inquiry into the Preconditions of Moral Performance* (University Park: Pennsylvania State University Press, 1994), p. 202.

not kill."[22] The preferred geography of sin is "the outside," where the wrongdoing can happen unnoticed and unhindered.

Second, there is the *ideology* of sin. Cain responds to the divine question "Where is your brother Abel?" with a lie: "I do not know" (v. 9). He denies the crime. Then he adds that, not being his "brother's keeper" (v. 9), he is not responsible for knowing where his brother is. To top it off, this comment is a subtle attempt to ridicule the question in order to deflect its challenge: "Does the keeper (of sheep) need a keeper?"[23] The ideology of sin functions to deny both the act and the responsibility for it, preferably with a touch of humor. Yet the ideology of sin is rarely simply an instrument of evasion, designed to silence the outside voice that accuses; perpetrators employ it also as an instrument of self-deception to hush the conscience inside.

In a way, the consequences of the murder correspond to the murder itself. By his crime, Cain robs himself not only of a brother but also of the possibility of belonging.[24] The land soaked with fraternal blood is inhospitable and no longer yields fruit (v. 12); he has killed, and now he may be killed (v. 14); he refused to look up to God (v. 6), and now he is hidden from God's face (v. 14). By his own act of exclusion he excludes himself from all relationships — from the land below, from God above, from the people around. No belonging is possible — only distance. The distance here does not mark a lifestyle of an ordinary nomad but denotes sheer transcendence ("wanderer") and anxious flight ("fugitive").

Why this rabbity vagrancy, we may ask? Why banishment into the land of unpredictability and fear, governed by the practice of exclusion that verges on chaos? Because belonging is home, and home is brother who is no more.

To have a brother, one must *be* a brother and *keep* a brother. Is there hope for Cain, who had a brother but was not a brother,[25] who

---

22. Emmanuel Lévinas, *Ethics and Infinity,* trans. Richard A. Cohen (Pittsburgh: Duquesne University Press, 1985), pp. 87, 89.

23. Wenham, *Genesis 1–15,* p. 106.

24. Zenger, "'Das Blut deines Bruders schreit zu mir,'" p. 19.

25. As Ellen Van Wolde has pointed out, Abel is regularly called Cain's brother, whereas Cain is never called Abel's brother. Cain has a brother but *is not* a brother,

killed the brother he should have been keeping? The hope lies in God and God's engagement with Cain's affairs. God's insertion before the wrongdoing — "Why are you angry?" (v. 6) — was ineffective; Cain turned away from God. The insertion did, however, underscore the fact that although Cain may have had "good reasons" to be angry, he had *no right* to be angry. After the wrongdoing, God's second insertion — "Where is your brother Abel?" (v. 9) — did not seem to achieve much, either; it elicited only self-justifying denial. But, again, God's question made clear that life in community means sharing a common social space and taking responsibility for the other. God's third insertion was an angry word of judgment — "What have you done?" (v. 10). Here we learn why God kept asking Cain questions. Yahweh, the God who hears the groans of the oppressed, saw the murder coming and warned against it; God, who attends to the harassed and brutalized, heard the innocent blood crying out and judged the perpetrator.

Divine Judgment

Divine judgment accomplished what divine questions did not: it elicited Cain's response. Commentators are divided on whether Cain complained about the weight of the sentence ("My punishment is greater than I can bear") or admitted the greatness of his transgression ("My iniquity is too great to be forgiven") or both. In any case, in addition to noting the danger of the chaotic land of exclusion to which he was consigned on account of his wrongdoing, Cain acknowledged his responsibility before God.

God's fourth and final insertion is a response both to Cain's acknowledgment of responsibility and to the weight of his punishment. In the land of exclusion, the Lord "put a mark on Cain," not to brand him as a perpetrator but to protect him as a potential victim.[26] The mark may symbolize a system of differentiation that pro-

---

whereas Abel is a brother but *does not have* a brother ("The Story of Cain and Abel," pp. 33, 36).

26. Lapide, *Von Kain bis Judas,* p. 14.

tects from "mimetic violence" of all against all, as Girard has suggested.[27] But more important than differentiation is the *grace* that undergirds it. The same God who did not regard Cain's scanty offering bestows kindness upon the murderer whose life is in danger. God does not abandon Cain to the cycle of exclusions he himself has set in motion. Labeled by the mark of God, Cain belongs to God and is protected by God even as he settles away from "the presence of the Lord" (v. 16).

We leave Cain protected in primal history; on Good Friday we will find him redeemed. Cain, the one who acted out the exact opposite of an embrace, whose body went "forth totally against the other body in an intention to . . . kill it,"[28] will be drawn near and embraced by the Crucified. Will the embrace of the Crucified heal Cain of envy, hatred, and the desire to kill? In de Unamuno's "Abel Sanchez," Joaquín Monegro tells his wife, Antonia, a saint, that she could not cure him because he did not love her.[29] In a sense, the same can be said of every Cain: the embrace of the Crucified will not heal him if he does not learn to love the one who embraced him. Cain, the anti-type who murdered his brother, will be healed by Christ, the type who laid down his life for us, only if he sets out to walk in Christ's footsteps (cf. 1 John 3:11-17).

CAIN, GOD, AND US

How do the issues of blame and moral order that we touched upon at the beginning of this chapter look in light of the above interpretation of the story of Cain and Abel? Does the story help us decide in the debate between typical "liberal" and typical "conservative" agendas? I suggest that instead of telling us simply which side to uphold, the story is pointing toward a still sparsely populated space between these two opposing views. It draws the contours of a cre-

27. Girard, *Things Hidden since the Foundation of the World*, p. 146.
28. Z. D. Gurevitch, "The Embrace: On the Element of Non-Distance in Human Relations," *Sociological Quarterly* 31, no. 2 (1990): 199.
29. de Unamuno, *"Abel Sanchez" and Other Stories*, p. 175.

ative middle ground that is shaped less by the pragmatics of cultural debates — in which opponents get forced into unnuanced polarities — and more by attentiveness to the deep convictions of the Christian tradition about evil as sin and about grace as the means of its redress. In conclusion, I want to sketch that creative middle ground by briefly revisiting Cain, who murdered, the God who cared, and those of us who have read the story.

Cain, Who Murdered

Notice the interplay in Cain's behavior between the pressure of the social environment and his internalization of its signals on the one hand, and the claim of moral demands upon Cain's freedom and responsibility on the other. Eve's exuberance over his sheer existence and his own economic success prepare the way both for Cain's inappropriate sacrifice and his reaction to God's unfavorable judgment. We expect him to act the way he did because his history has shaped him to act the way he did. Yet, the compelling inner logic of his behavior notwithstanding, he can act otherwise; his behavior is not predetermined but willfully executed. The divine "Why?" suggests this, and the call to "master" the deadly beast of sin implies this.

The original crime takes place in the space created by the pull of partly internalized signals from the social environment and the possibility of acting in accordance with moral demands; it emerges out of the interplay between compulsion and choice, between slavery and freedom, between the force of the crime's inner logic and the possibility of its mastery. The original crime is both high-handed and deeply tragic. Hence neither the typically liberal hesitation to ascribe personal blame nor the typically conservative disregard for the power of sin will do as a response.

The God Who Cared

God's primal care in response to the original crime fits the complex inner dynamics of the crime. God cares for victims and, therefore, condemns both the crime and the criminals. God does justice. An order without justice would be an unjust order; a peace without justice would not be peace but an oppressive calm, suffused with the suffering of the innocent. As God does justice for victims, however, He does not give up on criminals. He seeks to bring them to recognize the gravity of their deeds. And even in punishment, God does not cease to extend grace. The mark He placed on Cain's forehead is a reminder that no crime imaginable could exclude the perpetrator from God's care. And this indiscriminate care — a care as indiscriminate as God's sun, which rises on the evil and on the good (Matt. 5:45) — shows that God's grace has primacy over God's justice. God's grace is not an erratic exception to his justice; rather, God's justice is an inalienable dimension of His grace. The just grace of God is the shape of His primal care appropriate to the character of Cain's original crime.

We Who Have Read the Story

The story of Cain and Abel invites us to identify with the slain innocent brother. Although it seems obvious that we should do so, our deep proclivities are to do otherwise. Victims are always, by definition almost, weak losers; we prefer powerful winners. Moreover, criminals are shrouded in what has been called "the prestige of evil" (Laurence Selenick), whereas victims are burdened by the "dullness"

> The Church is, unfortunately, little different from society in its perspectives. If society is enthralled with evil and power, in a sense, the Church is as well. We don't like to hear the stories of the wounded. We recoil from dealing with wounded hearts, their struggles and questions. We want to deal with the power. And until we, as a church, get back to healing and ministering to the wounded, we are not a church.
>
> Lisa Lampman

of innocence. Hence a pervasive cultural obsession with criminals, and a rather quick forgetfulness of victims and their family members.[30]

The story of Cain and Abel, on the contrary, takes decidedly the perspective of the victim and condemns the perpetrator. At the same time, however, it underscores the imperative that we not demonize the perpetrator. True, justice must be pursued, and the punishment of the criminals must be appropriate. But even at their worst, criminals remain human beings and, therefore, "neighbors" for whom we must care. Each in their own way, both victims and criminals, are objects of our care. And if we are to betray neither the "blood of the innocent" nor "the blood of God's Lamb" shed for the guilty, both kinds of care must be pursued at the same time.

Inscribed both in the story and in the literary context in which it is embedded is the message that just as we must care for both Abel and Cain, so also we must see ourselves in the faces of both brothers. We cannot choose only one; each of us is both Abel and Cain. In different aspects and at different junctures of our lives, we are both innocent victims and guilty perpetrators. In our innocence, we should not forget our sinfulness, and in our sense of endangerment, we should remember to fear our own dark shadows. In "The Criminal among Us," Willie Jennings quotes an old Calvinist liturgy (1571) of the perpetrator's return that expresses beautifully the sense of the community's own sinfulness as it both names the perpetrator's deed as sin and receives him or her back into the community:

> We in the sin of this our brother accuse and condemn our own sins, in his fall we all lament and consider our sinful nature, also we shall join repentance, tears, and prayers with him and his, knowing that no flesh can be justified before God's presence, if judgment proceed without mercy. . . . We all here present join our sins with your sin; we all repute and esteem your fall to be our own; we accuse ourselves no less than you; and now finally,

30. Eric Schlosser, "A Grief Like No Other," *Atlantic Monthly*, no. 9 (1997): 39.

we join our prayers with yours, that we may obtain mercy, and that by the means of our Lord Jesus Christ.[31]

CRIME AND ITS REMEDY

Regina Schwartz used the story of Cain and Abel to indict the one God of the Bible and to exonerate Cain, the original criminal. How can we interpret the same story to respond to her assertion that monotheism, by requiring exclusive allegiance to the one God, sets up a system of rivalry and exclusion which leads inescapably to violence? More importantly, how should our belief in the God of the Scriptures impact our deliberations about the nature of both the "crime" and its remedy?

First, we recognize that all of us in various ways, at various times, and to various degrees participate in the original crime. And we do so not because God's judgments have created artificial scarcity but because we conspire with our environment to follow the inclinations of our sinful heart, which wants what it wants even when it knows that what it wants is evil.

Second, we remember that the only proper response to the original crime is not to abandon the God of the Bible but to imitate Him. Thus we pursue justice for the innocent and extend costly grace to the perpetrator, both at the same time.

Third, we never forget that there is an evil worse than the original crime. It consists of self-centered slothfulness of the mind, heart, and will that will not recognize one's own sinfulness, not pursue justice for the innocent, and not extend grace to the guilty.

31. Willie James Jennings, "The Criminal among Us," *The Other Side* 31, no. 5 (1995): 62.

CHAPTER THREE

The Mark of Evil

DAN B. ALLENDER

Evil. Tentacles from the kingdom of darkness wrap themselves indiscriminately around the hearts of God's created beings. The intent? To weaken and destroy the individuals; to cause us to doubt God's character and undermine His created order. How do we, with such limited vision, understand the nature of evil? What is at the heart of this horrible power of destruction? What is it seeking to accomplish — its ultimate goal? Amazingly, though it seems paradoxical, every dark touch of evil has the potential for helping us understand more perfectly God's power, His love, and His overwhelming goodness. Even in the face of evil's grip, we can regain our faith, rebuild our hope, and grow closer to the One who is sovereign over everything, even the dark heart of a very dark kingdom.

Joan sat in my office, her face red, puffy, and stained with tears. She had been crying for days, and in the first twenty minutes of our time together she wept uncontrollably. Every few moments she pounded her hands on her knees and turned her face toward me with a wet, fiery glare. In a hoarse whisper, she said, "Why — oh, God, why did He let my little girl be raped? Can't God do anything that matters, that really matters?"

A pastor sat with me by a hotel pool. Our children swam ten yards away, and we watched them paddle about with a carefree innocence that warmed our hearts. I began to talk about what God had been teaching me since we had seen each other last, but my friend stopped me: "Did you hear what happened to my brother?" I shook my head no. "He was murdered six months ago by a man who for no reason walked up to him and shot him in the head. Since that day I haven't been able to talk with God other than to yell at Him and then turn my back on Him."

Our next-door neighbor stood on her front lawn, dazed and frozen. At first I thought she was staring at some problem on the facade of her house, but it quickly became clear that she was lost in an aimless stare. I said, "Jane, are you all right?" She turned to me and said offhandedly, "They took all my jewelry. They took my stereo. And then they ripped everything to pieces for no apparent reason." She and her family had returned that morning from a weekend ski trip to find their home ransacked. Days later Jane told me, "The loss of some of my jewelry was heartbreaking, but what I can't get over is that they went through my drawers. It feels haunting to go into my bedroom knowing they've been there. My home feels unclean and unsafe."

In each of these situations, the victims — including those directly assaulted, their families, and friends — encountered evil. An evil deed may or may not be perpetrated by an evil person; nevertheless, the result is always diabolical. A good man might drink to excess and in a drunken stupor make a horrible decision to drive. On the way home he might hit and kill a child. He has committed an evil deed that has diabolical effects on countless people.

Some deeds are not only evil but are perpetrated by a person who is evil. The evil person may or may not consciously serve the kingdom of darkness, but his deeds ultimately serve the purposes of Satan. Harm of any kind, no matter what the motive or the intent of the person inflicting it, shatters our sense of safety, predictability, and trust in the goodness of our world. For many crime victims, an act of evil causes a loss of trust in God that is difficult to restore. But an evil act perpetrated by an evil person pierces the heart even more deeply.

Evil acts and evil people inevitably cause us to reckon with the nature of life, our place in the world, and the God who could have intervened to stop the harm, but did not. Often the victim of unexpected, unexplained harm asks a question raised by the psalmist many years ago: "Why, O Lord, do you stand far off? Why do you hide yourself in times of trouble? In his arrogance the wicked man hunts down the weak, who are caught in the schemes he devises. He boasts of the cravings of his heart; he blesses the greedy and reviles the Lord" (Ps. 10:1-3).[1]

The questions "Why, O Lord, do you stand far off? Why do you hide . . . ?" invite the worshiper of God to ask one of the hardest questions that can be posed: "How can an all-good and all-powerful God allow harm to occur to those He loves?" The answer to this question is called a *theodicy*, or a defense of God that usually addresses the issue of God's character and His freedom from sin alongside the nature of free will and its consequences. Our focus will be more selective. We will consider these questions: How are we to wrestle with evil? And what does an encounter with evil compel us to face about ourselves?

We begin with a simple assumption: To the degree we understand the nature of evil, not only do we better understand the human condition and our adversary, the Devil, but we also comprehend more about God. The result? We are not as startled and detoured by evil's harm, but instead are wooed to the Gospel in spite of and to some degree because of evil. We will focus on three issues: the heart of evil, the horror of evil, and the hope of redemption from evil.

---

1. All Scripture quotations are taken from the New International Version.

THE HEART OF EVIL

It is impossible to address the topic of evil without focusing first on the ultimate evil: Satan. Satan is called the accuser, the one who lies and deceives and prowls about the world to destroy anything that reveals the glory of God. The evil one hates the glory of God. He cannot destroy God: Satan is a powerful being, but he is a created being and not equal to God; therefore, his existence still depends on the activity of God.

The evil one cannot destroy God, but he can mar, distort, and nearly destroy the mark of God in creation. For that reason, his fury and hatred are spent against human beings who are made in the image of God and bear the mark of His glory more than any other created being (Ps. 8:5).

The evil one delights in severing relationships and demeaning dignity by setting up traps that strip a person of power, promise (trust), and pleasure in order to incite powerlessness, betrayal, and shame. A loss of power steals from a person a sense of future and hope. Betrayal cuts the cords of trust and makes faith seem foolish. And shame mocks desire and degrades pleasure, thus destroying the impetus and reward of love. Evil's plan is to destroy the glory of God in man by attempting to steal from him what is most sacred and most human: faith, hope, and love.

> If evil can destroy faith, hope, and love, then, in fact, it has to a large degree debilitated our capacity to function in the world, in relationships, and on behalf of God and others.

In order to gain a more accurate understanding of evil — be it supernatural evil or human evil — it is imperative to listen to the claims evil makes about itself and the assertions made about it by others. Self-reference or self-definition is the primary mode for attempting to understand another's motivation and mode of operation. The evaluations of those most affected also provide key insights into that one's character. Listen to the claims of those who are evil and those affected by evil.

> You [evil] said, "I will continue forever — the eternal queen!" But you did not consider these things or reflect on what might happen. Now then, listen, you wanton creature, lounging in your security and saying to yourself, "I am, and there is none besides me. I will never be a widow or suffer the loss of children." Both of these will overtake you in a moment, on a single day: loss of children and widowhood. They will come upon you in full measure, in spite of your many sorceries and all your potent spells. You have trusted in your wickedness and have said, "No one sees me." (Isa. 47:7-10)

> Give her as much torture and grief as the glory and luxury she gave herself. In her heart she boasts, "I sit as queen; I am not a widow, and I will never mourn." (Rev. 18:7)

Evil is distinguished by at least three internal qualities: it has no conscience, it feels no empathy, and it delights in doing harm.

Seared Conscience

"I sit as queen." "I am, and there is none beside me." "No one sees me." I am Royalty.

Evil is arrogant beyond comprehension. It is not mere selfishness, or even an advanced form of narcissism. It is an assumption of power that exceeds the demand to be first or the perception of oneself as greater than others; evil stands above all others, abrogating the power of others to determine their fate. In *People of the Lie*, Scott Peck remarks that the evil person has an "unsubmitted will" that refuses to bow before anyone, including God, because it must be the sole determiner of the future.[2] It will allow no one to influence or

2. M. Scott Peck, *People of the Lie: The Hope for Healing Human Evil* (New York: Simon & Schuster, 1983), p. 78.

shape its direction because to do so would be to place itself on the same level as others and thus share power. Evil undertakes the constant battle to gain more and more power over others and to enslave others to its will.

I am; and there are no others. Ultimately evil craves to be as independent and powerful as God. In fact, evil assumes the name of God: "I am who I am" (Exod. 3:14). In calling itself all-powerful, all-knowing, and capable of striking anywhere at anytime, evil refuses to take anyone else into account. It is as if no one exists but the evil being. There is no law that can bind evil, no person who can obligate it.

C. S. Lewis has pictured evil as a ravenous, vacuous, never-ending hunger that must be filled by eating or absorbing others. Marguerite Shuster brilliantly explains the emptiness of evil. She writes,

> God can will what is other than himself; thus He makes a universe and human beings with their own sphere of freedom (and thus, too, He can sacrifice Himself). The Devil, on the other hand, because he can will only himself, has and is nothing. By denying God, he lost the single Necessity and is therefore insatiable, destroying everything he gets because he no longer is.[3]

Evil may exist in community, but it joins with others only to gain a greater strength to disempower those with power. In fact, evil searches for someone to devour in order to fill that emptiness that comes from being dislocated from serving and loving others.

No eyes will trouble me. Evil feels little or no guilt or shame. Evil is capable of utterly inhuman acts of brazen, barbarous harm without any sense of distress or remorse. Peck has said that "the central defect of the evil is not the sin, but the refusal to acknowledge it."[4]

It is as if the inner witness of God, called the conscience, has been unplugged or, better described, seared. As a result, there is no sense

---

3. Marguerite Shuster, *Power, Pathology, Paradox: The Dynamics of Evil and Good* (Grand Rapids: Zondervan Publishing House, 1987), p. 134.
4. Peck, *People of the Lie*, p. 69.

of inner distress in violating others; there is no regard for the way one is seen by others. A conscience regulates not only our behavior but also our sense of place with others. Someone without a conscience is unable to serve others or be committed to anyone other than himself or herself. The only regulating force for evil is power.

When a normal, sinful person commits a clearly harmful deed, he or she will often fear being caught and the consequences that might ensue. Fear often stops normal sinners from committing evil deeds because they imagine how others, especially those they love and respect, will respond to their misdeeds. Normal sinners have the capacity to feel shame in anticipation of being caught and exposed. Evil has no connection with others; it refuses to lose power to anyone. Therefore, it is unable to be humbled by guilt or shame. In fact, the more shameful its deeds, the greater the power and glory it steals from others and God.

Deadened Empathy

"I am not a widow, and I will never mourn."

Never a widow, never a loss. An evil person will never lose power or suffer loss by deeply connecting to another person. Evil refuses to engage in normal intimacy where giving and receiving leave the heart open to disappointment and loss. In a fallen world, death hovers as the ultimate loss and destruction of intimacy. Death is both a reality and a symbol of separation, division, and divorce. Every person faces a legion of losses every day. Most people accept and embrace loss as inevitable and grow stronger as loss deepens hope for the future and intensifies gratitude for daily blessings. Evil refuses to bear the ordinary lot of humankind. It seems to be above daily losses and ultimately above the final loss of death.

Evil attempts to escape death by refusing to care. If I don't care about anyone, then I will not be troubled by his departure or death. Evil says, "I will transcend death (loss) because I have never been enmeshed in life." For that reason, evil has often had a love affair with death. Death symbols, dangerous rituals, and fearlessness in the face of harm are often the marks of evil. The greater the familiarity with death, the less terror it yields as a reality that will annul one's existence. Anything that draws the heart to life, to hope, and the essentials of humanity must be mocked and destroyed.

For instance, a child innocently playing with her adoring parents may draw hoots of derision from a pack of kids with skulls tattooed on their arms. It would be erroneous to assume that a specific teen with swastikas and the marks of decay reflected in his clothing and personal hygiene is evil, but the symbols of cultural derision and the taunting of tenderness reflect a hatred of loyalty and love.

Never a widow, never a sorrow. Evil refuses to feel pain or loss; it is dead to sorrow. Evil refuses to mourn; therefore, it has no (apparent) need of comfort. Consequently, evil will not be aware of or offer comfort to the pain or suffering of another. Evil does not feel the feelings of another. Evil does not act to ameliorate suffering. Instead, it stands immune to pain and disdainful toward the pain of the other. In that sense, it is not that evil is unaware of suffering, but it is unmoved to help. It is unwilling to suffer desire. Evil refuses to feel any passion that would obligate it to extend comfort or protection to another.

A woman I counseled described how, when she was a child, her father had regularly beat her until she was nearly unconscious, and when she began to come back to consciousness and moan, her father would say, "Stop whining. You sound pathetic. Just get up and clean yourself up." He did not feel shame for his brutality, nor did he suffer when she felt pain. The suffering of the other is at best an inconvenience and more often than not a source of pleasure. Evil feels no remorse, loss, or pain regarding the harm that is perpetrated; far more, evil enjoys the planning, the setup, the trap, and the physical and emotional consequences of the harm.

Delight in Cruelty

Nothing can heal your wound; your injury is fatal. Everyone who hears the news about you claps his hands at your fall, for who has not felt your endless cruelty? (Nah. 3:19)

43

Therefore pride is their necklace; they clothe themselves with violence. From their callous hearts comes iniquity; the evil conceits of their minds know no limits. They scoff, and speak with malice; in their arrogance they threaten oppression. (Ps. 73:6-8)

Endless violence. Evil delights in doing harm. Evil is cruel. Cruelty involves not just the extent of the harm but the manner in which the harm is perpetrated. It is, therefore, not sufficient for evil merely to steal; it must wreck. Not merely rape; it must prolong tension, mock, and debase. Not merely murder; it must torture and feign release before exercising the final power to determine another person's earthly existence. Evil loves to incite hope and then see it dashed in an instant. Nothing brings evil more joy than conquering the spirit of its victim by teasing her with the promise of rescue.

A client told me that many of her childhood days began in the same manner. Her mother would greet her with a smile, serve her breakfast, and then drive her to school. This would lull her into the innocent and naïve hope that her mother would be kind to her. Whenever her mother was generous and kind, she would doubt the previous night's outburst and forget the horror of her mother's humiliating assaults. When she got home from school, she would spend the first few hours doing homework and chores; occasionally she got permission to play with other children in the neighborhood.

But when evening descended and dinner was served, a gothic night of hell would begin. Often the mother would pick at her for some small failure, real or imagined, in a sarcastic tone. She would often serve her daughter from different dishes. She would insist her daughter wanted more spinach even when her daughter declined it. She would slap the spinach on her daughter's plate and bellow at her to eat it. When her daughter picked at the food, she would grab her hair and yank her head, demanding she eat more deliberately and quickly. The meal would end eventually when the mother left the table, leaving her daughter with the task of cleaning up.

Before she could finish, the mother would command her to undertake several more tasks. Whatever task she did, the mother would complain that she not only didn't do it well but that she was failing to get the dinner cleanup finished. The mother would call her from room to room, never permitting her to finish the task she had started. Then she would mock her daughter and physically abuse her for failing to do what was required.

The evening *coup de grace* involved taking a bath in front of the mother. The mother would criticize her weight or make jokes about her body. Then she would begin accusing her elementary school daughter of sexual impropriety, and the abuse would escalate until she was both physically and sexually assaulting her daughter. After the mother tired of the game, her daughter was left to cry herself to sleep most nights.

My client could not recall seeing a glow of devilish delight on her mother's face. But she could recall the intense focus and the sense of weary self-righteousness her mother had because she had to endure such a recalcitrant daughter, and the growing intensity of words or blows that ended in a climax of dark energy. An evil person like my client's mother is well versed in the masquerade of making evil appear like light. She would often finish her brutality by exclaiming about the high price of raising a child in those times and how exhausting it was to care about how a child turned out. She would then tell horror stories of parents who simply did not care for their children as she did for her daughter. Her daughter could only dream of being in one of those families.

As I mentioned earlier, evil delights in provoking fear and then feigning rescue. It comes alongside the victim, often with a keen sensitivity to the victim's plight and desires, and then pierces the hope with a blow that mocks the aroused desire. The victim of evil is left feeling exhausted and foolish, and knowing there is no hope of rescue.

Mocking, mean-spirited, threatening words. One might think that evil operates primarily within the realm of physical or sexual harm. This is not the case. Its preferred mode of operation, especially garden-variety evil, is through mockery, meanness, and threats. Evil speaks the language of shame and contempt.[5] Evil uses the power of the raised eyebrow and the smirking eyes with subtle

5. Ted Peters, *Sin: Radical Evil in Soul and Society* (Grand Rapids: William B. Eerdmans, 1994), pp. 217-62.

and almost indiscernible force. The twisting of the phrase "Did I hurt you?" with the inflection of feigned concern, punctuated with dancing, mocking eyes, is enough to send a shudder of horror through the heart of a vulnerable victim.

What makes mockery so powerful is that it is so subtle, but the message is so clear. If the victim does not address the mockery, he or she feels small and stupid. Yet if the victim directly addresses the stinging words, they can be effortlessly turned back on the victim, who is then criticized for being too sensitive or incapable of judging the situation accurately. It is part of the delight of seduction. Mockery, when confronted, becomes a web that entangles the victim more deeply in the inexorable, sticky threads of powerlessness.

Evil loves the catch-22 of a double bind. If the victim is silent, then he or she is a willing participant in the dance of darkness. But if the victim points out the injustice, then he or she is more deeply drawn into the lair and must either fight to the death or eventually give up, thus providing the evil person the pleasure of winning a more intense and exciting conflict.

> What you find in those who are evil is an absence of connection to the inner world of others. Although they comprehend what motivates and understand the potential of loss and shame in others, and in many ways are psychodynamically very accurate and intrigued, they do not feel the feelings of others.

Evil ultimately works to thwart the integrity of words. It speaks and not only does not mean what it says but longs to pervert meaning so that what was said is the opposite of what is meant. Evil parades as light. It offers help when it desires to destroy. It sings praise when it really despises. It encourages when it actually taunts. The result is overwhelming chaos, confusion, and not only pain but also a kind of craziness which tragically presumes that somehow the victim is not really a victim but is at fault for the crime.

46

What is the effect of evil on the heart of the victim? Evil longs to destroy intimacy and union with others; further, it intends to shatter a sense of personal wholeness. If it can tear at the integrity of the self and then destroy the bridge of trust to others, it has established a great beachhead in the assault on the desire to love and be loved, and is one step closer to severing the connection to God. We will now look at how it seeks to accomplish this.

THE HORROR OF EVIL

Satan is working to destroy hope through powerlessness, faith through betrayal, and love through ambivalence. His ultimate purpose is to destroy human glory and indirectly to mar the glory of God. Whether the evil is perpetrated by an evil person or is done by a mere pawn unwittingly in service to ultimate evil, the consequences will be nearly the same. Evil perpetrated by an evil person, however, intensifies the hopelessness, betrayal, and ambivalence of its victim to the extent that it seems that evil is utterly superior to good. When that is the case, the personal consequences for the victim include greater dissociation, distortion of reality, and distance from relationships.

Powerlessness and the Loss of Hope

Evil works to steal power and mar creativity.[6] As we have seen, it seeks to devour the life of its victim in order to fill an inexhaustible hunger that arises from its utter separation from God.

Powerlessness involves the awareness that nothing done now will change the future. "I am helpless to effect any change to improve my situation. I may be able to yell, but it doesn't change my imprison-

---

6. Dan Allender, *The Wounded Heart: Hope for the Adult Victim of Childhood Sexual Abuse* (Colorado Springs: NavPress, 1990). This book provides a more comprehensive picture of the damage of powerlessness, betrayal, and ambivalence with regard to sexual abuse.

ment. I may plead, but it falls on deaf ears." Eventually, when there is nothing one can do to change the horror, the natural response is to give up. It is easier to quit trying and grow numb than to hope and have that hope be dashed time and again. The Proverbs speak to this sense of despair: "Hope deferred makes the heart sick, but a longing fulfilled is a tree of life" (13:12).

My friend whose brother was randomly gunned down on a busy street lost hope in life. My friend was the younger brother who depended on the counsel and support of his older and wiser sibling. He was furious at God because he had always assumed his relationship with his brother would be a vital, living reality. Nothing he said or did could bring his brother back to life. His brother's death stole his sense of anticipation in life. The future seemed endlessly uncertain and dark.

> Hope is part of imagination. God has given us the capacity to image or imagine that which could come in the future, based on what we know of the past. The degree to which any being that is evil can destroy our capacity to imagine is the degree to which we lose the capacity to move forcefully and wisely into the future.

Hope is what propels us into the future. If hope is lost, then one is cast into a mechanical, rote existence that sees each day as nothing more than a repetition of what has come before. Hope lost spells the loss of vitality, passion, and creativity. Once people lose hope, they become robotic serfs that any person or regime can easily control. Evil labors to assume the power that is cast off by those who have lost hope and can no longer move creatively into the future.

Betrayal and the Loss of Faith

Evil works to sever relationships and destroy trust. It seeks to isolate the victim in order to gain power and destroy the intimacy and joy of connected, caring relationships. Evil refuses to allow anyone the unity and intimacy that it has forsaken with God.

Betrayal is the experience of being set up, violated, and then discarded. It is being used by someone who stains our dignity for their pleasure and then is unmoved by our pain. It is not merely being sinned against; it involves the further violation of facing a criminal who is cold in heart, untouched by remorse or shame. Thus the ultimate betrayal is not merely the harm but the refusal of the one who perpetrated the evil to repent. Repentance is the sole ground for trust or relationship to be restored.

There is a form of healing that can come with punishment pronounced and delivered, but it is never complete or restorative without repentance and forgiveness. Incomplete justice is not the sole province of the criminal justice system; we see it in everyday life, even among friends. For example, two friends have a serious altercation, and a rift occurs between them, but they do not address it. Over time the relationship returns to a forgetful resumption of activity, healing has been thwarted, and the wound remains. The wound may heal, but contrary to God's path. The long-term effect is a bias that interprets the other in light of the past and unresolved offense. Over time the backlog of suspicious assessment halts the normal flow of intimacy and care. Further, it erodes confidence in the restorative power of the Gospel.

Not only does broken trust sever the bridge of relationship with the one who committed the crime, but the fallout darkens the sky and clouds all other relationships. It particularly calls into question our relationship with God. Does He rescue? Does He protect? Will He let the guilty go free?

As hope focuses on the future, so faith looks to the past. Faith is founded on the memory of God's redemptive acts. For Jewish persons, it is the memory of the Exodus; for Christians, it is the cross. Faith dashed calls into question the veracity of God's past rescue. Even if one does not question the historical veracity of it, the loss of faith makes one unable to believe it personally. "God may have saved Israel, and He may have raised Jesus from the dead and broken the bondage of sin and death, but it isn't true for me."

Without faith, we are groundless and susceptible to the shifting winds of whim and fortune. Evil works with diabolical intensity to call into question the past goodness of God by stripping us of confidence in him today. When we lack a solid foundation and a sturdy confidence, we are more likely to rely on our own strength, which ultimately is the path of darkness.

AMBIVALENCE AND THE LOSS OF LOVE

Evil works to infuse shame and violate pleasure. It seeks to promote inner disintegration in order to gain power and destroy the integrity and beauty of the individual. Evil refuses to allow anyone peace or pleasure in the goodness of God.

Ambivalence is the experience of feeling torn in two. When an individual has a divided sense of self, he or she feels shame and self-hatred for having trusted someone who used intimacy to gain access to do harm. For example, many sexual abusers use gifts to lure their victims and gain their trust with promises of more. Sexual abuse, then, usually involves touch or interactions that arouse the body and/or the soul of the victim. Evil uses the arousal of pleasure to make the victim feel responsible for what happened and inculcate the horrible fear that a darkness exists within that can never be named or expressed to any other person. "How could I have felt any pleasure when he touched me? What does this say about me?"

The ambivalence of a sexually abused individual involves feeling some element of sensual/sexual pleasure while simultaneously despising both what is felt and the person perpetrating the crime. Eventually the ambivalence spills into the soul and fuels both shame and contempt. As difficult as this is to comprehend regarding sexual crimes, it is even harder to comprehend about other forms of victimization. Recall my neighbor who stood on her front lawn, numbly looking at her house. Weeks later, in a brief conversation we had on her porch, we talked about ambivalence without ever using that term. I asked her how she felt about her home and in particular her bedroom. She looked startled.

Jane: "Fine — sort of."

Dan: "Sort of?"

Jane: "Yeah, I'm fine now. The insurance gave us what we needed to pay for the losses. Of course, some things can never be replaced."

Dan: "Of course. But when you go into your house and your bedroom, is it the same?"

Jane: "Well, I'm not afraid like I was at first. For the first week or so, before I went in I had to have my husband go in first and make sure it was safe."

Dan: "I don't blame you. I suspect I would have wanted the police to go through first."

Jane: "I know. At first I wanted Hal to carry a gun, but over time I realized that wasn't what I wanted. So I feel a lot better."

Dan: "I'm thrilled. So, without the feeling of fear, it feels normal and really the same as it did before?"

Jane: "Not really. I'm not afraid, but — I don't know what to call it — I still feel kind of sick and sad, like the room will never be mine again."

Dan: "Yeah. They stole the room's innocence and beauty. I suspect it's hard to put into words. You still love your home, but on the other hand, it's lost something that you fear can't be replaced?"

Jane: "When you said that, I felt something sick inside. I'm not sure I want to talk about this."

Evil works to destroy innocence and pleasure. Further, evil wants a victim to feel dirty, cheap, stupid, or foolish for desiring or receiving pleasure. I worked with a woman who had been violently raped over the course of many hours. She recalled with horrible shame the sense of comfort she felt when the perpetrator tenderly held a bandage to her head to staunch the blood from a wound he had caused. "I must be so sick," she said. "How could I allow myself even a moment of pleasure in his care after what he did to me?"

Evil alternates between feigned solicitousness and brutal mockery of the aroused hope and pleasure. To the degree that evil can trap the victim in ambivalence, it will silence him or her in the cold, barren isolation of shame and hatred. Evil hates love. It hates the pleasure of giving and receiving. It despises the pleasure that comes from the joy of blessing another and the delight in receiving an unexpected and undeserved gift. Evil hates the play of intimacy and the sensual arousal that grows when beauty allures the heart to the wistful hope of heaven. Accordingly, evil works with a vengeance to numb the heart to the pleasures of love while also increasing shame in a pleasure that seems dark and dangerous.

Evil stands over its labor, content that many have succumbed to its power — or at least to its damage — and relinquished faith, hope, and love. Indeed, many have been lost because of the horror of evil. But it need not be that way. The quintessential cry of hope is found in the remark Joseph made after he had endured the physical, sexual, and emotional crimes committed against him: "You meant it for evil, but God meant it for good."

How is it possible for us to say the same words with equal passion?

THE HOPE OF REDEMPTION FROM EVIL

Evil is not the final word. It is not capable of creating or defining reality; it can only pervert, distort, and destroy. But in one sense evil serves as the dark backdrop on the stage where God's redemption shines with even greater brilliance and pronounced drama. What evil uses to destroy, God uses to expose, excise, and then heal.

It is impossible to make sense of evil. Evil is unexplainable. It does not make sense; it is non-being and non-sense. It is, therefore, contrary to logic to attempt to fully comprehend any evil act or any evil person. The factors that shape an evil person's character might be the same dynamics that form the character of a saint. Even more, it is hideous to attempt to find the "meaning" of pain in a staggering event like the Holocaust or attempt to comfort a victim of rape by trying to discover what those involved were meant to learn.

Nonetheless, it is the brilliance and the glory of humanity that we cannot live without meaning, even when an explanation for the individual or global harm is impossible.

Viktor Frankl, a physician who suffered through the Holocaust in Auschwitz, said, "If there is meaning in life at all, then there must be a meaning in suffering. Suffering is an ineradicable part of life, even as fate and death. Without suffering and death human life cannot be complete."[7] Even if we cannot find an explanation in the act of evil itself, we cannot live without meaning. And meaning can be gained only when one embraces "the last of the human freedoms — to choose one's attitude in any given set of circumstances, to choose one's own way."[8] It is the possibility of faith, hope, and love that propels us forward to consider how evil can draw us to greater humanity.

FAITH AND DOUBT

Evil is thwarted to the degree that we directly and boldly face darkness in the world, in others, and most profoundly in ourselves. The description of evil's mode of operation excludes most people. The few I have encountered who do fit the description are qualitatively different in character and being than even some of the most grievous sinners I have met. Nonetheless, it is quite disturbing for me to realize that I am more similar to an evil person than I am to the most holy. When He was delivering the Beatitudes, Jesus said to morally upstanding and religious people, "If you, then, though you are evil, know how to give good gifts to your children, how much more will your Father in heaven give good gifts to those who ask him!" (Matt. 7:11).

Jesus was not primarily discussing the character of the people He was addressing. He was contrasting the holy God to mere man. In contrast to God, we are all evil. And yet, we know how to give gifts —

7. Viktor E. Frankl, *Man's Search for Meaning: An Introduction to Logotherapy* (New York: Simon & Schuster, 1959), p. 76.
8. Frankl, *Man's Search for Meaning*, p. 75.

tangible expressions of genuine care — to our children. Jesus' point was that if we, who are capable of evil, can give, then how much more does God give good and perfect gifts. But Jesus didn't hesitate to imply that our hearts are full of darkness and deep-seated self-absorption. We are not evil in the sense of being radically hardened, cold, and cruel, but we are inflexible in our self-righteousness, distant when we fear being hurt, and mean when we feel our rights have been violated. We not only have the capacity to do evil, but at any given moment move toward being evil.

> Regarding the question of whether many offenders are sociopathic or can be reached, I am convinced that many can be reached. One way to do it is to provide some opportunity that will encourage them to recognize the impact of what they have done. A second way is more complex; it involves their coming to terms with their own experience or their interpretation of it. Most offenders either have been victims or think that they have been victims, and that their actions are a response to that perceived victimization. And we also have to come to terms with that. It can be a very complex issue because some of their experiences are legitimate. Some are victims and some are not, but they have to put that into perspective and come to terms with what responsibility means in that situation.
>
> Dr. Howard Zehr

So the question becomes, How does an intrusion of evil through the harm that may befall us in a fallen world open our eyes and change our hearts?

Any significant harm compels us to ask, "Why, O Lord, do you stand far off? Why do you hide yourself in times of trouble?" (Ps. 10:1). Harm rips off the facade that life is predictable, manageable, and good. As long as suffering is kept at bay, we are not compelled to ask hard questions of God and ourselves. But when evil or the harm of living in a fallen world intrudes, we find that our doubts about God's goodness surface with intensity.

It is when our faith collapses that He invites us to wrestle with Him. Christians in this era are unfamiliar with the long and surprising tradition of "arguing with God." Rabbi Anson Laytner comments on how remarkable it is that God allows us to take Him to court to make a protest against Him.[9] Almost every prophet and figure of note in Scripture struggles with God. The most prominent struggle, of course, was the wrestling match that Jacob had with God, after which God changed Jacob's name to Israel, which means "he struggles with God" (Gen. 32). God named the ancestor of His people Israel. God loves those who fight with Him because it is only when we enter into battle with Him that our eyes and hearts can be opened and we can surrender to His purposes.

Elie Wiesel writes about this struggle in his book *The Town Beyond the Wall*. Wiesel presents Pedro, a man who suffers unspeakable affliction. At one point Pedro cries out, "I want to blaspheme and I can't quite manage it. I go up against Him, I shake my fist, I froth with rage, but it's still a way of telling Him that He's there, and He exists, that He's never the same twice, that denial itself is an offering to His grandeur. The shout becomes a prayer in spite of me."

Doubt opens the heart to the core demands we have made of God. When trust is broken, it compels us to ask the fundamental questions: What did I depend on Him for? What did I expect of Him in order to retain my trust in Him?

Facing our doubt leads either to hardness or to the most human, wrenching prayer in the New Testament: "I do believe; help me overcome my unbelief!" (Mark 9:24). It is when we are caught in the middle between faith and doubt that our hearts are most deeply called to surrender to His provision. Earlier I mentioned the woman I counseled whose daughter had been raped. She cried out, "Can't God do anything that matters, that really matters?" Eventually she had to ask whether her own salvation "mattered." She came to the point of facing the hard fact that her trust in God depended on the

---

9. Anson Laytner, *Arguing with God: A Jewish Tradition* (Northvale: Jason Aronson, 1990) p. xxi.

preservation of her upper-middle-class, predictable, pleasurable, profitable life.

God had failed her; she felt justified in hating Him. But eventually she relinquished her demand to understand why. Instead, she heard her own cries in the agony of Jesus. And in His surrender to His father, she found a path that did not deny her agony or confusion but reflected her conviction that in spite of evil, God is good.

HOPE AND DESPAIR

Faith falters when our predictions — even more, our presumptions — about God are shattered. Faith is the foundation that provides stability and balance; hope, which builds on the security of faith, is the lure that moves us into the uncertain, unknown future. Hope is faith in the future. When faith crumbles, hope dissolves. For many, the loss of hope begins a spiral into despair or depression. Depression involves a biological breakdown that adds great, seemingly inescapable weight to the existential experience of despair. Few who have faced evil and its consequences will escape an encounter with depression.

Despair and its biological brother, depression, seize the heart and send it into a hot, airless region that smothers hope. No one has described this better than William Styron. He writes, "It may be more accurate to say that despair, owing to some evil trick played upon the sick brain by the inhabiting psyche, comes to resemble the diabolical discomfort of being imprisoned in a fiercely overheated room. And because no breeze stirs this cauldron, because there is no escape from this smothering confinement, it is entirely natural that the victim begins to think ceaselessly of oblivion."[10]

Evil labors not only to take away hope but also a reason to live. Viktor Frankl noted that many prisoners with strong physical constitutions did not survive the concentration camps, while others who were frail but who found meaning and hope in a sunset or a small gesture of humanity often survived.

10. William Styron, *Darkness Visible: A Memoir of Madness* (New York: Vintage Books, 1990), p. 50.

Hope is essential to life. It appears that despair is hope's enemy, but despair is actually the dark, fetid soil where fruit best grows. Evil intends to use despair to destroy; God intends for despair to drive us to our only true hope.

Isaiah addresses the potential of growing hope through despair. He says,

> You were wearied by all your ways, but you would not say, "It is hopeless." You found renewal of your strength, and so you did not faint. Whom have you so dreaded and feared that you have been false to me, and have neither remembered me nor pondered this in your hearts? Is it not because I have long been silent that you do not fear me? (57:10-11).

God actually wishes for us to know despair, a despair that comes from hope's deflation. This despair is an exhaustion that brings us face to face with those whom we have most deeply dreaded and feared more than God. Each of us is, as Calvin noted, an "idol-making factory." We are attached to countless gods whom we delight in more than God. It is through God's mercy that when evil strikes, He uses the experience to destroy the idols that we unwittingly serve.

My friend whose brother was murdered eventually came to acknowledge that he trusted his brother more than God. When he was young, his father had abdicated any paternal interest in him or guidance of him, and his older brother had stepped in to mentor him. Their relationship was godly and enviable. My friend almost never made a decision without running it past his brother first. They were the antithesis of Cain and Abel, but the murder sent my friend wandering into the future as an alien, bearing the mark of loneliness. He killed hope rather than face the agony of remembering and pondering God in the midst of his loss.

My friend allowed his heart to be filled by anticipating "The Day of the Lord," when all evil will be repaid, all tears will be wiped away, and all who are divided will be reconciled (Isa. 25; Rev. 19). His despair lasted nearly a year, but now he bears not the mark of Cain but the stripes of the cross. What appears to be death itself can mysteriously open the door to resurrection. When one's biblical hope is restored, one not only regains a future; one lives with a loan from heaven itself to cover the debts and losses of this life.

LOVE AND DIVISION

Faith and hope are the bookends of love that enable it to stand in a turbulent world. One simply cannot love unless one remembers redemptive goodness in the past and anticipates redemption in the future. Any loss of faith or hope will put love in jeopardy.

Love is the primary weapon against evil. Evil is committed to devouring, to absorbing others in an attempt to fill an insatiable emptiness. It despises both light and the invitation to humbly receive forgiveness. Therefore, the nature of true love involves revelation and invitation. Godly love exposes darkness with a strength that reveals God's righteousness and a tender mercy that invites the heart to repent and receive forgiveness.[11]

Psalm 62:11-12 describes God's character: "One thing God has spoken, two things have I heard: that you, O God, are strong, and that you, O Lord, are loving. Surely you will reward each person according to what he has done." These two verses tell us that mercy does not eradicate justice, nor does justice preclude mercy and reconciliation. The mystery is great and the application to those who have done grievous harm difficult; nevertheless, love and forgiveness enter the breach between justice and mercy without denying either, and simultaneously reveal and invite.

Love that exposes evil's hardness, coldness, and cruelty must cut to the core of its refusal to feel, desire, and grieve, while exposing its hatred of humility. Love does not merely proffer forgiveness; it must expose the human bent to justify oneself and blame the victim while feeling little or no remorse. Oddly, love exposes first one's own pro-

---

11. Dan Allender and Tremper Longman III, *Bold Love: The Courageous Practice of Life's Ultimate Influence* (Colorado Springs: NavPress, 1992). In chapter 10 of this book, "Loving an Evil Person: Siege Warfare," the authors consider in greater detail the nature of love defined as offering a taste of both God's strength and mercy to an evil person.

clivity to evil and sin in order to clarify that no one has escaped the great divide between the heart and God (Matt. 5:21-28).

Even more strangely, love acknowleges that the sins of the other are not as great as one's own. Jesus cautioned us, "Do not judge, or you too will be judged. For in the same way you judge others, you will be judged, and with the measure you use, it will be measured to you. Why do you look at the speck of sawdust in your brother's eye and pay no attention to the plank in your own eye?" (Matt. 7:1-3). In God's economy, our ownership of sin always begins with an assault on our self-righteousness. You may have stolen from me; I am the thief. You may have raped me; I am the adulterer. You may have killed my son; I am the murderer. To write those words causes my hands to shake. To speak those words to one who has suffered such an assault makes me mute. To address that eventuality in my life causes me to turn white with furious indignation. How could God call me to bear the loss and then respond as He did on the cross?

When asked if we are to forgive our enemies, Elie Wiesel said, "No, 'You shall love your enemy' is not written. The Torah, the Bible, knows the limits of the human heart. You must not go too far. One does not forgive one's enemy, unless he asks one's forgiveness. We do not have to love our enemy. Why should we? He seeks only to kill us. To love him would be unnatural."[12]

It is unnatural; it is beyond human comprehension and capacity, unless we have been caught in the throes of grace. The unspeakable barbarity of certain crimes seems to compel a refusal of grace. How could one approach Eichmann, smirking in the dock, with the good news that he could have life with God if he confessed his sin and received forgiveness? How could the rapist who butchered your daughter be offered reconciliation with God and the victim and her family?

Love begins with faith. One must recall clearly the price of redemption: it is purchased with the blood of Christ. The Father turned against and away from His Son in order to put upon the perfect, unblemished Lamb the sins of the world. For a terrifying, in-

---

12. Philippe de Saint-Cheron and Elie Wiesel, *Evil and Exile* (Notre Dame: University of Notre Dame Press, 1990), p. 46.

comprehensible moment, the righteousness of God required severing the bond of perfect intimacy enjoyed in the Godhead for eternity. Mercy toward the sinner exacted a price of infinite value. For the sake of glory, God allowed the Trinity to be divided. Love willingly enters the terrifying breach between justice and forgiveness and offers the hope of dignity, respect, and new relationship with God.

To love as God loves is to offer righteous strength and merciful tenderness in an intricate tapestry of fierce beauty. Strength does not back away from the reality that travesty and harm must be accounted for, and that a price which is not inconsistent with mercy must be exacted. But justice meted out without sorrow and the constant offer for mercy replicates the evil originally perpetrated. Justice restores respect, but mercy offers healing for the heart as the breach is spanned by the only one who can reach that far into an evil heart.

It is our privilege to offer that which is inconceivable and impossible by human power alone: the offer of a bridge to span the divide between shame and worship, between darkness and light, between evil and goodness. To offer to walk with another by first acknowledging one's own need for grace today, even when one is a victim, assails the kingdom of darkness with a love fueled by remembered faith and visionary hope. It is the provision of life rather than assent to death. It is the Gospel. It is the death of evil.

CHAPTER FOUR

Responsibility toward Victims' Rights

CARL F. H. HENRY

A modern — and skewed — view of victimization can leave us somewhat bewildered. When it becomes the norm for criminals to point blaming fingers elsewhere and deny responsibility for their actions, we are left wondering just who the victim really is. Meanwhile, those who have suffered at the hands of another's aggression can be "imprisoned" by their own bitter thoughts and eroded faith. We can be too quick to judge the rights and wrongs of oppression. It is not until we take a hard look at the meaning of crime in the shadow of the cross that we comprehend a greater spiritual reality.

onfusion is common today over the term *victim*. By standard definition a victim is one who suffers loss, pain, or death through another person's assault or aggression. The term also applies to those who suffer from natural catastrophes, such as earthquakes or tornadoes, but at its heart, *victimization* has long implied distress — mental or emotional or physical — suffered because of an invader's perversity.

The confusion comes because many moderns choose a broader-based definition in which the "blame" becomes more nebulous. No longer is it fashionable to attribute base motivations and behaviors to the actual perpetrators of crimes. The beginning or the initiation of cruelty must lie elsewhere, with something or someone less personal.

This line of thinking not only allows anyone with a grievance to claim victimization, but also redefines the prevalent notion of a "victim" as actually having "victimizing" consequences. In other words, the traditional emphasis that society is aggrieved and wronged by crime is inverted. The offender is regarded as a victim of structural injustice and is not questioned for railing freely against a society that seems to stand in need of alteration and rectification.

And not only is society at fault. In like fashion, God himself is blamed for one's psychic dispositions and physical lusts: "God made me that way." Thus, in the disorderly condition of modern life, the offender appears to suffer the consequences of a society that has not contributed to his betterment and a God who has actually contributed to his delinquency.

Beneath this distortion of responsibility, the offender is regarded simply as the victim of prejudices that one segment of society imposes on another. We no longer acknowledge that a perpetrator of crime is alienated from God and from society. Instead, a skewed attitude emerges that depicts this rebellious human as a virtuous victim of corruptive influences, and the secular world's presuppositions about crime become humanity's norms.

This elevated view of victimizers is nurtured, unfortunately, when power is misused by those who are charged with the public enforcement of justice and are presumed to champion it. One thinks here of charges that federal authorities used excessive power in the

1994 confrontation of Waco cultists. Such an event nourishes the grievance that innocents may be too readily considered suspects and that suspects can be treated prematurely as criminals.

In addition, some schools of thought reinforce this view by considering the present structures of society inherently unjust. Revolution theology and liberation theology posit, for instance, that poverty is crime's root cause. A redistributionist view of material goods is, therefore, regarded as a potential solution to lowering the crime rate and to decriminalizing humans.[1]

BUT FOR THE GRACE OF GOD . . .

Thus, for most of us, two walls seem to stand divided by a great chasm. On the one side, we affirm that every individual is influenced by the world in which he or she lives. On the other, we stress that regardless of the influences of "nature or nurture," it remains the individual's ultimate right to choose how he or she behaves.

But here we must back away a bit for a clearer view. Does such a separation really exist? Or do the steep walls seem to converge as we look at them from higher ground?

While we criticize the victimizer for his or her destructive choices, we remain part of the society that helps shape individuals. Any failure to care about deplorable social conditions accommodates a state of affairs that our public participation might have altered constructively. We acknowledge this when we confess in our congregational prayers that we have sinned against God "by what we have done, and by what we have left undone." We haven't "loved our neighbors as ourselves," and this must encourage us to question whether or not each of us is somehow — however remotely — involved in the offender's misdeeds and hence also in the victim's plight.

Accepting this presupposition, but without diminishing the ap-

---

1. The collapse of Communist theory multiplied doubts about this particular reading of history, however. Modern society attests that the possession of material goods is no guarantee of noncriminal behavior.

propriate grievances of those who have been violated, we must take things a step further. Not even the victim is permitted to detach his or her own spirit from all personal responsibility within the totality of humanity. An evangelically orthodox view of life emphasizes — through its doctrine of sin — that the same potentiality for evil that lurks in the heart of the worst criminal could, but for the grace of God, overtake and implicate others of us also. But for divine providence, any one of us could be the guilty offender rather than the astonished sufferer.

Original sin engulfs all of us. We are not merely potential victims but actual perpetrators of sin that encroaches on our mental life, on our emotional desires, and on our volitional commitments.

THE ULTIMATE VICTIM

The ultimate victim of crime and violence is not the aggrieved person whose rights have been infringed upon, nor is it society in general whose laws have been scorned at the expense of social unity and public order.

In this "larger picture" view of victimization and the responsibility that we all must share, we see crime for what it is: an offense against God, the Creator of life. It is a repudiation of His honor, a violation of the dignity of the Sovereign of the universe, a rejection of transcendent divine law, a thumbing of one's nose at God's revealed will.

Our view of punishment of the criminal then takes on a new perspective as well. It serves an altogether different purpose from our usual goals: reformation of the offender and promotion of the safety of society. Laudable though these efforts are, the true purpose of punishment is to acknowledge God's Lordship, to vindicate His honor, to preserve His dignity, to recognize that law is not merely majority opinion but is grounded essentially in the self-revealing Creator, who discloses His Word and Will. It anticipates the final decisive judgment of evil and the universal vindication of right.

God stands as the unrequited victim of a criminalized society. Criminals are engaged not only in promoting the overthrow of social stability and of cosmic cohesion, but, even more fundamentally, in banishing from human relevance the King of glory.

Shall we then say that Christ Jesus — God self-revealed, incarnate, crucified — is the supreme Victim in a universe that was created flawless and stained by human revolt? Is it proper to speak of Him in such terms? Do not some theories of atonement insist He be properly designated solely as Victor, never Victim?

CHRIST: THE INNOCENT "CRIMINAL"

In the broadest sense, the antonym for *victim* is indeed *victor.* Here the notion of conqueror comes into its own and with it an emphasis on moral mastery. The profoundest context for use of the terms *victim* and *victor* is therefore ethical. One speaks of the virtuous victim, of the principled victor, of vanquisher and vindicator in a theological framework.

Yale postliberal theologian George Lindbeck notes that in the Church's development of Christian atonement doctrine, "the themes of Christ as victor and victim stand out."[2] Both themes are necessary facets of the doctrines of redemption and reconciliation. The Church accordingly has viewed Jesus on earth as victim although more especially as victor.

We see this reflected, on the lay level, in our hymns in which the various theories of Christ's death for sinners focus now on one aspect and then on another. In our great Easter anthem "Christ the Lord Is Risen Today," Christians sing of "the Paschal Victim," and in the Mennonite hymn "Alleluia, Alleluia," they affirm that "on the cross a Victim for the world's salvation bled." The words of the familiar "O Sacred Head, Now Wounded" emphasize both the injustice of Jesus' condemnation to crucifixion and the stunned gratitude of recipients of God's grace attained through the Redeemer's voluntary substitutionary atonement.

---

2. Lindbeck, in *The Nature of Confession: Evangelicals and Postliberals in Conversation,* ed. Timothy R. Phillips and Dennis L. Okholm (Downers Grove, Ill.: InterVarsity Press, 1996), p. 19.

The apparent clash of perspectives arises from the fact that Jesus was dealt with as a criminal although He was sinless. Yet anyone who finds in this terrible miscarriage of justice only an allusion to undeserved suffering misses the central point: that God came in the flesh to save penitent sinners and that Christ sacrificed Himself voluntarily in offering atonement for human sin.

One seriously distorts the scriptural understanding of Jesus' life and death by reducing its explanation to the sociocultural fortunes of justice and injustice. To interpret the slaying of Jesus only in the context of legal and political factors is to reject in principle the transcendent significance that Christianity assigns the death of the crucified Jesus.

If we focus on the truth that we are all sinners deserving of punishment and that Christ has taken that punishment, we then respond to the problem of crime in a different way. We expect punishment to be appropriate. We expect it to be meted out.

At the same time, we work to care for the offender, to bring him into relationship with Christ. If we take as our starting principle that the work of God is to create a faithful community, and if we recognize that a conversion isn't simply an instant but is a process, then we might begin to think of crime victims in a different way. We begin to realize that here is a process that we all have to go through in learning to forgive, in learning to come to terms with evil — not only the evil that we do but the evil that others do to us as well.

Dan Van Ness, forum participant

Although the procedures of criminal trials, including the producing of evidence and the testimony of witnesses, are among the relevant features of New Testament accounts, the terminology of crime and its victims carries meanings too shallow to comprehend the death of the Nazarene biblically. Nowhere is Jesus presented as merely a prey or quarry of criminal aggression. Indeed, never is He depicted as technically a victim at all. His life, although stripped from Him "by wicked hands" (Acts 2:23, KJV), was given voluntarily: "No man taketh it from me, but I lay it down of myself" (John 10:18, KJV).

The New Testament views the death of Jesus as the gift of God. His life is given, not taken. Jesus is presented as the righteous incarnation and manifestation of the supernatural Creator and the final judge of all rebellion and unrighteousness.

Here is no suffering victim of unpredictable violence. Jesus voluntarily yielded himself to the intention of Judas. Willingly He went to the cross to bear our penalty and guilt and to break sin's power. Christ became undeservedly a prisoner reserved for death so that we who deserve to die need not do so. Woefully outnumbered by sinful humanity, Jesus, who was the exemplar of personal and social righteousness, died alone in our stead. Now He calls us to stand for justice even if we must stand alone amid prevalent temptations to discount law and social order.

THE TRANSCENDING RESPONSE

As we answer Jesus' call to stand for justice, we must sharpen our focus. The need is not only found in the community at large but also in the solitary resident whose life has been shattered, whose privacy has been violated, and whose routines have been thrown into turmoil by an intruder's unexpected invasion. Many victims of crime never recover from the psychological scars. By clinging to the unforgettable pain, the victim never ceases to be a victim. The loss of a treasured heirloom, the violation of one's privacy, the assault upon and ravishment of the person — all can strip the individual of confident existence and daily security. The deepest hurt of all is the disregard of personal dignity and the gnawing fear that one may be vulnerable to its repetition at any moment.

When social critics contend that contemporary legal interest is more concerned with the rights of accused criminals than with the rights of crime victims, the resentment can worsen. Concerns that our judicial system favors the interests of criminals above those of victims are not completely unwarranted, just as concerns about inadequate police protection are not unfounded. Every random, frustrating report of a policeman who is involved in a drug scandal or a judge whose decisions are swayed by political considerations erodes faith in the ultimate triumph of the right.

The victim who comes to faith in God as an indirect consequence of criminal invasion and assault faces a Herculean test of spiritual growth and maturity. The temptation to hold on to resentment can bring him in principle to the same spiritual and moral vacuum as the transgressor. He can forget that his own sins have been redeemed by the blood of the Savior.

Rather than fall to the same level of disregard for human life and liberty exhibited by the criminal, the sufferer can rise above it. He must come to realize both that our Creator God has been aggrieved by criminal abuse in a way that we cannot fathom, and that He loves the offender not one bit less than the victim. To be sure, God hates the crime and rebukes the villain. That does not imply, however, that He loves the transgressor less than He loves the one whose pain He wants to heal. If the victim never comprehends this, then walls of hatred may well block his spiritual enlightenment.

The message that Prison Fellowship founder Charles Colson carries to death row is that God loves the murderer and stands as ready to forgive him or her as to forgive an impenitent victim. Offenders are exhorted not only to show compassion to victims while pursuing restitution, but also to avail themselves of the benefits of biblical atonement so that they may share in the free gospel of redemptive grace.

Many a victim lives a solitary existence for long years, unattended and even abandoned by the world, until a welcome intruder suddenly penetrates the walls of isolation, and a door swings open to a new circle of healing relationships. Finding friends, new friends, morally concerned and spiritually devout friends, can make a city or a village and a congregation within it a new environment with a new horizon. To find God is to imbue that circle of people with a transcendent quality. When the victim becomes actively engaged in reestablishing order through the transformation of the apprehended criminal and through the appropriation of forgiveness and reconciliation, the dynamism of a Christian society is dramatically at work.

Much as when Paul returned the now twice-born runaway slave Onesimus to Philemon and urged the wronged master to embrace his slave as a brother, so also the moral powers of the Christian religion are operative when the penitent villain comes to terms with transcendent ethical claims. Miracles happen when villain and victim are reconciled, and both reach out for a just society through the renewing forces of biblical Christianity.

To treat the offender as a human being does not require his or her exemption from penalty for dereliction, nor does it preclude adequate restitution. But it does require a courtroom exhibition of equality with respect to both the victim's and the defendant's rights. Moreover, to treat the villain as a spiritual being is to be aware that his or her moral regeneration will multiply his or her worth to society. But perhaps most important, victim and villain alike can, through the power of the cross and the sacrifice made there, discover an access to healing that transcends all human losses.

CHAPTER FIVE

Go and Do Likewise: The Church's Role in Caring for Crime Victims

HAROLD DEAN TRULEAR

The Church has long understood the importance of certain aspects of crime-related ministry: witnessing to those in prison, for instance. In a less-than-holistic approach, however, ministry to those who have suffered from victimization has been less visible. Yet the practical care and understanding that the Church can offer victims of crime is profoundly important. Following the example of the good Samaritan, we can open the doors of our hearts — and our churches — to help those who are suffering.

A practical biblical perspective on the Church's ministry to crime victims might best begin with the experience of a writer whose theological encyclicals and inspired wisdom have influenced the lives of literally millions of people.

We know him today as John, the beloved disciple whose strongly theological recountings make sharp, clear doctrinal points about the one called Christ. We also know that the beloved one, who taught that love was the true mark of those who would follow Christ, was himself called upon to show love. Indeed, compassion was among the first recorded acts of his ministry and models the call of the Church. It is in his reaching out to Mary, the mother of Jesus, as and after she witnesses the killing of her son, that we see a picture of holistic witness. The apostle of love does not learn love as a theological construct. He experiences the love of Christ firsthand in his witnessing of the crucifixion, and he heeds the call to manifest that love in the immediate context of the pain and anguish of Mary (John 19:26-27).

The initiation of John's ministry through a significant act of compassion teaches that theological rigor and human kindness are not options within the framework of Christian discipleship. Rather, they flow from the same heart of the Savior who launched the vocation of this disciple with the words "Behold thy mother."[1] Thus, we approach crime victimization in the same manner. We engage in acts of compassion motivated by compelling biblical theological witness. Both are integral parts of Christian ministry; they cannot be bifurcated into what Ronald J. Sider has called "one-sided Christianity," where one or the other holds primary authority as the "badge of Christian fidelity."[2]

There are numerous ways for the Church to express compassion in instances of victimization, and all are important. Two avenues of

1. The Reverend Stacey Townsend (now pastor of Second Antioch Baptist Church, Philadelphia) pointed out this initiation of John's ministry in his sermon on Good Friday, 1988, at Mount Zion Baptist Church of Germantown, Philadelphia, Pennsylvania.

2. In his book entitled *One-Sided Christianity: Uniting the Church to Heal a Lost and Broken World* (San Francisco: HarperCollins, 1993), Ronald J. Sider makes this point forcefully. See especially pages 81-118.

help stand out in particular as important ministries within the Church.

First, Jesus himself offered the concept that prison visitation is an integral part of Church witness (Matt. 25:31-46). To that end, many churches have begun ministries to and with prisoners. Organizations such as Prison Fellowship Ministries work with churches, chaplains, and inmates in fulfilling this crucial dimension of the Church's witness. Educational institutions such as the Center for Urban Theological Studies, Spring Arbor College, and New York Theological Seminary have committed themselves to the Christian and even ministerial education of women and men in prison.[3]

Second, the Church is called upon to be a prophetic presence in society, embodying the call to social righteousness and holiness characteristic of the Old Testament prophets. As such, it exists in creative tension with the criminal justice system, seeking to call that system to accountability before the God of the universe. As God has ordained every government official to be "the minister of God . . . for good" (Rom. 13:1-4, KJV), so the Church keeps prophetic watch to see that governments administer justice, and that people are treated with fairness and dignity at every intersection within the criminal justice system. Justice Fellowship and the Black Men in Prison project of the Interdenominational Theological Center in Atlanta join with the witness of denominations and local churches in keeping this witness alive.

In the push to minister to the incarcerated and the mandate to be prophets of justice in society, however, the Church has given proportionately less attention to ministry with crime victims. Countless women, men, and children have been scarred, injured, and suffered loss of property and even life with little attention coming from the household of faith. As we approach the biblical perspective on the Church's mission to these victims, we do not diminish the need for ongoing ministry to prisoners and the call for justice; no dimen-

3. Spring Arbor College in Spring Arbor, Michigan, and the Center for Urban Theological Studies in Philadelphia have offered courses in the prison and jail systems of their respective venues. New York Theological Seminary offers a Master of Professional Studies degree in Pastoral Care to inmates in the New York State correctional system.

sion of Kingdom building should be slighted. But we do need to develop ministries that aid victims of crime.

It is the tendency of the American church to sacrifice holistic ministry for ministries of specialization, which unintentionally further the divide between theology and ethics on the one hand and the various tasks of ministry on the other. Precisely because of this, I propose a "tripartite" context for ministry with crime victims. The three parts of this focus are these: (1) attitude — religious devotion, empathy, compassion, and listening; (2) action — intervention and networking; and (3) monitoring — seeing to the victims' aftercare and establishing methods of prevention.

Each of these components is reflected in the Parable of the Good Samaritan and its biblical context. In this parable, found in Luke 10, Jesus recounts actions that constitute the love of neighbor in the new Kingdom. Attitude — the compassionate expression of God's love — often stands as a biblical prerequisite to action. Jesus' parable shows us, however, that even an imperfect love for humanity can be deepened by participation in acts of compassion. This is implied when Jesus tells the lawyer with whom He has been speaking to "do likewise," even though the lawyer's attitude is clearly not fully formed in love at this point.

So we acknowledge both that ministry to crime victims should flow from a loving, compassionate heart — the love of God shed abroad in our hearts by the Holy Spirit (Rom. 5:5) — and that people should not use lack of compassion as an excuse to exempt themselves from getting started. This is why the Church examines itself in preparation for ministry: not to get the perfect attitude but to plant the seeds of love that will grow into the fruit of the Spirit (Gal. 5:22). Only then will ministry develop into all God has called it to be.

The other two parts of this tripartite approach to helping crime victims should be understood less as sequential and more as points of entry into ministry. In other words, acting is not a prerequisite to monitoring. In a holistic approach, the first involvement of a church might involve prevention, such as a neighborhood watch or a safe corridors program.[4] A church might begin by speaking out on

4. Many African-American churches have found that these types of programs

the need for the care of crime victims, "breaking the silence" concerning the seemingly hidden reality of the countless neighbors who are primary victims (those who suffered the crime) or secondary victims (those close to the victims who were directly affected by the crime). Both of these, as we will see, are functions of monitoring. Once attitude is in operation, a church's discernment process helps determine the point of entry into the dialectic between acting and monitoring, and the various phases involved. A holistic approach recognizes the importance of all phases in the care of persons victimized by crime.

Let's return to the Parable of the Good Samaritan to study all three parts in action. This is a story with plain, commonsense applicability to the Church's ministry to crime victims; it carries the same weight of holistic witness and resists the tendency to freight with importance any work of ministry outside the context of Kingdom building.

ATTITUDE: HOW WE SEE "OUR NEIGHBOR"

Luke sets the story of Jesus' encounter with the lawyer "wishing to justify himself" squarely between two events that point to the ultimate significance of Kingdom ministry. The Gospel writer seeks to provide a context of religious devotion for the encounter between Jesus and the lawyer so that the command to "go and do" is seen properly as a dimension of eternal life and not as an act in and of itself.

---

combine both a visible concern for the potential victims of crime and an opportunity for the significant involvement of men in the ministry of the church. Churches such as Bethel A.M.E. in Baltimore, Second Baptist Church of Perth Amboy, N.J., and Mount Sinai Christian Church of Staten Island, as well as the African-American Interdenominational Ministers of Philadelphia, have launched successful "security ministries" designed not only to protect life and property at church functions and neighborhood events (like the passageways to public schools in the inner city), but also to let vulnerable populations in those neighborhoods know that there is a caring presence in the community of the people of God. (This is discussed later.) Interdenominational Theological Center ethicist Riggins Earl deems this part of "re-neighboring the hood."

The Parable of the Good Samaritan immediately follows Jesus' conversation with disciples returning from the mission field (and His attendant prayer to God on their behalf) and immediately precedes the story of Jesus in the home of Mary and Martha. The parable, an admonition to works, follows an episode in which salvation is given primacy over ministry and precedes an event in which time with Jesus supersedes the claims of ministerial activities.

In the story before the parable, Jesus sends His disciples out on a mission as laborers into "the harvest" (Luke 10:1-24, KJV). When the disciples return "with joy" that demons "are subject unto us through thy name," Jesus responds that their joy should reside in their names being "written in heaven." He then offers prayer to the Father with joy of His own, grateful for the disciples' participation in God's work of salvation. It is the revelation of the messianic Kingdom that Christ has in view, and this offers theological introduction to the Parable of the Good Samaritan.

The story after the parable shows Martha anxious and "troubled about many things" (Luke 10:38-42, KJV). The ministry of serving has her complaining of lack of help, comparing her work to that of others, and commanding that Jesus re-orchestrate the division of labor in the fellowship. These are all temptations that plague the Christian activist whose focus on the good deeds of ministry eclipses the importance of strengthening our relationship with Christ through marked times of devotion and study. The placement of the story here suggests that as the Church in its Samaritan outreach heeds the call to "Go and do likewise," it must never forget to spend time at the feet of Jesus, the "good part, which shall not be taken away from her."

Mother Teresa enlightened our understanding of the relationship between discipleship and ministry. When asked about how God had called her to work among the poor, she replied that God had not called her to work among the poor. He called her to follow him and led her there.

God So Loves the City: Seeking a Theology for Urban Mission

The parable, thus contextualized, gains value not from an overly allegorized interpretation but from its connection to the Kingdom-building enterprise. The compassion revealed in the parable points to the revelation of the Kingdom and the acts associated with it. Here is a new definition of *neighbor* that stretches beyond the immediacy of family, friend, and tribe; and the compassion for the victim demonstrates this new "re-neighboring" effort. In his commentary notes on the passage, Walter Liefeld argues that the lawyer "needed to learn that God does not bestow the life of the kingdom on those who reject the command to love."[5] The acts of compassion by the Samaritan clearly demonstrate the principles of the Kingdom — the "things" that Jesus speaks of in His prayer for His returning disciples.

The lawyer, an expert in religious dogma, asks Jesus a theological question: "What must I do to inherit eternal life?" (Luke 10:25, NIV). Jesus turns the question back to him, calling on the lawyer's considerable theological skills to interpret the law on the question. The lawyer's reply demonstrates his theological acumen: "You shall love the Lord your God with all your heart, and with all your soul, and with all your strength, and with all your mind; and your neighbor as yourself" (Luke 10:27, NIV).

The central focus of his theology, however, is self-justification; he seeks doctrinal support for his current lifestyle. "Who is my neighbor?" (Luke 10:29, NIV) he asks in his quest for a biblically based sanctuary for his altar of self-interest. The parable, then, answers his question by opening his eyes to the vast dimensions of the Kingdom (remember, the "hero" is from the hated Samaritan ethnic group) and the lawyer's responsibility within the new definition of the neighborhood.

Herein lies the starting point for the Church's ministry with crime victims: *an honest conversation with God that raises the question of why, with our theology and current lifestyle, ministry to crime victims has received such a low profile.* The local church that seeks to become involved in ministry to crime victims begins its outreach with honest prayer and soul-searching in order to discern the true nature of its

---

5. *The Expositor's Bible Commentary,* vol. 8, ed. Frank E. Gaebelein (Grand Rapids: Zondervan, 1984), p. 944.

mission. This is not just another program. Rather, the encounter with Jesus in prayer, study, and reflection yields a response to his command to "Go and do likewise" (Luke 10:37, NIV). Otherwise, we participate in what Jacques Ellul calls the "false presence of the kingdom," where Christians of goodwill participate in worthy, even biblically based causes because of fad or fashion rather than a clear directive from God.[6]

Ellul bemoans churches that get involved in the "issue of the day" as it becomes known through the media. In such cases, the primary stimulus for mission becomes the media rather than the prayerful discernment of the church and its leadership. When the media initiate mission, the work often ends when the cause is no longer front-page news. If the church takes initiative based on its desire to participate in the new Kingdom, however, the ministry lasts, whether the issue be hunger, land mines, lepers, AIDS, or crime victims.

So the Church confesses its self-interest and wonders how it ever came about. Is it because we have pressed for a gospel of self/community justification? Is it because the burning theological question for us has been how we might get God to sanction our current commitments to be good, moral, ethical people? The lawyer's question supposes that love is a theologically acceptable — even required — notion. The real question raised concerns the sphere of love's operation. The Church would never quarrel with love as a biblical proposition. The contested ground lies in the general topography marked "us" and "them." Where is the line drawn between those deserving of help and those not so? To whom have our ministries of compassion been mandated?

Both the crime victim and the Samaritan provide answers to this question. Neither one would be a neighbor in the traditional sense of the term. The victim is unclean — hence the ceremonial avoidance of the priest. The Samaritan is also unclean — hence the surprise that he is the one who shows neighborly love. The Church, therefore, after its process of discernment, moves beyond traditional defi-

---

6. Jacques Ellul makes this point clearly in *The False Presence of the Kingdom*. Martin Luther King also made reference to America's preoccupation with issues generated by the media that lasted a sum total of "ten days."

nitions of clean and unclean to offer aid and assistance. This is crucial because generally we strive to avoid acknowledging that crime victims are "like us" — suburban, middle-class "good folks" who are unfortunate victims of criminal violence and activity. But crime victims are these — and more. Indeed, African-American and Latino men and women are far more likely to be victims of violent crime than are their white counterparts.[7]

Such a move across the boundaries between "us" and "them" calls for empathy. *The Westminster Dictionary of Christian Ethics* defines *empathy* as the ability to put "oneself in the place of the other, understanding and sharing the other's experience, and seeing the world as he or she sees it."[8] It is a process of intimate identification with the situation of the other. God himself sets the precedent for empathic engagement with those who suffer victimization when He tells Moses that He has heard the cry of the Hebrew slaves and knows their suffering (Exod. 3:7). God's assertion that He "knows" their suffering is the ultimate declaration of empathy. He feels what they feel, and it becomes an impetus for His movement to action on behalf of the Israelites.[9]

In her book entitled *Empowerment Ethics for a Liberated People*, Church of God pastor and Howard University ethicist Cheryl J. Sanders calls *empathy* that which keeps the privileged and comfortable from losing sight of the plight of the broken and hurting. It "tempers the tendency of empowered persons to divest themselves of concern for less empowered others under conditions of oppression."[10] Sanders is not solely concerned about the larger context of victimization; she also focuses on the way in which empathy en-

---

7. See, among other references, K. Tarcliff, P. M. Marzuk, A. C. Leon, C. S. Hirsch, M. Stajic, C. Portera, and N. Hartwell, "Homicide in New York City: Cocaine Use: Firearms," *Journal of the American Medical Association* 272 (1994): 43-46.

8. *The Westminster Dictionary of Christian Ethics*, ed. James Childress and John Macquarrie (Philadelphia: Westminster, 1986), pp. 190-91.

9. The Hebrew concept of "knowing" implies a very real acquaintance with and an intimate knowledge of the situation. Indeed, the same Hebrew word is used to describe the sex act.

10. Cheryl J. Sanders, *Empowerment Ethics for a Liberated People* (Philadelphia: Fortress, 1995), p. 118.

gages persons in ministries of compassion, citing the work of black churches in history and their ministries of charity.[11] She cites the rooting of empathy in "the moral reciprocity in the Golden Rule, Jesus' admonition to treat others as you would like to be treated if you, in a way of speaking, had to trade places with them."[12]

Empathy involves listening. In ministry to crime victims, the church must pay attention to the cries, the hurt, and the pain of the victim. In binding up the wounds of the victim he finds along the road, the good Samaritan observes the hurt and bleeding places. When he carries the victim to the inn, he takes into account the need for personal sacrifice, economic investment, and long-term care. This is the Church in a listening posture, a process of discernment that identifies with the suffering of victims but begins with hearing their stories and coming to some understanding of their situations.

When the text notes that the good Samaritan "took pity" on the wounded man, it points to his ability to empathize. The phrase "took pity" *(esplanchnisthe)* indicates a deep level of sympathy: one claims to feel inwardly the suffering of another. This is not always easy in a culture that has lost some of its capacity to mourn and has misdirected what capacities remain.[13] Yet the Church must recapture a serious "mourners" posture that recognizes the true nature of victimization and the forms of suffering it brings. Indeed, the Church is called upon to stimulate a response of mourning in others — much like the "professional weeping women" of Israel. It was the job of these women to attend funerals and cry aloud in order to symbolize the community's grief and help those who had suffered loss to get in touch with their own grief and pain (Jer. 9:17-20). In their ministry it was just as important for them to stir up empathy among the congregation as it was to provide consolation to the bereaved.

---

11. Sanders, *Empowerment Ethics for a Liberated People,* pp. 43-60.

12. Sanders, *Empowerment Ethics for a Liberated People,* p. 118.

13. See Harold Dean Trulear, "Meaningful Death and the Possibility of New Life," *Transformation* 12, no. 1 (January/March 1995): 17-22.

ACTION: LIVING OUR ATTITUDES

The presence of such empathic mourning provides the context for the Samaritan's action, which takes two basic forms. He begins, first, with a work of *intervention,* interrupting the trajectory of one left to die with acts of compassion intended to help him recover and live. He pours healing salve on the wounds and binds them up. Here he uses resources at his disposal to care for an immediate need.

Then, second, in taking the victim to the local inn, the good Samaritan models a *networking* of resources between those immediately at his disposal (the oil and wine that he used as salve, and the strips of cloth — presumably torn from his own garments — that he used as bandages) and those outside of his personal holdings.

The Church likewise performs both functions as it identifies the immediate need and the resources for care. A number of training programs offer help in identifying the needs of crime victims; churches can both access and help resource them. National organizations for crime victims, such as the National Organization for Victim Assistance (NOVA) and Neighbors Who Care; local associations, such as the Dallas-based Mothers Against Teen Violence; and federal, state, and municipal assistance agencies for crime victims all provide churches with training. They also help identify resources available to persons directly and indirectly affected by crime.

Neighbors Who Care has identified nine areas of potential problems for crime victims in which the church can both discern needs and identify resources for help.[14]

First, there are physical problems. These include both "obvious physical injuries" as well as less apparent problems such as "nightmares; changes in sleep patterns; extreme fatigue; impotence; extreme weight changes and chemical dependency . . . an exaggerated startle response"; and "emotional stress."

Second, there is the potential for problems in the mental area — problems ranging from trouble concentrating to flashbacks, anxi-

14. "Crime Victimization Overview" (n.d.), produced by Neighbors Who Care, P.O. Box 16079, Washington, D.C. 20041-0500. Used by permission.

ety, and memory loss. In addition, victims often feel the need to make sense of what has happened to them and raise questions about safety, prejudice, and crime in society.

In the spiritual realm, a third area of concern, victims can begin to re-evaluate their beliefs, positively or negatively, sometimes suffering a "loss of faith because of their inability to cope with pious platitudes sometimes offered by clergy and church members." Some ask, "Why did God let this happen to me?" Others may wonder what they "did" to cause such a tragedy and suffer feelings of guilt. Joyce Strickland, the founder of Mothers Against Teen Violence, states that such is often the case with mothers (and other family members) of murdered youth. Some feel guilty because they think they didn't provide the youth with enough protection; others feel guilty because they think they didn't show enough love when the youth was alive.[15]

A fourth, closely related area is emotional trauma. The victim has suffered the violation of "the sanctity and security of . . . life" and might experience a possible attendant "loss in [his/her] sense of purpose for life." This emotional toll, which may be difficult to detect, includes "feelings of loneliness, depression, sadness, fear, self-pity, and helplessness," and can lead to the desire to escape and withdraw or to exact revenge.

Fifth, crime victims experience "disruption of interpersonal relationships," including the potential for "reduced parenting skills, divorce, isolation from family networks, increased risk of family violence, and chemical dependency" and its attendant influence on friendships. "Often, a victim is pressured by friends and family to 'get on with your life,' and is rejected when he or she cannot comply with others' expectations." Also, family members can become "overprotective" and not allow victims to heal, grow, and become restored.

Sixth, crime victims suffer financially. There are expenses for

---

15. From an interview with Joyce Strickland in September 1997 in Dallas, Texas. Indeed, Ms. Strickland was moved to found Mothers Against Teen Violence, which works in the areas of both prevention and intervention, after her own son, while home from college, was murdered in a random robbery in 1993.

"medical treatment and hospitals, funerals, psychological counseling, cooperation with the investigation, and prosecuting costs." In burglaries and robberies, of course, there is the loss of property. In addition, there can be "hidden expenses due to changes in lifestyle . . . such as [a] college scholarship given up because of an inability to concentrate on studies; moving expenses to get away from painful memories of the crime; and a home or car repossessed because of non-payment."

Seventh, employment-related problems can include alterations in work habits ranging from an inability to function in the workplace to forms of "workaholism" that affect social and familial life.

Eighth, media involvement can bring unwanted publicity or invasion of privacy. On the other hand, some victims are angered by "the media's lack of concern for their story."

Finally, there is the strain associated with legal and judicial processes, ranging from the victim's unfamiliarity with the criminal justice processes to the pain of facing the defendant in the courtroom. In cases where the crime is not solved, various forms of resentment can hold sway.

In these nine areas the Church is called upon to exercise care and sensitivity in the processes of intervention and networking. In some cases a church will possess the resources to begin the healing process, just as the good Samaritan could go into his travel bag for oil and wine. Here a church can benefit from training programs that help members understand the oil and wine at their disposal, ways of pouring out the "salve" of human kindness and godly compassion. In developing a core of volunteers to minister to crime victims, the Church makes use of its standing resource, people anointed by the Holy Spirit to do the works of the Paraclete. Indeed, the term *paraclete* can be translated as "one called alongside to help," and we, having been baptized into Christ's body, are called to a ministry of advocacy.[16]

16. When Jesus teaches that we will do "greater works" because He "goes to the Father," He shows the greater works to be those of the Spirit. The Spirit is "another comforter" — another paraclete — and as such, Jesus demonstrates that His ministry has been one of the paraclete/advocate. Because we are baptized into His Body to do His works, we are called to ministries of advocacy as well.

God gives us a model to follow in His compassionate response to Elijah when the prophet, a victim of harassment, runs for his life when threatened by Queen Jezebel.

Elijah speaks of his fear and weariness before God: "It is enough; now, O Lord, take away my life; for I am not better than my fathers" (1 Kings 19:4, KJV). God does not scold Elijah for his fear. Rather, He asks him, "Why are you here?" An omniscient God knows why His prophet has came to Mount Horeb: his powerful adversary has threatened him with death. But God recognizes Elijah's need to talk through his pain and the threat that stalks him.

God listens to Elijah so that Elijah might speak what is in his heart. Just so the Church must listen to the stories of crime victims, that we might hear what is in their hearts and be a comforting presence to them. In an age where the average listener is quiet just long enough to figure out an "answer" to offer, the real work of listening builds trust and confidence that the one telling the story can know that she or he is cared for. Also, listening to the specifics of the complaint demonstrates that God is strong and open enough to care about the true nature of the situation.

Elijah reveals his feelings, and God affirms his feelings by offering not correction ("Elijah, don't feel that way"; "Get on with your life"; "Go back to prophesying") but real comfort ("Arise and eat"), real presence (in the still small voice), and real company (in the 7,000 who had not bowed their knees to Baal and in the intimate friendship of Elisha). The Church can provide listening ears, comforting words, a supportive presence, and intimate company in the hours of distress for victims of crime.

This ministry of coming alongside, of offering comforting presence, is a particularly valuable opportunity for churches. The National Organization of Black Law Enforcement notes, for instance, the immediate importance of staying with a victim until the police arrive.[17] This is a time for an assuring presence, representing the sure presence of the Father, who sits with us in times of intense pain and suffering. Neighbors Who Care notes that victims do not need advice or well-intended pronouncements after a crime, especially comments that "could shut down communication, such as 'I know just how you feel' . . . 'I can't believe you feel that way' . . . 'You should count your blessings' . . . 'Why did you/didn't you' . . . 'Everything will be all right' . . . and 'It must be God's will.'"[18] Offering a caring presence does not mean trying to give advice or "fix" the situation.

Churches can also become resource centers for members and the general community as they arm themselves with information on referral institutions that deal with crime victimization. Taking victims "to the inn" consists of enabling persons to make contact with local, state, and federal government departments and agencies that work with crime victims. Many private agencies are dedicated to victims' services; a networking church will find out which ones operate in its community. Neighborhood associations, such as the West Mount Airy Neighbors of Philadelphia, often have restitution funds for crime victims. There are also some organizations and associations that operate missions of a greater scope but that give some attention to crime victims' concerns. Churches can contact community clubs and organizations to see what programs and resources are available.

Those called alongside to help can also offer hands-on assistance, such as financial provision to offset losses; property repair and cleanup after burglaries; help in developing new security measures; temporary provision of meals, clothing, and shelter; and technical assistance in filling out forms and navigating the variety of encounters within the legal system. Having a basic knowledge of the laws in one's community concerning victim restitution is an indispensable tool for networking. This is particularly important for crime victims from poor and ethnic-minority communities, who constitute a disproportionately high percentage of the total number

17. See their "Minority Community Victim Assistance: A Handbook" (1989).
18. "Surviving Crime" (Neighbors Who Care, 1997).

of crime victims. A church's presence can be a crucial mediating force in the minority victim's engagement with a law enforcement community, which, through the warp and woof of American cultural history, has often come to be distrusted by marginalized communities.[19]

A well-trained church ministry to crime victims will explore all of the options with a victim to ensure that maximum restitution occurs. The church takes the victim to the inn and says, "Take care of him; and whatsoever thou spendest more, when I come again, I will repay thee" (Luke 10:35, KJV).

MONITORING: GOING THE DISTANCE

This brings us to the third and final part — monitoring. In going to the inn, the good Samaritan recognizes that the victim has long-term needs as well as short-term needs, and finds the proper agency to care for the victim for an extended period of time.

Ongoing Support

Churches can help victims find counseling programs and support groups whose resources can be of benefit over the longer haul. Churches can also form support groups in their own communities that encourage victims to share their stories and continue to heal in the aftermath of trauma. When John took Mary, the mother of Jesus, to his own home (John 19:27), he made available to her a space of refuge and comfort where she could grieve, talk, and heal.

---

19. See the especially helpful "Minority Victim Assistance Handbook," produced by the National Organization of Black Law Enforcement. In a section discussing barriers to crime-victim assistance, they note that many "minorities do not trust the 'system'" and that victims' assistance programs can be helpful bridges between wary victims and the necessary authorities in a case. In addition, in their discussion of "things you can do without money," they stress the importance of community organizations, including churches, inviting police officers and service providers to attend local gatherings to discuss available services.

Many support groups have specific qualifications for group participation. The support groups formed by Mothers Against Teen Violence, for instance, provide a context of forgiveness for family members who have lost a loved one to street violence. As mentioned earlier, family members, especially mothers, often suffer from guilt over the loss of a child. They wish that they had "done more" to protect their loved one, or they grieve that the last conversation with their teen was an argument. Sometimes parents question whether they did all that they could to raise the child correctly. According to Joyce Strickland, family members need to forgive themselves for things said and done in past relationships with loved ones so that they can avoid being emotionally paralyzed by guilt.[20] Indeed, persons in such a state of guilt need to find the resources to accept the forgiveness that God offers and to believe that it really applies to them. Support groups provide a place for that process to take place.

Another specific venue for long-term care is the residential facility for persons with handicaps. Individuals involved in ministries to these people have been trained to deal with a variety of needs. Recently, however, a new group has begun growing exponentially in these facilities, one for whom their training has provided no help. Young African-American and Latino males represent a growing percentage of the disabled, largely due to street violence.[21] The needs of young adults are complex: the frustrations of being forced to live with permanent motor or mental disabilities are compounded by the anger produced on the streets of the inner cities. One residential-facility chaplain has called for local churches that have some experience with inner-city youth and young adults to become involved in the lives of the young men in his facility.[22] He is not alone in voicing a need for the Church's help.

There are a number of successful youth programs, such as the Ten Point Coalition in Boston. There a partnership of churches,

20. Interview with Joyce Strickland in September 1997 in Dallas, Texas.

21. See Harold Dean Trulear, "To Make a Wounded Wholeness," in *Human Disability and the Service of God,* ed. Nancy Eiseland and Donald Saliers (Nashville: Abingdon, 1998).

22. Interview with the Reverend Scott Simmons at Inglis House in July 1996 in Philadelphia, Pennsylvania.

government, and law enforcement officials has helped effect a pronounced decline in the number of young victims of crime: in the last three years there has been only one juvenile homicide. Still, not enough groups are involved in long-term victim care, a crucial element in the monitoring process.

Part of the reason may be that churches are reluctant to consider these persons as victims, because a number of them have become disabled while engaged in some counterproductive, criminal, and/or evil activity. Yet, the love of Christ must be ministered to people who are complicit in their victimization.

Prior to his intervention, the good Samaritan seeks no information on the circumstances leading to his act of compassion. Indeed, Christ's intervention of grace in our lives comes to us while we are undeserving: "While we were yet sinners, Christ died for us" (Rom. 5:8, KJV). Churches called to minister in high-crime neighborhoods will need to deal with the challenge to minister to crime victims whose lifestyles have contributed to their victimization. Since all have sinned and fallen short of God's glory, and since His love extends to the whole world, the Church will need to offer ministries of grace and compassion to these victims as well.

Prevention

Monitoring also involves forms of prevention, and speaking is one of them. Speaking out on the issue of crime, crime victimization, and crime prevention within the Church context breaks the silence and lets crime victims know that they have a friend in the Body of Christ. Marie Marshall Fortune, in her landmark textbook entitled *Sexual Violence,* notes that many survivors of child abuse and many of those currently suffering spousal abuse are hidden from the eyes of the Church because of the Church's failure to speak about this problem.[23]

Speaking, preaching, and teaching builds an awareness that the

23. Marie Marshall Fortune, *Sexual Violence: The Unmentionable Sin* (New York: Pilgrim Press, 1983).

problem does exist, even within the Church, and encourages survivors and current victims to come to a church or a pastor to seek help. A church with a good networking system can refer victims to the proper agencies for help. Liaisons with local police departments' divisions on sex crimes and domestic disputes are becoming common in Brooklyn churches as law enforcement officials and congregations launch a joint venture in their mission to end domestic violence. As a pastor, I kept a licensed pastoral-counseling center on retainer with the church for just such situations.

A further contribution to the cause of prevention is the neighborhood watch program. This form of prevention helps those already victimized to know that someone cares for them and their neighborhood. It also ministers to those gripped by fear in their neighborhoods by creating safe streets and by giving persons a sense of security in their homes and surrounding areas. Churches in cities across the country are developing security ministries that offer safety for church and community members, and provide unique ministry opportunities church members.

A NEW OPPORTUNITY

When Jesus tells the lawyer to "Go and do likewise," He offers a mandate to engage in acts of compassion that demonstrate the presence of a new Kingdom. The growing attention paid to crime victims over the past twenty years provides a similar "new opportunity" for churches to open their doors so that victims may enter and volunteers may be dispatched. Compassion, listening, intervening, networking, aftercare, prevention — all are mobilized by the desire to fulfill the mandates of the new Kingdom that God has ushered in through Jesus Christ. Now the Word comes to us today: "Go and do likewise."

CHAPTER SIX

Victimization and Healing: The Biblical View

ELIZABETH ACHTEMEIER

What is our response toward those who have suffered from victimization? How do we address their needs? And what about our feelings toward the offenders? Do we demand recompense, or does this negate our call to love our enemies? Answers can be found in God's plan for His created humanity and relate to the goal of His working in our world. We therefore turn to the Scriptures for our guidance.

It is possible to view the victims of crime from a secular point of view and to ask for aid for them out of purely humanitarian, retributive motives. The Scriptures tell us, however, that all of life is to be understood in relation to God and that apart from that relationship, it cannot properly be understood. First, therefore, I want to put the discussion of this topic in the context of the purposes of God and to make some general remarks by way of introduction.

What is the goal of God's working in our world? According to the testimonies that we find in the Scriptures, God is at work to establish a community of faith, a community of trust in and obedience to His lordship.

When God created the world, He made it very good. But human sin corrupted every aspect of God's creation. Daily, we human beings attempt to shake off our creaturely dependence on our Creator and to be our own gods, creating our own future and our own right and wrong. The result is that our relation with God, with the natural world, and with every human being has been distorted — male with female, sibling with sibling, society with society, nation with nation. All possibilities for individual and corporate community have been shattered, and we now live on a planet where we simply cannot get along with one another.

The result is that God, in the history of salvation that is recorded for us in the Bible, sets out to make a new community, living in a land flowing with milk and honey, that knows how to live in righteousness and justice under His guiding lordship. He chooses for His special community the people of ancient Israel. And it is God's intention to draw all peoples and nations into that chosen community, in order to establish over all the earth a new order known as the Kingdom of God.

When Israel rebels and fails to be the instrument for God's recreation of a good world, God sends His only begotten Son to be the vinestock of a new community, growing out of the root of Israel — a community called the Christian Church that will be the forerunner and firstfruit of a universal people who live in faithfulness to God. Once again, God's desire is to create "one great fellowship of love" — love for Him and love for neighbor — "throughout the whole wide earth." God is at work in our world, as He always has been, to make a new people, and we Christians, who call ourselves after the name of our Lord Christ, are members of that people.

In the context of that worldview, then, how are we Christians, as members of God's people, to regard victims of crime? Certainly we are to give aid and comfort and healing to all such victims, as Neighbors Who Care has pointed out to us by focusing on the story of the Good Samaritan in the New Testament. But there is much more to be said from the standpoint of the Scriptures.

By way of parentheses, let it first be said that we are concerned with true victims. Victimhood has become a fad in our society, in which individuals claim they have been victims of one or another of society's structures in order to shed their own responsibility for what they are or have done. They then ask for special privileges to make up for their persecution. But this chapter is not dealing with such irresponsible claims. Rather, we are concerned with true victims, who have been subject to some sort of crime.

The viewpoint of the Scriptures, then, is that we are to exhibit love and care for such victims, because God has shown love and care for us. For example, love and concern for the victims of poverty are to be shown to the poor, the stranger, the fatherless, the widow, according to Deuteronomy, because God came to our aid when we were helpless. "Remember that you were a slave in Egypt and the Lord your God redeemed you from there," reads the text (Deut. 24:18, 22). "We love, because He first loved us." (1 John 4:19).[1] When we were helpless victims of slavery to sin and death, God in Christ loved us and redeemed us. And so as members of God's new community, we are to extend the same mercy and aid to others who are helpless.

Always we need to realize, too, that the goal of aid to the victim of crime is not simply to help the individual but also to restore the health of the community as a whole, including the criminal himself. Contrary to the individualism of our time, the Scriptures never understand individuals to be separate from their communities. To be sure, the value and responsibility of the individual are always held in

---

1. Scripture references in this chapter are taken from the Revised Standard Version of the Bible, 1946, 1952.

honor: The Ten Commandments, for example, are addressed to individuals: "Thou shalt..." addresses you personally. But individuals are never totally separated from their communities, and six of those commands from the Decalogue to individuals have to do with communal relations.

As a result, when a crime was committed in Israel, God's punishment for that crime was believed to return not just on the individual criminal but on his community as a whole. For this reason, the Priestly Writers were anxious that atonement be made for every crime. And a wrong perpetrated against an individual festered and infected the whole body politic until the victim was vindicated and made whole again. That is a profound thought. Crimes within our communities are not isolated incidents that can be ignored if they don't occur in our suburb. Rather, crime lames not just its victim and its perpetrator but the community as a whole. "If one member suffers, all suffer together," writes Paul (1 Cor. 12:26). And the goal is the restoration of the whole community.

Finally, by way of introduction, the community of faith understands a healthy community not as one in which just any human order prevails. The prophet Zechariah points out that a totally godless community may have achieved a peace and order that is, in Calvin's words, "an accursed happiness" (Zech. 1:11). A healthy community in biblical terms is one in which God's *mispat*, God's order, prevails. Christians are not to live by the ways of the sinful society around them (cf. Lev. 18:1-4). They are not to be conformed to this world (Rom. 12:2). Rather, Christian communities take as their measure of good the commandments and will of God. And it is when God's will for human life is disrupted by some act that a crime occurs, in the Bible's view. We should, therefore, note that when crimes are detailed in the Scriptures, their condemnation is based on the fact that they are wrong in the sight of God.

FORMS OF VICTIMIZATION IN THE SCRIPTURES

Specifically, what are the forms of victimization that are mentioned in the Bible? By listing those, we may be alerted to forms of victimization in our own communities. Certainly because the Bible is the most realistic book in the world, portraying our lives as they actually are, its list of crime victims is almost endless.

On a nationwide scale, there are those who are victims of slavery, and the primary example, of course, is the bondage of the Israelites in Egypt. But the Scriptures also have a great deal to say about the treatment of individual slaves, as we shall see.

The population may be the victim of an unjust government that requires of them burdensome taxation and forced labor — crimes against which the prophets frequently pronounce the judgment of God (cf., e.g., Jer. 22:13-19). Or the nation may suffer extreme cruelty in warfare or in captivity, as Amos condemns at the beginning of his book, and as Obadiah decries. And of course there is the government persecution of the faithful at the hands of Rome, as we find in Hebrews, 1 Peter, and Revelation.

On the commercial level, we frequently have portrayals in the Old Testament of those who are victimized by false weights and measures, and there are few commands more emphasized in the Old Testament than that which Moses gives in Deuteronomy:

> You shall not have in your bag two kinds of weights, a large and a small. You shall not have in your house two kinds of measures, a large and a small. A full and just weight you shall have, a full and just measure you shall have; that your days may be prolonged in the land which the Lord your God gives you. For all who do such things, all who act dishonestly, are an abomination to the Lord. (25:13-16; cf. Lev. 19:35-36; Prov. 20:10, 23; Isa. 1:22; Amos 8:5; Mic. 6:11)

Such dishonest commerce led often to the poor falling into debt, for which they sometimes lost all of their property and were thrown into prison or subjected to slavery. And most of the prophets condemn such oppression of the poor (cf. Isa. 5:8; Amos 8:4-6; Mic. 2:1-2; Hab. 2:6; et al.).

When the poverty-stricken sought redress in the courts, they often became the victims of corrupt elders and judges, who decided cases according to the wealth and position of the defendants or on the basis of bribes (cf. Isa. 1:23; 5:23; 59:4, 14; Jer. 5:27-29; et al.). Thus Isaiah could pronounce,

> Woe to those who decree iniquitous decrees, and the writers who keep writing oppression, to turn aside the needy from justice and to rob the poor of my people of their right, that widows may be their spoil, and that they may make the fatherless their prey! (Isa. 10:1-2)

"Justice, and only justice, you shall follow," commands Deuteronomy (16:20), for God is a God of justice.

One of the surprising scriptural emphases is also on the harm done in society to those who are victims of lying and slander. Even in biblical times, many suffered under slander, a crime of which the Psalmists frequently complained (e.g., Ps. 4:2; 62:7). And Jeremiah, among the prophets, was especially concerned that honest speech had disappeared from Judah:

> Let every one beware of his neighbor,
> and put no trust in any brother;
> for every brother is a supplanter,
> and every neighbor goes about as a slanderer.
> Every one deceives his neighbor,
> and no one speaks the truth;
> they have taught their tongue to speak lies;
> they commit iniquity and are too weary to repent.
> Heaping oppression upon oppression, and deceit upon deceit,
> they refuse to know me, says the Lord.
> (Jer. 9:4-6; cf. Isa. 28:15; Mic. 6:12; 1 Pet. 2:1)

In the face of such doublespeak in society, James could write that "the tongue is a fire. The tongue is an unrighteous world among our members, staining the whole body" (James 3:6).

Similarly, the populace of Israel was frequently the victim of false prophets, who prophesied lies and "the deceit of their own hearts" (Jer. 23:26), who said "thus says the Lord" when the Lord had not sent them, who milked their hearers for money, and who sometimes turned to magic (Ezek. 13:17-18), much like some cult figures in our own day. Because the people often turned to them for guidance, and because it was difficult for the people to distinguish between true and false prophecy, deceitful prophets often worked great hardship on their communities. For this reason, Deuteronomy gives two tests of true and false prophecy (Deut. 13:1-5; 18:21-22), and both Jeremiah and Ezekiel have extended judgment oracles leveled against phony prophesying (Jer. 23:9-32; Ezek. 13:1-23), while our Lord tells us that we are to beware of false prophets who come to us in sheep's clothing, but inwardly are ravenous wolves. "You will know them by their fruits," our Lord tells us (Matt. 7:15-16).

Finally, among those crimes of society that victimized the populace, we might mention that of conspicuous consumption, that pride of wealth that was gained through oppression of the poor. Isaiah has devastating words to say of the wealthy women with their headbands and crescents, pendants and bracelets, perfume and rings, and glorious robes and handbags, who are haughty and mince along (Isa. 3:16-26). And Amos condemns those who loll about leisurely on beds inlaid with ivory, who eat the best food, and sing idle songs, and drink quantities of wine from bowls, but are not grieved over the ruin of the populace (Amos 6:4-6). Thus, Jesus can admonish us not to lay up treasures for ourselves on earth, but rather treasures in heaven (Matt. 6:10-20; cf. James 5:1-6), and 1 Timothy admonishes us to set our hopes not on uncertain riches but on God, who richly furnishes us everything to enjoy. Do good, be rich in good deeds, liberal and generous, writes the author, and thus lay "a good foundation for the future" (1 Tim. 6:17-19).

Over and over again, throughout the Scriptures, it is the poor who are the primary victims in corrupted society.

Having said that about God's preference for the poor, of which we hear so much in social discussions, it should also be pointed out, lest we become unrealistic, that poverty victims are by no means considered always righteous in the Scriptures. Jeremiah searches Jerusalem for one righteous person who does justice and seeks truth and correction from God, and he tells us that he finds such persons neither among the poor nor among the rich (Jer. 5:1-5). "None is righteous; no, not one" (Rom. 3:10; Ps. 14:3). Human sin is universal, and victims of societal sins cannot claim for themselves pure righteousness in the sight of God or of their fellow human beings.

Obviously, in any sinful society, there are also individuals who are victimized by specific instances of crime, and the case is no different in the Scriptures. We hear of theft, of the loss of property, of bodily injury, of rape and adultery and divorce. There are instances of harshness toward servants and violations of familial relations, of oppression of the handicapped, of slavery, of persecution of individual prophets.

It should also be pointed out that criminals themselves could become victims of an unjust judicial process and excessive punishment. Thus, alongside the calls for just and fair courts in the Scriptures, there is the stipulation that there must be two or more witnesses to a crime in order to convict, and if false testimony is given, the one giving it shall be subject to the punishment that would have been given to the accused (Deut. 19:15-21; Matt. 18:16; 2 Cor. 13:1). Similarly, if a guilty man deserves to be punished by beating, the punishment must be administered in the judge's presence and be in proportion to the nature of the offense. "Forty stripes may be given him," says Deuteronomy, "but not more; lest, if one should go on to beat him with more stripes than these, your brother be degraded in your sight" (Deut. 25:1-3).

VENGEANCE, RECOMPENSE, AND
THE MEANING OF LOVING YOUR ENEMY

When we read of crimes in the Scriptures or in our morning headlines, probably our first sinful reaction is to cry out for vengeance upon the criminal. Habakkuk's prayer at the beginning of his book could characterize that of any upstanding citizen:

O Lord, how long shall I cry for help
and thou wilt not hear?
Or cry to thee "Violence!"
and thou wilt not save?
Why dost thou make me see wrongs

and look upon trouble?
Destruction and violence are before me;
strife and contention arise.
So the law is slacked
and justice never goes forth.
For the wicked surround the righteous,
so justice goes forth perverted.

(Hab. 1:1-4)

We grow very weary of crime, and our base reaction to criminals is "Lock 'em up." We want vengeance, retribution, or at least just punishment. At the same time, we want recompense for those who have been victims of criminals. On the other hand, we know Christian teaching about forgiveness and about loving our enemies. At this point, sometimes our thoughts grow very confused, and so it is necessary in this discussion to talk about the difference for the Christian community between vengeance, retribution, and recompense.

Throughout the Scriptures, while certainly criminals were punished, all vengeance toward criminals was left to God. There is no book in the Scriptures which contains more calls for punishment of enemies than does the collection of Psalms, but with a very few exceptions, the Psalmists do not take that punishment into their own hands. Rather, they pray to God to level the punishment against the wrongdoers. A similar prayer of Jeremiah's is typical:

O Lord of hosts, who judgest righteously,
who triest the heart and the mind,
let me see thy vengeance upon them,
for to thee have I committed my cause.

(Jer. 11:20)

The case is turned over to God. As Paul writes, "Beloved, never avenge yourselves, but leave it to the wrath of God; for it is written, 'Vengeance is mine, I will repay, says the Lord.' No, 'if your enemy is hungry, feed him; if he is thirsty, give him drink; for by so doing you will heap burning coals upon his head. [Paul means that the enemy may repent.] Do not be overcome by evil, but overcome evil with good" (Rom. 12:19-21).

That is what the Scriptures mean when they talk about loving your enemies and turning the other cheek — those teachings that Martin Luther King Jr. applied so effectively to race relations. Christian victims are not to take vengeance against those who have wronged them. Rather, they are to love their enemies and pray for those who persecute them, even offering aid to those in need. All vengeful punishment of crime belongs to a merciful God, whom we trust to deal with wrongdoers as He wills. And while our society may put criminals in prison, we are not to use prisons as instruments of hatred.

Certainly, in the Scriptures, there is no doubt among the faithful that God will punish evildoers. Israel learned that when she was sentenced by God to languish in Assyrian and Babylonian exile, just as, much earlier, the Egyptians learned it at the site of the Reed Sea. The task of the faithful, then, becomes first of all that of trusting in and waiting for God's retribution.

For example, both Titus (3:1-2) and 1 Peter (2:13) admonish Christians to be subject to the governing authorities. That is especially remarkable when we remember that the audience of 1 Peter was a church undergoing the "fiery ordeal" of persecution by the Roman Empire. First Peter reminds its readers that when Christ was reviled, "He did not revile in return; when He suffered, He did not threaten; but He trusted to Him who judges justly" — namely, God (1 Pet. 2:23). Rather, the church was to suffer for "doing right" (3:17). For "after you have suffered a little while, the God of all grace, who has called you to His eternal glory in Christ, will Himself restore, establish, and strengthen you" (5:10).

In light of that, I was struck by a recent statement by Cardinal Ratzinger, who is head of the Vatican's Congregation for the Doctrine of the Faith. Ratzinger had harsh words to say about the World Council of Churches and those priests in Latin America who were "harming the life of the Gospel" by giving financial support to "subversive moments," all on the basis of Marxist liberation theology. The World Council representative replied that "systematic torture of political opponents and assassinations were widespread" in Latin

America in the 1970s. But Ratzinger's reply was, "We need not theology of liberation but theology of martyrdom."[2] In short, Ratzinger was advocating what 1 Peter sets forth — acceptance of suffering in order to do the right, while waiting for God's deliverance of the faithful and His just punishment of the wicked.

That raises the question as to whether or not victims of crime should work to punish and overthrow those who have harmed them. In short, should we take retribution into our own hands? Certainly there are instances in the Scriptures in which evil and repressive governments are overthrown, most notably the Omri dynasty in the ninth century B.C., whose downfall is instigated by the prophet Elijah and finally implemented by his successor, Elisha. And in our own century, there are few of us who objected to the defeat of Nazi Germany and the Nuremburg trials of its war criminals.

THE BASIC QUESTION

Let us therefore ask the basic question of this study. Should victims of crime passively wait for God's punishment of evildoers and for their own deliverance, or is there specific human recompense that should be made to crime victims that would contribute to the restoration of God's intended community? Is there some reward and aid that should be given to the victims of crime beyond that retribution and deliverance that God will work? Or is God's work sufficient?

THE REWARDS OF THOSE WHO WAIT ON THE LORD

Certainly the Scriptures are full of the testimonies of those victims of crime who find their only compensation and aid in the work of God. If one studies only the Psalms, it becomes clear that those who rely solely on God find in their fellowship with Him rewards far greater than any human compensation for suffering might give. The Psalmists speak of the refuge and protection that they find in God's

2. Reported in *Christian Century*, 18-25 June 1997, pp. 582-83.

presence (Ps. 9:9; 12:5-8; 27:5; 31:19-20; 33:20; 59:16-17; 113:6-9), and of the strength that they find in the Lord (Ps. 10:17), whose right hand upholds them and provides for their needs (Ps. 68:8, 10). In God, the integrity (41:12) and honor (61:7) of the faithful are upheld, and they find that God delights in their welfare (35:27). God's consolations cheer them (94:19), and they experience a joy and a peace that the wicked cannot know (Ps. 4:7-8; 5:11). Indeed, God becomes for such victims a fountain of delight and life and light beside which all human experiences and rewards pale (Ps. 36:8-9). Psalm 73 beautifully sets forth such satisfaction:

> . . . I am continually with thee;
> thou dost hold my right hand.
> Thou dost guide me with thy counsel,
> and afterward thou wilt receive me to glory.
> Whom have I in heaven but thee?
> And there is nothing upon earth that I desire besides thee.
> My flesh and my heart may fail,
> but God is the strength of my heart and my portion for ever.
>   (Ps. 73:23-26)

Surely the Christian Church can offer victims of crime such comfort, such strength, such companionship with God from its Gospel.

It is from the Gospel itself that Christians can find their best recompense.

Psalm 73, which I just quoted, also points us to the future rewards that will be given by God to victims of crime who wait faithfully for God's recompense. "The meek shall possess the land, and delight themselves in abundant prosperity," says Psalm 37:11, that verse from which Jesus took one of His Beatitudes. Indeed, Jesus' blessings in the Beatitudes all look for future reward for the righteous: the Kingdom of heaven for the poor in spirit, comfort for those who mourn, satisfaction for those who hunger and thirst for righteousness, mercy for the merciful, the vision of God for the pure in heart, sonship for the peacemakers, great reward in heaven for those who are persecuted for righteousness' sake (Matt. 5:3-12). In this vein, Paul can write that "the sufferings of this present time are not worth comparing with the glory that is to be revealed to us" (Rom. 8:18), and the persecuted churches of Hebrews in 1 Peter and Revelation are urged to endure for the sake of the future joy that is set before them in the Kingdom. Victims who are faithful to the Lord will have their future recompense from His hands.

BIBLICAL RECOMPENSE FOR VICTIMS OF CRIME

Nevertheless, there is ample evidence in the Scriptures that victims of crime are to be recompensed here and now for the suffering they have experienced. And the basis of that recompense is the value and dignity that the Scriptures find inherent in human life.

The High Value of Human Beings

God has made all human beings "a little less than the elohim," that is, the heavenly beings (Ps. 8:5), in the image of God Himself. God has crowned humanity with glory and honor and given it dominion over all the works of His hands (Gen. 1:26-28; Ps. 8:6-8). As a result, our Lord teaches, human beings — all human beings — are of more value than anything in the natural world, of more value than the birds of the air that God feeds, of more value than the lilies of the field that are clothed in a glory exceeding Solomon's (Matt. 6:25-30). God constantly extends to His human creatures intimate care and concern, numbering the hairs on our heads, noting when we sit down and when we rise, seeing all our ways, and knowing aforetime all that we speak (Matt. 10:30; Ps. 139:1-4). God wants nothing less for us than abundant life (John 10:10), and His love for us so overflows that He gives His only beloved Son to die that we may live eternally.

Such value and dignity afforded to human beings are therefore to be preserved in human relationships. A poor man is not to be demeaned by those to whom he owes a debt (Deut. 24:10-12), nor is the rich man to be accommodated instead of the man in shabby clothing (James 2:1-6). A divorced wife is not to be humiliated (Deut. 21:14), and indeed, the prophet Malachi tells us that God hates the violence that divorce inflicts on all parties (Mal. 2:16). Escaped slaves, according to the Old Testament, are not to be returned to their masters; rather, they are to live free from oppression in Israel at the place which they themselves choose (Deut. 23:15-16), while in the New Testament, Paul wants the slave Onesimus to be considered a brother like himself (Philem. 15-18).

"You shall not curse the deaf or put a stumbling block before the blind," commands Leviticus (19:14), and the lame, the maimed, the blind, the dumb, and the diseased are the recipients of great love and restoration from Jesus, as well as those promised a place in the future Kingdom of God. Servants are to be paid promptly for their labors (Lev. 19:13; Deut. 24:15). And in all circumstances, parents are to be honored and esteemed (Exod. 20:12; Lev. 19:3; Mark 7:10-13; Eph. 6:2).

In both Old and New Testaments, the worth of individuals is to be exalted by love toward them (Lev. 19:7-8), whether they be friends or enemies (Matt. 5:38-48). So if a neighbor's ox or ass is lost or has fallen by the way, the animal is to be restored to its owner (Deut. 22:1-4), but the same is true also of the animals belonging to an enemy (Exod. 23:4-5). And the love for neighbor as oneself is to be extended even to unknown foreigners and strangers who dwell in our midst (Lev. 19:33-34).

The Scriptures are quite clear that love toward others is motivated by the love that God has for us. But they are also certain that we return God's love by loving our fellow human beings. Indeed, the commandments in the book of Deuteronomy as a whole are intended as instructions about how to love God. We love God by exalting and loving our fellows, who are made in the image of God. And that can take some interesting forms in Deuteronomy. For example, Deuteronomy 22:8 commands that the Hebrews build railings around their flat-roofed houses. Why? Because a neighbor might fall off and be killed. All sorts of means are to be taken to insure the well-being, the honor, and the dignity of others in our society. Human beings are valuable in God's sight. And we love God by considering all persons valuable in our sight as well. Thus, Jesus pushes that value to its ultimate height by teaching that we are in danger of hellfire if we even are angry or insult someone else (Matt. 5:21-22).

Recompense for Victims of Crime

Despite the fact that God punishes criminals and that the faithful have rewards running over from their fellowship with God, there is nevertheless ample biblical evidence that crime victims should be extended human recompense for their suffering in order that the wholeness of the community be restored.

For example, in Luke 19, the chief tax collector, Zacchaeus, in whose house our Lord decides to remain for a day, is prompted by that fellowship with Jesus not only to continue to give half of his goods to the poor but also to restore fourfold to anyone who has been defrauded. And Jesus replies, "Today salvation has come to this house" (Luke 19:1-10). The hated Jewish tax collector, by his fourfold restoration of that which has been unjustly gained, experiences the wholeness that belongs to saved relationships. And that restoration not only aids those who have been defrauded — the victims of the crime — but also helps restore health to the community at large, and indeed, to the tax collector himself. All benefit from recompense — the victim, the community, and the one who has committed the crime. Criminals themselves are helped by repenting of what they have done and by making repayment for it.

So there are a multitude of commandments in the Old Testament requiring restitution. Thieves must pay double for what they have stolen of money or goods from a house (Exod. 22:7). If that stolen is an ox or an ass, five animals must be given back to make restitution (Exod. 22:1). Any breach of trust concerning that which has been lost and claimed by someone else must be doubly recompensed; Israelites were expected to return lost property (Exod. 22:9). If the carelessness of a person results in the loss of another's property or animals, always the loss must be covered (Exod. 21:33-36; 22:5, 6, 14).

This protection of private property extended to a neighbor's land and its produce. Deuteronomy commands that a neighbor's landmarks not be removed; land is that which has been given to each by the Lord (Deut. 19:14). The prophet Isaiah delivers a harsh judgment from God upon the rich who take over the land of the poor: "Woe to those who join house to house, who add field to field" (Isa. 5:8); and Zechariah saw God uttering a curse upon anyone who stole (Zech. 5:3). When someone even strolled through a vineyard or grain field, according to Deuteronomy, they could pluck what they wanted to eat, but they could not put any of the grapes or grain into a vessel, because that would constitute stealing (Deut. 23:24-25). Leviticus gives a general summation of the recompense that had to be made for theft:

> The Lord said to Moses, "If any one sins and commits a breach of faith against the Lord by deceiving his neighbor in a matter of deposit or security, or through robbery, or if he has oppressed his neighbor or has found what was lost and lied about it, swearing falsely — in any of all the things which men do and sin therein, when one has sinned and become guilty, he shall restore what he took by robbery, or what he got by oppression, or the deposit which was committed to him, or the lost thing which he found, or anything about which he has sworn falsely; he shall restore it in full, and shall add a fifth to it, and give it to him to whom it belongs, on the day of his guilt offering. (Lev. 6:1-5)

As for bodily harm, the man who struck another had to pay for the injured person's loss of time and for his thorough healing (Exod. 21:18-19). If a man wounded his own slave, he had to let the slave go free (Exod. 21:26-27). Recompense was made to the victim who had suffered loss.

This was true also in the case of a miscarriage. If two men were fighting together and accidentally struck a pregnant woman so that she miscarried and yet the child lived, the one who hurt her had to pay a fine. If the child died, then the man who caused the mishap

104

forfeited his life (Exod. 21:22-25). The unborn too were not to be injured, and Amos tells us that the Lord himself would personally kindle the fire of judgment on the Ammonites who savagely "ripped up" pregnant women in warfare (Amos 1:13-15).

If a virgin who was not betrothed was raped, then the criminal had to give the marriage present for her — Deuteronomy stipulates fifty shekels of silver — and make her his wife (Exod. 22:16-17); he could not subsequently divorce her (Deut. 22:28-29).

Crimes in Israel were not only punished, but recompense was made to their victims by the criminals, because Israel was the people of God, who wisely knew that injury to victims disturbs not only the relationship of criminal to victim but also relationships within the community and the relationship of the whole community with God.

Now many rightly would say that these are all Old Testament laws and that Christians are no longer under the law. Christ is the fulfillment of the law, and Christians are to live by grace through faith alone. Further, they argue, Christians are to forgive those criminals who have wronged them rather than asking restitution from them.

As I have argued above, however, forgiveness — loving your enemies — means that we do not take vengeance into our own hands toward those who have wronged us. Vengeance belongs to God; he will repay. But the God of the New Testament, as of the Old Testament, seeks a righteous community, one in which we bear one another's burdens in the love and law of Christ (Gal. 6:2). And victims of crime have been burdened. They have suffered material loss or bodily injury, degradation, and the sense of uncleanness that often follows a theft of their property, or the terrible fear and loss of self that is so characteristic of rape victims. They suffer, and in New Testament terms, the church suffers with them (1 Cor. 12:26). Victims not only need to be comforted — and the church can give enormous comfort from the Gospel. Victims also need the full restoration to them of what they have lost.

More than that, however, the criminal needs the specific repentance that comes from recompensing the victim for the crime committed. And the entire community needs both the criminal and the victim restored to wholeness through the victim's recompense and the criminal's repentance. Only then are all parties restored to health and the faithful community healed in all its parts. And only then can God continue to use such a community and every individual in it as instruments for furthering His good and loving purpose for His world.

CHAPTER SEVEN

The Contours of Justice:
An Ancient Call for Shalom

NICHOLAS WOLTERSTORFF

The concept of justice was carved out by the hand of God Him-self. God's love for justice is unbending, a conviction that should guide us as we carry messages of hope to those who suffer from victimization. Yet we are not without questions about justice. How is it relevant for us today? Justice is rarely mentioned in the New Testament; is this simply an Old Testament idea that roughly parallels the concept of it in modern life? This chapter is written for Christians who desire to better understand the biblical concept of justice and its application. For, as we will see, in both Old Testament and New the contours of justice fit our mandate — to bring God's shalom to a needy world.

O ver and over the Old Testament confronts us with the declaration that God loves justice. To read Isaiah 61 is to hear God saying, "I the Lord love justice" (v. 8).[1] To join Israel and the Church in taking on one's own lips the words of Psalm 37 is to find oneself saying that "the Lord loves justice" (v. 28). These are but two examples of many.

This love of God for justice is declared to be an active love. God does not simply *admire* justice, as one might admire a fine painting. God's love for justice is the love of one who *does* justice; God is Himself just. "The Lord works vindication and justice for all who are oppressed," we sing when we bless the Lord with the words of Psalm 103:6. When we cry for deliverance with the words of Psalm 140:12, we say, "I know that the Lord maintains the cause of the afflicted, and executes justice for the needy."

God commands us to be lovers and practitioners of justice as He is — and pronounces judgment on those of us who are not. Indeed, how could God actively love justice and be indifferent to whether you and I do justice? "Justice, and only justice, you shall follow," says Moses in his great farewell speech recorded in Deuteronomy, "that you may live and inherit the land which the Lord your God gives you" (Deut. 16:20). The command is intensified in the prophets. In a passage from Amos (5:21-24) that by now has entered into the consciousness of humanity, God says,

> "I hate, I despise your feasts,
> and I take no delight in your solemn assemblies.
> Even though you offer me your burnt offerings and cereal
>   offerings,
> I will not accept them,
> and the peace offerings of your fatted beasts
> I will not look upon.
> Take away from me the noise of your songs;
> to the melody of your harps I will not listen.

---

1. Unless otherwise indicated, Bible quotations in this chapter are taken from the Revised Standard Version.

But let justice roll down like waters,
and righteousness like an ever-flowing stream."

The same command to do justice occurs in an equally well-known passage from Micah. The passage opens with intense poignancy, as God expresses pained lament to Israel — not now humanity lamenting to God but God lamenting to humanity:

"O my people, what have I done to you?
In what have I wearied you?
Answer me!
For I brought you up from the land of Egypt,
and redeemed you from the house of bondage. . . ."

The prophet then imagines someone, stung by this divine lament, asking what would please God and ease God's sorrow:

"With what shall I come before the Lord,
and bow myself before God on high?
Shall I come before him with burnt offerings,
with calves a year old?
Will the Lord be pleased with thousands of rams,
with ten thousands of rivers of oil?"

We all know the prophet's answer:

He has showed you, O man, what is good;
and what does the Lord require of you
but to do justice, and to love kindness,
and to walk humbly with your God?

(Mic. 6:1-8)

THE FOUNDATIONS OF GOD'S JUSTICE

I suggested above that God's command that we do justice and God's judgment on those of us who do not are to be seen as manifestations of God's active love of justice. How could God actively love justice, I asked, and be indifferent to whether you and I do justice? But quite clearly there's more than this to the connection between God's active love of justice on the one hand, and God's command and judgment on the other hand. The command and the judgment are also grounded in the general divine imperative that we are to imitate God, image God, become icons of God — in short, that we are to conduct ourselves in a God-like manner. We are to model ourselves after God. And since God actively loves justice, our being God-like requires our doing so as well. That same farewell speech of Moses can be used to make the point: God "executes justice for the fatherless and the widow, and loves the sojourner, giving him food and clothing," says Moses. And then he draws the application: "Love the sojourner therefore; for you were sojourners in the land of Egypt" (Deut. 10:18-19). And in another passage: "You shall not pervert the justice due to the sojourner or to the fatherless, or take a widow's garment in pledge; but you shall remember that you were a slave in Egypt and the Lord your God redeemed you from there; therefore I command you to do this" (Deut. 24:17-18). As God has heard our laments and satisfied our longings, so we are to hear the laments of the poor among us, the weak and oppressed.

Why does God love justice? I daresay that every member of the Church has some degree of familiarity with the words from the Old Testament that I have quoted, and others of the same sort. But I want, on this occasion, to go beyond recalling the words, to consider into what larger pattern God's love of justice fits.

An ancient, enduring, and prominent strand of Christian theology sees God's love of justice as grounded in God's anger with those who disobey God's commands. God's love and practice of justice is God's love and practice of retributive justice. But I think it is starkly clear that the passages which speak of God's love of justice are not pointing to God's delight over the misery of those who are justly punished; God has no such delight.

Having said that, I must note, however, that judgment does have an indispensable place in the relation of God to justice. Though God's love of justice is not God's love of wreaking on wrongdoers

110

their just dessert, nonetheless, God does pronounce judgment on those who perpetrate injustice. That's because God's active love of justice is not a love which confronts a good but incomplete world, but a love which confronts a *fallen* and incomplete world — a world in which injustice is perpetrated. Given such a world, how could God love justice without pronouncing judgment on all the actual injustice? Given such a world, the love implies the judgment.

GOD'S PREFERENCE FOR THE POOR

Once again, then, why God's love of justice? One way of approaching the answer is to probe further a point just made — namely, that given the actual condition of our social world, God's love of justice inevitably implies God's hatred of the injustice that is to be found in that world. A striking feature of Old Testament literature, noted rather often in recent years, is the repetitious citation of widows, orphans, and aliens as categories of persons especially likely to be victims of injustice in ancient Israelite society — to which is often added the overlapping category of "the poor." Just one example of many is the passage, already cited, from the farewell speech of Moses: God "executes justice for the fatherless and the widow, and loves the sojourner, giving him food and clothing."

For me as a philosopher, this is very striking indeed. It's clear from Plato's *Republic* that, for him, the most fundamental indicator and root of injustice in society is people not doing what they are best at doing, and in particular the chain of authority in society not having wise people — philosopher kings — at the top. For John Locke, the most fundamental indicator and root of injustice is the violation of a person's property in his own body and in the fruits of his labor. By contrast, for the songwriters and prophets of the Old Testament, the salient indicator of injustice in society would appear to be the presence of persons in society who lack the material and other goods necessary for flourishing; in ancient Israel, the groups who were especially vulnerable in that regard were widows, orphans, and aliens. It's for this reason that the love of justice attends especially to their fate.

Thus, I don't think there can be any doubt that there is "a prefer-

111

> When the Bible talks about justice and injustice, it doesn't start giving us a litany of the perpetrators. It gives us a litany of the victims, the wounded ones — the widows, the orphans, and the aliens.

ential option for the poor" in the Old Testament. The claim, characteristic of the liberation theologians, that there is such an option has enraged a good many writers in North America and Europe; but if one comes to the prophets and songwriters of the Old Testament after reading Plato and John Locke on justice, the presence of such an option slaps one in the face, as it were. The live question is not whether there is such an option, but what we are to make of it. God, says the psalmist, is the One

> who executes justice for the oppressed;
> who gives food to the hungry.
> The Lord sets the prisoners free;
> the Lord opens the eyes of the blind.
> The Lord lifts up those who are bowed down;
> the Lord loves the righteous.
>
> The Lord watches over the sojourners,
> the Lord upholds the widow and the fatherless;
> but the way of the wicked the Lord brings to ruin.
>
> (Ps. 146:7-9)

I submit that in all of Plato and Locke, there is nothing remotely similar to this.

Loving "Each and Every"

Let me single out three elements in that part of the thought of the Old Testament, which constitutes, so far as I can tell, the background for this preferential option for the poor. There is, in the first place, the haunting theme of "each and every." It must, of course, be granted that there are some passages in the Old Testament which make it appear that it is only justice within Israel that is of any concern to God. But there are plenty of passages that strike a universal note; and in any case, this is the Christian reading of the Old Testament. God loves each and every one of God's human creatures. Thus it is, for example, that in the New Testament we get the parable of the shepherd not being satisfied with the fact that ninety-nine of his sheep are safely in the corral, but going out to look for the hundredth one. Evidently justice has something to do with God's love for each and every one of God's human creatures.

Pursuing Shalom

Second, the rationale for connecting the love of justice with the triad of widows, orphans, and aliens remains, so far as I can see, inscrutable unless we bring *shalom* into the picture; and, of course, there are plenty of passages in which justice and *shalom* are mentioned in the same breath — as, for example, in Psalm 85, where we read that "Justice and *shalom* will kiss each other." The state of *shalom* is the state of flourishing in all dimensions of one's existence: in one's relation to God, in one's relation to one's fellow human beings, in one's relation to nature, and in one's relation to oneself. Evidently justice has something to do with the fact that God's love for each and every one of God's human creatures takes the form of God desiring the *shalom* of each and every one. Not merely the freedom from violation of one's property, but the flourishing of each and every one. That's why God's justice, and ours, is manifested in getting food to the hungry, liberating prisoners, curing the blind, lifting up the sorrowing and humiliated, being welcoming to the stranger, and supporting widows and orphans.

Honoring "Rights"

What I see as the third element in the relevant background thought of the Old Testament will take just a bit longer to explain. What I have said so far illuminates the *scope* of justice as it is understood in the Old Testament writers. But it does not, to my mind, explain what in all this constitutes *justice*. Justice, as I see it, has to do with *rights*. A social situation is *just* when the *rights* of the people in that situation are honored. In turn, a person or group has a *right* to some good just in case they have a legitimate claim to that good. The legitimacy in question may be legal, social, or, more fundamentally, moral. Thus, to have a moral right to some good is to have a morally legitimate claim to that good. For example, to have a moral right to sit on a bench in the park is to have a morally legitimate claim to sit on a bench in the park.

The appeal to rights has come under heavy attack within the Christian community in recent years, with a good many writers arguing that we who are Christians should renounce all appeal to rights and abolish the concept from our conceptual repertoire. I think that would be a calamity of first proportion. So let me do what I can to clear away what I regard as the misunderstandings that have led to this radical and misguided conclusion.

> When we fail in our obligations, we are guilty. When we fail to enjoy our rights, we are morally wounded. So obligations have to do with guilt, and rights have to do with woundedness. I have come to think that these are two irreducible sides of the moral life.

Apparently most people, when they hear the word *rights*, think immediately of so-called natural human rights. I propose that we think of such rights *last of all*. Begin instead by noticing that the conviction that we human beings have morally legitimate claims to

114

goods of various sorts pervades the fine texture of our ordinary lives: we all operate with the conviction every day. If a student writes a paper for me of top-notch quality, she has a *right* to receive from me a grade of A for the paper. My giving her an A when I judge her paper to be of top-notch quality is not an act of charity or goodwill on my part; it's granting her what she has a right to. Neither is it merely an obligation on my part — though indeed it is that. If it were merely an obligation on my part, then the only morally significant consequence of failure to award her an A would be moral guilt on my part. But in fact that would not be the only morally significant consequence. I would be morally guilty, indeed; but she would be morally injured. Given that she was morally injured, it would be appropriate for her to be angry, whereas if my guilt were the only morally significant consequence, pity for me would be the appropriate response on her part.

Or suppose that I have bought a ticket for a seat on a plane and that the plane is not oversold, nor are there any other extenuating circumstances that make it right for those responsible to keep me off the plane. Then I have a *right* to a seat on the plane. If I'm allowed on the plane, that's not an act of charity or goodwill on the part of those responsible; it's granting me what I have a right to. Neither is it purely a matter of obligation on their part to allow me on the plane — though it is *also* that. For should they fail to allow me on the plane, not only are they morally guilty, but I am morally injured.

Suppose there were no rights. Then the student could ask me for an A, request an A, beg for an A, and so forth; and I could ask, request, beg to be allowed on the plane. But the student would not be entitled to claim an A, and I would not be entitled to claim a seat on the plane. Furthermore, if there were no rights, then if I awarded the student an A, the appropriate response on her part would be to thank or praise me; and if I was allowed to take a seat on the plane, the appropriate response would be for me to thank or praise the people manning the ticket desk. If there were no rights, what would be missing in the moral life would be the moral propriety of insisting on the enjoyment of goods. Jesse Owens, having won the 100-yard dash at the Berlin Olympics, had the right to the gold medal. It was morally appropriate for him to insist on receiving it. He did not have to beg or ask for it; indeed, it would have been inappropriate for him to do so. And when he received it, he did not have to thank Hitler for giving it to him, praising his moral character. All he had to do was take it. For it belonged to him. To have a right to some good is for that good to *belong* to one — whether or not one actually possesses it, whether or not one is in a condition to enjoy it.

I hope I have said enough to make it clear how deep and pervasive in human life is the assumption that we human beings have rights — and what a profound alteration would occur if we no longer acknowledged the existence of rights. No longer to recognize rights would be no longer to acknowledge that "the other" comes into my midst bearing claims on me. It would be no longer to acknowledge that by my actions and inactions I may not only besmirch my own moral character but morally injure "the other." It's often said that evangelical humility requires of us that we not insist on our rights — and for that reason we who are Christians ought to have nothing to do with the notion. But that conclusion is plausible only if one insists on looking at the situation entirely from the first-person perspective. Consider it from the second- or third-person perspective. You now stand before me, feeling desperately hungry, feeling humiliated, having written a top-notch paper, having won the race, or whatever. The question then is whether you have any claim on me, or whether it's all a matter of charity or obligation on my part. The question is whether it's possible for me to morally injure you, or whether it's only possible for me to morally besmirch my own character. When seen from this second- or third-person perspective, the denial of rights seems anything but an act of evangelical humility; it seems, on the contrary, like an act of intolerable arrogance on my part. A refusal to let anything count but my own virtue.

Of course, not everything whose enjoyment or realization would be a good for me is something to which I have a legitimate claim. A seat in business class is, to my mind, a genuinely good thing. But if I've only bought a tourist-class ticket, I'm not entitled to that particular good. Should the person at the ticket counter decide, for whatever reason, to place me in business class, it is appropriate for me to thank him or her.

Now to pull things together: The thought that appears to me to lie behind the statements about justice made by the writers of the Old Testament is that each and every human being has a morally legitimate claim to the fundamental conditions of *shalom* — that is, of human flourishing. Not everything that can rightly be seen as an element of flourishing is something to which one has a legitimate claim; there will, accordingly, always be room for discussion as to where exactly the line is to be drawn. That discussion will have to be a situated discussion; what each of us can legitimately claim depends very much on personal and social circumstance. But what comes through loud and clear in the Old Testament writers is that the impoverishment of a minority within a society which as a whole is relatively well-to-do is a violation of justice. So too is arbitrary imprisonment and humiliation.

An objection that will certainly be forthcoming to this line of thought is that I am overinterpreting. Perhaps our contemporary concept of *justice* is connected with legitimate claims in the way I have suggested; but no such concept is to be found in the Old Testament. The words regularly translated with the English word *justice* simply don't have that meaning. So it will be said.

> Why are rights important? Part of the reason is that they ground requirements. They mean that we don't have to be beggars in life. And the next step is justice — the situation in which people enjoy their legitimate rights.

The possibility that I am overinterpreting does indeed have to be taken seriously. But I don't think I am. The question is whether the widows, the orphans, and the aliens were understood as having a legitimate claim to at least the fundamental conditions of flourishing — to means of sustenance. Suppose they were deprived of those means: would they then be morally injured, or would it only be the case that the powerful in society were guilty of failing in their obligations? To me, at least, the thought seems clearly to be that they would be morally injured. The widows, the orphans, and the aliens, in conducting their plea for means of sustenance, were not limited to urging the powerful to fulfill their obligations. It was appropriate for them to *claim* those means as rightly theirs.

THE CLAIM TO *SHALOM*

Our question was this: Why does God love justice? And in the course of my suggesting an answer, we've gotten a glimpse of the essential contours of justice as understood by the Old Testament writers. My suggestion is this: God's love for justice is grounded in God's love for each and every one of God's human creatures. God's love for a human being consists of God desiring *the good* of that being — the good for a human being in turn being understood as the *shalom,* the flourishing, of that human being. Justice consists of enjoying those goods — those components of one's *shalom* — to which one has a legitimate claim. So of course God loves justice — and hates injustice.

Loving Justice

And you and I: Why should we love justice? Well, as we saw earlier, because our doing justice is instrumental in God's bringing about justice — and because God asks of us that we imitate Him in His doing of justice. But now we can give a somewhat deeper answer: because we are to love as God loves, and because we are to love because God loves. "The other" stands before me as a creature whom God loves; that's why I have to do what I can to see to it that justice is rendered to that person. How can I be a party to wreaking injury — moral injury — on someone God loves?

An ever-beckoning temptation for the Anglo-American evangelical is to assume that all God really cares about for human beings here on earth is that they are born again and thus destined for salvation — to assume that the only kind of lostness which God cares about is religious lostness. God leaves the ninety-and-nine and goes out in search of that one who is not a believer; God does not go out in search of the one who is poor, does not go out looking for the one

118

who is oppressed. But if we understand the *shalom*, the flourishing, for which God longs in this narrow, pinched way, then all those biblical passages about God's love for justice must remain closed books to us.

What God desires for human beings is that comprehensive mode of flourishing which the Bible calls *shalom*. *Shalom* includes religious reconciliation; but it includes vastly more as well. Insofar as someone is suffering injustice, one of the goods to which that person has title, a good essential to her flourishing, is not being enjoyed by her. God's love of justice is grounded in God's longing for the *shalom* of God's creatures and in God's sorrow over its absence. The contours of *shalom* can be discerned from the contours of the laments to which God gives ear:

Father of the fatherless and protector of widows
is God in his holy habitation.
God gives the desolate a home to dwell in;
he leads out the prisoners to prosperity.

(Ps. 68:5-6)

Who is like the Lord our God,
who is seated on high,
who looks far down
upon the heavens and the earth?
He raises the poor from the dust,
and lifts the needy from the ash heap,
to make them sit with princes,
with the princes of his people.
He gives the barren woman a home,
making her the joyous mother of children.

(Ps. 113:5-9)

BECOMING A HOLY PEOPLE

There's a long tradition of Christian reflection that grounds certain, at least, of the claims of justice in the fact that each and every hu-

119

man being calls for respect and honor on account of being made in the image (or *as* an image) of God. The thought is that what is required for honoring a person as an icon of God is what she has a right to. Or, to put it the other way around: What a person has a right to is what she has to enjoy if she is to be honored as an icon of God. So far as I can tell, this line of thought is not to be found in the biblical writers. What we do find, as I have suggested, is the thought that the doing of justice (partially) constitutes our imaging of God — rather than the thought that the doing of justice is required by respect for a person as an image of God. Nonetheless, I do embrace this line of thought. Resting content with the impoverishment of widows, orphans, and aliens is incompatible with honoring them as icons of God. On this occasion, however, I will have to forego developing this line of thought further.

There is, however, one additional line of thought in the Old Testament that I do wish to say just a word about. Several times over in his farewell address, Moses says to his audience that they are a people *holy* to the Lord their God, for God has chosen them to be a people for His own possession (Deut. 7:6; 14:2, 21; 26:19). It is in this context that all the regulations of Deuteronomy are set: the regulations concerning clean and unclean animals, the regulations concerning cleanness and uncleanness of persons, the regulations concerning the dismissal of those soldiers from battle who have large, unfinished projects back home, the proscriptions against idolatry and various forms of immorality, the regulations stipulating that the sacrificial animals be unblemished, the regulations whereby the community is to purge itself — and the regulations concerning justice.

The Bible tells us that God is the God of justice and asks you and me to do justice as well, in order to bring about God's justice, in order to imitate God, and in order to make a holy society. That really takes us aback, that society can be holy only if it is just.

Holiness was not only set-apartness; holiness was also unity, purity, completeness, perfection. And the idea behind the Mosaic legislation seems to have been that Israel's being holy to God is as much task as status: Israel is to *become* holy and to *institute* into its life memorial remembrances of God's holiness. Its life is to become unified, pure, complete, and perfect like unto God's; and it is to incorporate quasiliturgical memorials of God's holiness in its life. In its life it is to imitate and celebrate the holiness of God. And for that, it must do justice. Injustice is a form of desecration. Justice is sacral. The call to justice is grounded in the call to be holy even as God is holy.

What's the connection? Why is an unjust society an unholy society? What's unholy about injustice? In what way does an unjust society not reflect God's holiness? Obviously it does not reflect God's justice. But why, in addition, does it not reflect God's holiness?

The writers don't say; we are left to surmise. The clue, however, is right before us. The thought is that there is something incomplete, disunified, fractured, broken about the unjust society — in particular, about the society in which widows, orphans, and aliens do not enjoy the conditions of flourishing. And it's obvious what that is: The unjust society is one whose *shalom* is fractured, partial, incomplete, and thus incapable of reflecting the holiness of the divine.

NEW TESTAMENT JUSTICE

My discussion thus far has been based exclusively on the Old Testament. I have delineated the place of justice in Old Testament piety and avoided mingling New with Old Testament evidence. I have done so in order to be able to address myself to that rather large group of Christians who assume or insist that the propriety of such piety has passed away. New Testament piety, they say, in contrast to Old, does not include to any significant degree the doing of justice and the struggle for the undoing of injustice here in this present age. The New Testament doesn't talk about justice. It talks about other things: about sin, about salvation, about love, about evangelizing. It's true that God's heart goes out to the world's weak ones; it's true that God longs for *shalom;* it's true that God longs for a community which will reflect and celebrate God's own holiness. But God does not command you and me to fulfill these divine longings by trying to change society. Justice and injustice pertain to social structures and practices. The New Testament doesn't tell us to go out and reform society; it warns us, on the contrary, to stay away from that. It tells us that the struggle for such reform is always futile. It tells us that this present evil world is hopeless, that it may and will pass away. In hope and prayer we are to fasten our hearts on the coming of the New Jerusalem. No doubt in the New Jerusalem there will be justice, there will be *shalom,* there will be holiness. Nobody doubts that. In heaven there is no injustice. But for that New Jerusalem, we do not work. We wait. God and God alone will bring it about. The fundamental posture of the Christian in the world is hopeful, patient, suffering, prayerful, waiting, coupled with witnessing to the worth of such waiting. As Paul says in Romans 8:19-25,

> The creation waits with eager longing for the revealing of the sons of God; for the creation was subjected to futility, not of its own will but by the will of Him who subjected it in hope; because the creation itself will be set free from its bondage to decay and obtain the glorious liberty of the children of God. We know that the whole creation has been groaning in travail together until now; and not only the creation, but we ourselves, who have the first fruits of the Spirit, groan inwardly as we wait for adoption as sons [and daughters], the redemption of our bodies. For in this hope we were saved.... But if we hope for what we do not see, we wait for it with patience.

Now there can be no doubt that expectant waiting is indeed a fundamental component of New Testament spirituality. But that scarcely settles the issue before us. The issue is rather of the *form* that our waiting is to take. Are we to resign ourselves to the injustice of the world while patiently waiting for the coming of God's reign to sweep it all away; or are we to struggle for its alleviation while patiently waiting for the coming of God's reign to bring our efforts to fruition? Are we to tolerate our human injustice while waiting for God's justice; or are we to await God's justice as the fruition of our struggle against human injustice? Are we to await the fulfillment of our social endeavors as well as of our social hopes; or are we to await only the fulfillment of our social hopes?

Let me begin with the claim that the New Testament is silent about justice. At first glance it does indeed appear silent. But in part it appears so because of how it has been translated. The New Testament, as you know, was written in Greek. The standard Greek word for justice is *dikaiosune,* and almost always, when the word *dikaiosune* occurs in Greek literature from antiquity, it is translated *justice.* Now as a matter of fact the Greek word *dikaiosune* (along with the adjective *dikaios*) occurs rather often in the New Testament. Almost never, however, does it get translated in our familiar English translations as "justice." Let me give just one example of many — though I think a rather striking example.

The Beatitudes of Jesus are reported in both the Gospel of Matthew and that of Luke. In Matthew they occur at the beginning of chapter 5. Verses 6 and 10 of that chapter go as follows in the translation of the Revised Standard Version:

"Blessed are those who hunger and thirst for righteousness, for they shall be satisfied. . . .
Blessed are those who are persecuted for righteousness' sake, for theirs is the kingdom of heaven."[2]

Now the Greek word translated here as "righteousness" is actually *dikaiosune.* So let's replace "righteousness" in the translation with "justice":

"Blessed are those who hunger and thirst for justice, for they shall be satisfied. . . .
Blessed are those who are persecuted for the sake of justice, for theirs is the kingdom of heaven."

2. The New Revised Standard Version only changes the "shall" of verse 6 to "will."

It's obvious that these Beatitudes carry very different suggestions when the key word is thus translated not as "righteousness" but as "justice." "Righteousness" carries suggestions of individual piety. Beyond that, its connotations in contemporary English have become negative; most of us, if we heard someone described as very righteous, would not take that as a compliment. "Justice," by contrast, carries social connotations; when *dikaios* is translated as "justice," we feel intuitively that in this Beatitude we are dealing with an extension of the Old Testament rather than with a repudiation of it.

I submit, then, that part of the reason we have come to think that justice is not a theme in the New Testament is that our translations conceal from us the presence of the theme, and thereby conceal from us some of the continuity of the New Testament with the Old. If someone asked me whether it's flat-out mistaken to translate *dikaiosune* as "righteousness," I would say No — provided that "righteousness" is thought of as *going right*, or *doing right*, or something of that sort. Yet when it is never translated as "justice," when it is always translated with some such word as "righteousness," then continuity with the Old Testament is obscured, and the translation as a whole becomes misleading.

THE ARRIVAL OF *SHALOM*

But let's dig beneath the words. Another reason the presence of the theme of justice in the New Testament is obscured from us is that we think of the contours of justice along modern Western lines: we think of justice as present within society when people enjoy their rights to individual freedom. We don't think of justice along Old Testament lines: justice is present in society when people enjoy the fundamental conditions of *shalom* — and, in particular, when the widows, the orphans, and the aliens are no longer deprived and treated as outsiders.

With that understanding of justice in mind, let me address what usually proves to be the central issue when people say that the New Testament is not concerned with justice: Did Jesus teach that the holy, just, and peaceful reign of God which the prophets foretold and for which Israel was commanded to work is to remain unseen until the coming of the New Jerusalem, or did He teach that already in His work that holy, just, and peaceful reign was breaking in? And more than that: *Was* it breaking in? Did Jesus bring about justice? No Christian denies, I trust, that God will fully bring about that prophetic vision of the just and holy *shalom*. But do we await its implementation while enduring its absence, or do we await its completion while discerning its coming in Jesus?

After John the Baptist was arrested, says Mark in his Gospel, "Jesus came into Galilee, preaching the Gospel of God, and saying, 'The time is fulfilled, and the kingdom of God is at hand; repent, and believe in the gospel'" (1:14-15). Matthew records the same events: Jesus, after hearing that John had been arrested, "began to preach, saying, 'Repent, for the kingdom of heaven is at hand'" (4:17). However, Matthew adds an important detail to his narration. After hearing of John's arrest and before beginning to preach, Jesus withdrew to Capernaum in the region of Zebulun and Naphtali, so as to fulfill Isaiah's prophecy:

> "The land of Zebulun and the land of Naphtali,
> toward the sea, across the Jordan,
> Galilee of the Gentiles —
> the people who sat in darkness
> have seen a great light,
> and for those who sat in the region and shadow of death
> light has dawned."
>
> (Matt. 4:15-16)

Luke's report of the beginning of Jesus' ministry adds yet other details. In the course of his tour through Galilee, Jesus maintained His practice of going to synagogue on the Sabbath. One Sabbath, upon being handed the book of Isaiah in the synagogue, He read the opening of chapter 61:

> "The Spirit of the Lord is upon me,
> because he has anointed me to preach good news to the poor.
> He has sent me to proclaim release to the captives

125

and recovering of sight to the blind,
to set at liberty those who are oppressed,
to proclaim the acceptable year of the Lord."

(Luke 4:18-19)

He then sat down, and with the gaze of all the worshippers fixed on Him, He said, "Today this scripture has been fulfilled in your hearing" (v. 21).

One more specimen of Jesus' self-interpretation of His ministry is important. John the baptizer, while sitting in prison, began to hear news of the doings of Jesus, the one whom he had himself baptized. These reports led John to turn over in his mind the question of whether Jesus was or was not the expected one. So he sent some of his followers to ask Jesus Himself the question, "Are you He who is to come, or shall we look for another?" (Luke 7:20). Jesus' answer came in two stages. First, "in that hour he cured many of diseases and plagues and evil spirits, and on many that were blind he bestowed sight" (v. 21). Then, with a clear allusion to Isaiah, he said to John's followers,

"Go and tell John what you have seen and heard: the blind receive their sight, the lame walk, lepers are cleansed, and the deaf hear, the dead are raised up, the poor have good news preached to them. And blessed is he who takes no offense at me."

(Luke 7:22-23; cf. Matt. 11:2-6)

In short, Jesus interpreted his ministry in terms of the messianic expectations of Isaiah; the long-expected reign of God was, in His person and work, decisively breaking in. Those expectations were expectations for the coming of full-orbed *shalom,* for the arrival of holiness upon earth. And as we have seen, *shalom* and holiness include justice. Jesus' ministry was not the ministry of telling us patiently to await the sight of God's *shalom;* it was the ministry of displaying that *shalom* by healing those blemishes incompatible with *shalom:* blindness, lameness, leprosy, hopelessness, onerous religious obligations, social exclusion.

And this in turn explains the content of the songs, recorded in

126

Luke's Gospel, with which Jesus' birth was greeted — for example, Mary's song:

> "My soul praises the Lord and my spirit rejoices in God my
>   Savior,
> for he has been mindful of the humble state of his servant. . . .
> He has brought down rulers from their thrones but has lifted up
>   the humble.
> He has filled the hungry with good things but has sent the rich
>   away empty."
>
> (Luke 1:46-48, 52-53, NIV)

Of course we all know painfully well that the coming of God's reign was not completed by Jesus, and is not yet completed. Jesus did not produce that reign in its fullness. We have to interpret His work in the light of that fact. The category, which John regularly uses in his Gospel, is that of *sign;* Jesus performed signs. Traditionally these signs have been interpreted as proofs or evidence: Jesus produced miracles as evidence of his divine authority. But surely if we take seriously those passages to which I have pointed, in which the justice and *shalom* envisaged in the Old Testament are said to be breaking into our existence in the work of Jesus, then we have to interpret the signs as more than this. What Jesus produced were not just proofs of his divinity but *signs of the Kingdom.* And these signs are samples. The works of Jesus were cut from the cloth of the Kingdom to which they pointed. In them, justice and *shalom* were signified by being manifested.

THE PHARISEES AND THE WILL OF GOD

To get the full picture, we must remind ourselves of one more thing. Pervasive in Jesus' ministry was His polemical interaction with the Pharisees. *Pharisee* has acquired for us the connotation of *hypocrite.* No doubt there were hypocrites among the Pharisees. But that's not the first thing we should think of when we hear the word *Pharisee.* The Pharisees were a party in first-century Judaism who were deeply religious; their piety took the form of being intensely concerned with holiness. They believed that to become holy, one had to become a member of a holy community in which the regulations of the Torah were scrupulously followed, and to separate oneself from all those who were in any way unclean. They believed that this was also the best way to resist Roman oppression.

The conflict between Jesus and the Pharisees was not caused first of all, then, by Jesus' uncovering of the hypocrisy of some of them, but by His preaching and practicing a totally different message concerning the will of God. The Roman enemy, He said, should be loved rather than hated; He Himself had meals with those traitors among the Jews who collected taxes for Rome. And those who lived unclean lives, such as prostitutes, should not be ostracized but befriended; Jesus shared meals with them, too. Thus when Jesus went one Sabbath day to a feast in the house of a Pharisee who had brought together a few of his well-to-do friends, Jesus shattered the peaceful pleasantries by saying that a dinner party such as the one at which he was present was all wrong. Here there was respect for social status, whereas at God's feast, the little people would be invited to the head of the table to converse with the host — surely an echo of Psalm 113, where it is said that God "raises the poor from the dust, and lifts the needy from the ash heap, to make them sit with princes" (vv. 7-8). And then Jesus told the Parable of the Great Banquet, to which all the excluded and broken people from the byways of the world get invited, whereas all those who are more concerned with holiness regulations than with presence at the banquet are told to stay away.

In short, over and over the concern of Jesus is with those people that the Old Testament calls the widows, the orphans, and the aliens — and with all those that the holiness regulations of the Old Testament classified as unclean. Over and over Jesus brings them back into community. Once we understand the contours of justice as described in the Old Testament, and once we compare that to the pattern of Jesus' own actions, it is impossible to say that Jesus did not care about justice. Jesus did the works of justice.

Those who say that we must wait rather than work for justice regularly claim that Jesus did not struggle to change social structures or explicitly command us to do so. But in fact Jesus attacked the whole social structure of Pharisaism, attacked it for all the exclusions that it practiced, attacked it in word and deed. And He did so in the context of embracing that whole *shalom* vision of the Old Testament. He did not exclude from that vision the references to justice — indeed, how could one? On the contrary, He said that He had come to proclaim release for the captives and to set at liberty those who are oppressed.

CARRYING ON THE WORK

What remains to consider is how you and I are to participate in this coming of the Kingdom of justice and *shalom* that Jesus both announced and signified by manifesting. The answer can be approached from many different angles. One of the most important, it seems to me, is from the angle of the New Testament declaration that the church is the body of Christ on earth. Jesus is no longer physically present among us. Yet we are not to think of Him as simply absent from earth. The church on earth is to be seen as His body; and in that body His Spirit is present. The conclusion seems to me unavoidable: that we are to carry on, with such means as are given to us, Jesus' work of proclaiming the coming of the Kingdom and producing samples of its justice and *shalom*. We are to live with the outcasts, we are to console the brokenhearted, we are to heal the lepers, we are to lift the burdens of legalistic religion, we are to release the captives, we are to liberate the oppressed. And we are to do all these as signs — as *sampling* signs — in lives that are lives of discipleship. Obeying and imitating God now acquire the new quality of following Jesus. While enjoying such bits of health and justice as there are in our world, and struggling for their increase, we are always to say to ourselves and to all humanity, "Remember, there is more."

I have said that God's longing for justice and God's practice of justice are grounded in God's love for each and every, and in God's longing for a human community that will reflect God's holiness. Jesus, I said, showed us what it is to live that love and struggle for that holiness by himself thus living and struggling. And I have suggested that Christian piety will incorporate the struggle to imitate God and follow Jesus in these respects. Let me close by referring you to the picture sketched out in Psalm 72 of the good ruler who imitates God in His justice.

> Give the king [your] justice, O God,
>   and [your] righteousness to the royal son!
> May he judge [your] people with righteousness
>   and [your] poor with justice!

> Let the mountains bear prosperity for the people
>   and the hills, in righteousness!
> May he defend the cause of the poor of the people,
>   give deliverance to the needy,
>   and crush the oppressor!

> May he live while the sun endures,
>   and as long as the moon,
>   throughout all generations! . . .
> May all kings fall down before him,
>   all nations serve him!

> For he delivers the needy when he calls,
>   the poor and him who has no helper.
> He has pity on the weak and the needy,
>   and saves the lives of the needy.
> From oppression and violence he redeems their life;
>   and precious is their blood in his sight.

CHAPTER EIGHT

Restoring Justice

HOWARD ZEHR

The original concept of shalom, as we have seen, did not exclude the victims of society. Through the centuries, however, the Church, like the legal system, has shifted the focus from the hurting individual to intolerance for breaking the rules. Today's criminal justice system charges the offender with a crime against the state — not against the victim. In many cases the ensuing process is actually a hostile environment for victims. Can a more restorative form of justice — one that takes into account the victim's role — find its way into our legal system? Fortunately, changes are taking place. But unless churches take up their vital parts, change will be slow in coming.

To deal with wrongdoing, society must decide how it will administer justice. The choice generally falls among three predominant responses — what might be somewhat simplistically characterized as the "three R's" of justice: revenge, retribution, and restoration. In order to offer an appropriate answer to the victim's cry for justice, we need first to look at these three types of justice.

First is *the justice of revenge*. If society does not respond adequately to wrongdoing, there are those who will take justice into their own hands. As we have seen in Rwanda and the former Yugoslavia, revenge is a deadly spiral, incompatible with organized society, the Hobbesian nightmare. Fortunately, the two other "R's" of justice offer themselves to the world today.

Second, then, is the response of the predominant Western legal system, expressed through the criminal justice system. This is *the justice of retribution*. Its strengths — such as the encouragement of human rights and the promotion of the rule of law — are substantial. As a system of justice, however, it has flaws.

Criminal justice tends to be punitive, impersonal, and authoritarian. With its focus on guilt and blame, it discourages responsibility and empathy on the part of offenders. The harm done *by* the offender is balanced by harm done *to* the offender.[1] In spite of all this attention to crime, criminal justice basically leaves victims out of the picture, ignoring their needs. Rather than promoting healing, it exacerbates wounds. Retributive justice often assumes that justice and healing are separate — even incompatible — issues.

The third approach to justice is more reparative in focus. *The justice of restoration* is essentially harm-focused, meaning that victims' needs and rights are central, not peripheral. People — not the state — are seen as the victims of the crime, and offenders are encouraged to understand the harm they have caused and to take responsibility for it. Dialogue — direct or indirect — is encouraged, and communities play important roles. Restorative justice assumes that justice can and should promote healing, both individual and societal.

1. This approach to justice is today fueling a crime-control industry that has no discernible limits and may actually be undermining democratic society. For a frightening analysis, see Nils Christie, *Crime Control as Industry: Towards Gulags, Western Style* (New York: Routledge, 1994).

Restorative justice is, in fact, an older form of justice than our more predominant retributive style. It is the dominant theme of African customary law, of the indigenous Maori culture of New Zealand, and of the aboriginal people of North America. For those of us from European backgrounds, it is the core justice of our ancestors as well. Restorative justice is also the essence of biblical justice. The current assumptions of justice — that rules are more important than the harm done, that the state rather than the victim is the primary stakeholder in justice, that focus should be on guilt and punishment — are relatively recent.

The Western legal system has often repressed this more traditional restorative approach in the interest of uniformity and state control. Fortunately, people today in various parts of the world — including here in North America — are finding ways to draw the best from both retributive and restorative justice.

Some basic assumptions about retributive justice and restorative justice are outlined in Figures 1 and 2 (on pp. 134-35). Retributive justice and restorative justice may appear to be poles apart. They are perhaps best viewed as "ideal types" on opposite ends of a continuum. Our goal should be to build upon the strengths of the retributive, criminal-law process in order to move it closer to the restorative, victim-centered approach.[2] We can visualize this continuum as a gas gauge. At present, the needle is near "empty." Our job is to move it toward "full" by making justice more restorative.

WHY VICTIMS GET SIDELINED
IN THE LEGAL PROCESS

As we look more closely at the retributive criminal-justice system of our time, we see that there is a logical reason for its neglect of crime victims: They are not part of the crime equation, that is, the defini-

---

2. For a fuller discussion of restorative justice, see Howard Zehr, *Changing Lenses: A New Focus for Crime and Justice* (Scottdale, Pa.: Herald Press, 1990/95); and Dan Van Ness and Karen Heetderks Strong, *Restoring Justice* (Cincinnati: Anderson Publishing Co., 1997). See also Paul McCold, *Restorative Justice: An Annotated Bibliography* (Monsey, N.Y.: Criminal Justice Press, 1997).

Figure 1. Restorative vs. Retributive Justice		
	Retributive	**Restorative**
The Definition of Crime	A violation of the law in which the state is the victim	A violation of people and relationships
The Aim of Justice	To establish blame (guilt) and administer pain (punishment)	To identify reponsibilities, meet needs, and promote healing
The Process of Justice	A conflict between adversaries in which offender is pitted against state, rules and intentions outweigh outcomes, and one side wins while the other loses	A process that involves victims, offenders, and community in an effort to identify needs and obligations (dialogue, mutual agreement)

tion of crime. Crime is an offense against the state. Consequently, the primary "players" are the state, which is active, and the offender, who is passive and self-protective. The victim is legally on the sidelines, called in primarily when needed as a witness or when mandated by special legislation. Victims are not intrinsic to justice as we know it.

To further add to their separation, the historical processes that moved victims to the sidelines in the social-political realm have been paralleled within the Church in the theological realm. In a provocative essay, Julian Pleasants argues that, breaking from its earliest traditions, the Church also came to view criminal behavior as a violation of a higher authority.[3] Offenses became not violations of individuals but sins against God, a God who would punish unless appeased. From there it was a short step to the idea that salvation is gained primarily by making things right with God in order to avoid punishment. We who offend are encouraged to seek forgiveness

3. Julian Pleasants, "Religion that Restores Victims," *New Theology Review* 9/3 (August 1996): 41-63.

Figure 2. Restorative vs. Retributive Justice		
	Retributive Justice	**Restorative Justice**
Definitions	Defined narrowly, abstractly, a legal infraction	Defined relationally as violation of people
	Only legal variables relevant	Overall context relevant
	State violated	People violated
Actors	State (active) and offender (passive)	Victim and offender primary along with state and community
Process	Adversarial, authoritarian, technical, impersonal	Participatory, maximizing information, dialogue, and mutual agreement
	Focus = guilt/blame	Focus = needs and obligation
	"Neutralizing strategies" encouraged	Empathy and responsibility encouraged
Outcomes	Pain, suffering	Making things right by identifying needs and obligations; healing; problem-solving
	Harm by offender balanced by harm to offender	Harm by offender balanced by making things right
	Oriented to past	Oriented to future

135

from and reconciliation with God quickly, before we are punished severely. Our obligations to human victims can be minimized. Not surprisingly, chaplains often encourage prisoners to seek forgiveness from God with little reference to their obligations to the people they have harmed.

In short, traditional Christianity has worked to release the offender from guilt while leaving the victim still hurting. In contrast, Pleasants notes, God's plan was to reinforce the importance of human victims by identifying with them: that is a core meaning of the cross. Referring to Andrew Wung Park's book entitled *The Asian Concept of Han and the Christian Concept of Sin,* Pleasants argues that God's heart is wounded by the hurt of the victim more than by the sinner's breaking of the law. In contrast, Western concepts of justice make law-breaking central to both justice and salvation.

All of this is part of a larger process in which Christian thought has been shaped by secular law and philosophy. In what Dutch law professor Herman Bianchi has called a "historical short-circuit," concepts originally formulated within the broader context of *shalom* were taken and used piecemeal within a framework set by Roman law.[4] Rules became predominant, and God became a stern judge. Punishment and retribution took precedence over restitution. Victims were thus relegated to the margins.

Biblical justice envisions God's intention for humankind as a condition of *shalom,* a world in which people live in right relationship, a condition of "all-rightness."[5] The wrong of crime is less that it breaks rules than that it damages relationships, making the right relationships of *shalom* impossible.

To a large extent, crime is defined as harm. When the focus is on the harm that has been done, victims and their needs — and the obligations of offenders to victims — become central to the process of justice. In order to explore what justice means in practice, we must

4. Herman Bianchi, "Justice as Sanctuary," unpublished manuscript. See also Herman Bianchi, *Justice as Sanctuary: Toward a New System of Crime Control* (Bloomington: Indiana University Press, 1994).

5. My understanding of *shalom* draws especially upon Perry B. Yoder, *Shalom: The Bible's Word for Salvation* (Newton, Kan.: Faith and Life Press, 1987). See also Zehr, *Changing Lenses,* chapter 8.

begin by reviewing victims' experiences and emotions. Then we can look at what they deserve from justice and from their communities.

THE VICTIM'S REACTION TO CRIME

Let us begin to do that by listening to some voices:

This is crazy
I am crying
screaming
hiding my face in shame
I am weak
and can't rest.
My stomach is like a stone and
my fingers ache from clenching.
I suffer.
You!
You walk calmly
among people, relatives
They don't know you
as I do.
You smile
and feel no guilt
no shame.
You walk away from my pain.
This is crazy.
I carry the weight of the sentence
but you are the killer.[6]

If the perpetrator of the crime came into this room right now
I . . . would want to kill him for what he did to me.
I would shake him until I could kill him with all my strength —

6. Martha Janssen, "Crazy," in *Silent Scream* (Minneapolis: Augsburg, 1983).

how dare he take away from me what I have worked for, struggled for?
How dare he destroy my library card, union drug card?
What did he do with my personal possessions that mean so much to me?
I would want him to pay for his crime.
I feel his potential can be rape, robbery,
that he is dangerous, noncaring, an animal let loose in society.[7]

Set up a prosecutor against this criminal,
someone to bring my accusations against him.
Let him have a trial, but find him guilty,
for even his prayers are a crime.
I hope he doesn't live long, that someone else
gets his job, that his family is left without him.
I'd like to see his creditors take everything he has.
I hope he is left alone, without love, with no
descendants, cut off even from God.

Who are these voices? The first, as you may have surmised, is the voice of an abused woman. The second you might assume is from a victim of, perhaps, a deadly assault; in fact, it is from the victim of a theft. Did you recognize the third? It is from the Bible: I have paraphrased Psalm 109:6-15 in modern language.

These are anguished and angry voices. They speak words we do not often hear in polite company, certainly not in church settings, for several reasons. Our society is organized around the pursuit of happiness. Suffering is to be avoided; pain is a bad thing. For Christians, moreover, pain often represents failure: a failure of faith, a failure of God's presumed control over the world. And the anger in these voices seems a failure to love and forgive, a contradiction of Christ's commands. So we try not to listen to these voices.

Yet, as these voices remind us, victimization is a devastating experience that affects many areas of a person's life. Seemingly minor offenses can be deeply traumatic, even life-altering. The similarities

---

7. Quoted by Shelley Neiderbach in *Invisible Wounds: Crime Victims Speak* (New York: Haworth, 1986), p. 57.

in responses to so-called minor crimes and those commonly termed serious crimes are often more important than the differences. Many result in a form of traumatic stress.

Bruce Shapiro, editor of *The Nation,* was the victim of a nearly lethal knife attack. He describes his experience as "a profoundly political state in which the world has gone wrong, in which you feel isolated from the broader community by *the inarticulable extremity of experience*" (emphasis added).[8] This captures well the sense of disorder, the sense of isolation, the feeling of being out of control and cut off from others who have not shared the experience.

Basic human relationships are called into question. Along with that come many doubts — about faith, about relationships, about oneself. When others do not acknowledge the victims' trauma, the doubts may extend to the validity of their feelings and their interpretations of the events that have affected them.

A major reaction is fear — intense fear. That fear may lessen, but it can be associated with events or people — strangers, men, people of other races — for years to come.

Victims also have to face their vulnerability, their helplessness. Anger is usually part of the experience — anger at the perpetrators, anger at themselves (self-blame is a normal response), anger at "the system," anger at friends who refuse to listen or who blame victims for what happened, anger at God, who "allowed" this to happen. In fact, many victims experience a religious crisis as they try to reassess their assumptions about a God who could allow or even cause this to happen. Questions add to the turbulence: Who did this? Why? Will they try it again?

Frightening, unsettling dreams are common. Victims may relive the crime in their sleep. As Judith Lewis Herman has noted in her important book, *Trauma and Recovery,* they may experience unpredictable mood swings — between rage and the intolerance of aggression, between intimacy and the fear of it, between the repression of feelings and the sense of being overwhelmed by them.[9]

8. Bruce Shapiro, "One Violent Crime," *The Nation,* 3 April 1995, pp. 444-52.

9. Judith Lewis Herman, *Trauma and Recovery: The Aftermath of Violence — from Domestic Abuse to Political Terror* (New York: Basic Books, 1992), pp. 37-50.

There is no escape, awake or asleep, from the memories and feelings.

> Judith Lewis Herman points out that crime may force victims to struggle with the same developmental issues that they faced in childhood: identity, autonomy, self-control, aggression, social relationships. That, in turn, occasions a deep grieving process, not only for the person or things that actually may have been lost in the crime but also for the part of themselves that has died, their shaken sense of trust in God and the world, the damage done to their sense of place and identity. The sense of loss may be profound and requires mourning. The descent into mourning, warns Herman, is both dreaded and unavoidable.

Victimization involves profound grief — grief at the loss of property, of loved ones, of one's sense of security and identity, of faith, of innocence. In marriage, the fact of this grief and the differing ways that partners deal with it can lead to serious relational problems; the divorce rate among victims of serious crimes is unusually high. Diane Leonard, one of the survivors of the Oklahoma City bombing, was asked to testify during Timothy McVeigh's sentencing trial. She described her sense of grief like this: "I think the best way to describe it is I feel like I died, too, on April 19. I feel like my heart looks like that building. It has a huge hole that can never be mended. . . . There is nothing in my life that is the same."[10]

We see through these reactions that the crisis of victimization is *all-encompassing*. It can be described as three overlapping circles that touch every part of one's being: a crisis of self-image (Who am I really?), a crisis of meaning (What do I believe?), and a crisis of relationship (Whom can I trust?).

10. Quoted in *NOVA Newsletter* 17/2 (1997): 2.

THE PERVASIVE CRISIS

The crisis of victimization is also *fundamental* because it undermines three underlying assumptions or pillars upon which we build our sense of safety and wholeness: autonomy, order, and relatedness.[11]

First, all of us need to feel that we control our own lives. This need for *autonomy* reveals the reason for the dehumanizing nature of slavery: a lack of personal power undermines a sense of wholeness. Likewise, when a crime occurs, someone has taken control over the life of another. In fact, victims may feel that their feelings and memories are out of their control for years afterward. Such loss of control is deeply dehumanizing and demoralizing.

Second, all of us also need the sense of safety that is rooted in a feeling of *order:* we need to believe that our world is basically orderly and that events can be explained. Cancer victims want to know why they have this disease just as crime victims want to know why they were victimized. Answers restore order, and order is one of the pillars on which we base our lives. We will discuss answers more completely in a later section.

(These two "pillars" help explain why victims so often blame themselves. Victims need to know why the crime happened. Blaming themselves is one way to provide those often-elusive answers and restore some sense of order. Also, blaming oneself is a way to achieve a sense of autonomy; if we attribute the crime to something we did, we feel some control because we can try to avoid that behavior in the future.)

Third, all of us need a sense of *relatedness.* Healthy relationships with other people are essential; indeed, it is through interaction with others that we form and affirm our sense of identity. We all need to be accepted by others. We need to know whom we can trust, where we fit in. Crime undercuts this sense of relatedness. Crime victims often become suspicious of strangers, even neighbors. When family and friends do not respond as helpfully as they might — and many times we do not — victims often become alienated from them as well.

---

11. See, for example, Robert Johnson, *Death Work: A Study of the Modern Execution Process* (Pacific Grove, Calif.: Brooks/Cole Publishing, 1990), pp. 128-30.

Victimization represents a profound crisis of identity and meaning, an attack on the self as an autonomous yet relational individual in an orderly world.

Another way to understand the violation of crime is that it represents an attack on meaning. As Robert J. Schreiter has written in *Reconciliation: Mission and Ministry in a Changing Social Order,* we construct our sense of identity and safety to keep from feeling vulnerable.[12] We do this by creating symbols of people, objects, and events and preserving them in narratives or stories about who and what we are. These are our truths.

Suffering — whether through victimization or oppression — is essentially an attack on these narratives and thus erodes their meaning. To heal, victims have to recover their stories, creating new narratives that take into account the awful things that have happened. The suffering must become part of the story.

To recover this sense of meaning, it is important to express the pain. For many, that requires the repeated retelling of the "narrative of violence." This retelling and venting allows some easing of the trauma and begins the construction of a new narrative; it puts boundaries around the story of suffering in order to allow victory over it. According to Schreiter, this means reconstructing one's own story, but it also means hooking that story onto a larger narrative of meaning. Here the Gospel may provide an essential framework.

Through these processes, victims learn that they can face the pain without going insane. They make it part of their own story, a painful but distant episode in the larger narrative of their lives. This is why the words "forgive" and "forget" do not belong together; if anything, the pairing should be "remember and forgive," as the Truth and Reconciliation Commission of South Africa has repeatedly emphasized.

12. Robert J. Schreiter, *Reconciliation: Mission and Ministry in a Changing Social Order* (Maryknoll, N.Y.: Orbis Books, 1992).

In short, crime is a denial of the personhood of victims, a failure to value them as individuals. When we as friends or family members or caregivers fail to respect their needs, we perpetuate this disrespect for victims. When the legal system ignores victims, the cycle of disrespect is further perpetuated.

THE CRIMINAL JUSTICE PROCESS: A HOSTILE ENVIRONMENT FOR VICTIMS

Victims often feel that the criminal justice process not only leaves them out but also steals their experience and reinterprets it in foreign legal terms. For instance, if an offender pleads guilty in a plea bargain, the offense is usually renamed as a different or lesser charge. If victims are involved at all, their participation is usually limited to the role of witness. In that role, what they can contribute to the process is tightly circumscribed and emotionally very unsatisfying. Indeed, victims and survivors who were asked to be witnesses in the Oklahoma City bombing trial of Timothy McVeigh had to petition Congress to be allowed into the courtroom when they were not testifying.

Judith Lewis Herman observes that the adversarial setting of the court is a hostile environment. She describes the courtroom as an organized battlefield in which the strategies of aggressive argument and psychological attack replace the physical force of the medieval duel. "If you set out to design a system for provoking intrusive post-traumatic symptoms," she writes, "one could not do better than a court of law."[13] Is it any wonder that healing is so elusive?

On their journey toward justice and healing, victims have many needs. While only they themselves can define and address some areas of need, the larger community — including the criminal justice system — has a major role to play in creating a context where healing is facilitated. As Shapiro reminds us, victims often feel utterly isolated and alone. In Herman's terms, "disempowerment" and "disconnection from others" are the core of the trauma of victimization. Recovery,

---

13. Herman, *Trauma and Recovery,* p. 72.

All justice processes involve rituals. Unfortunately, the rituals of the criminal justice process are not aimed at healing; they may serve certain needs of the state and the larger society (including the need for scapegoats), but they rarely serve victims well. Victims often need rituals of lament and mourning. Rituals of vindication, remembering, and testimony are also essential.

Those who participated in a day-long "palaver" on rituals of justice and healing at Eastern Mennonite University in the spring of 1997 identified five categories of ritual that seem important to the justice process: lament, atonement (confession, remorse), reparation, re-entry, and reordering of one's life. Others could be added: participant Sam Doe of Liberia told of the ritual of cleansing used after massacres in his homeland. A similar kind of ritual was performed by members of my own church in the home of a woman who had been attacked there.

therefore, is based on empowerment and new connections, and these things can happen only in relationship to others.[14]

Neither the community nor the justice system can do anything that can substitute for the individual work that victims must do, but both can dramatically facilitate or impede the process of healing. We will look first at what victims deserve from the justice system, and then make some suggestions about what we as the Church can do.

WHAT DOES JUSTICE REQUIRE?

As we have observed, victims feel profoundly disrespected by crime. A respectful and just response to victims should therefore be organized around their needs. Among these are the five crucial needs that follow.

Most urgent, at least initially, is the creation of a safe space,

14. Herman, *Trauma and Recovery*, p. 133.

emotionally as well as physically. Victims want to know that steps are being taken to prevent the recurrence of this experience, for them as well as for others. This safe space includes a place to express, without judgment or blame, their anger and fears. It also includes a place to mourn; as Herman notes, mourning and reconstruction go together.[15]

Crime victims also want restitution. In part this means repayment for losses, but more important is the symbolic statement involved. Restitution symbolizes a restoration of equity, and it states implicitly that someone else — not the victim — is responsible. It is a way of denouncing the wrong, absolving the victim, and saying who is responsible. Accordingly, restitution is about responsibility and meaning as much as or more than actual repayment of losses.

Restitution helps with the need for validation *and* vindication, both of which are extremely important to most victims. Often it is assumed that victims want vengeance. Various studies suggest, however, that this may not be an inevitable response. Victims do want vindication, but vengeance is not the only or even the most satisfying form of it. In fact, Herman warns that revenge is the mirror image of the offense.[16] It might seem like it would be satisfying, but in fact it often retraumatizes the victim. The demand for vengeance may often be the result of justice denied, a failure to find vindication in more healing forms.

More important than restitution, surveys tell us, are answers to questions. Victims want to know what happened and why, because, as noted earlier, answers restore the sense of order that is essential to health. They want answers that are real, not conjectured; they want answers that are as multilayered as real life, not the simplistic, binary answers that emerge from the legal process. Some of these answers are interpretive and have to be discovered by victims asking themselves certain questions, such as "Why did I react as I did? Why have I acted as I have since that time?" Factual answers, however, generally come from asking key questions of others: "What happened? Why did it happen? What is being done about it?"

15. Herman, *Trauma and Recovery,* chapter 9.
16. Herman, *Trauma and Recovery,* pp. 189-90.

Also important is what people who work with victims of domestic violence call "truth-telling," and what we have discussed earlier as narrative or story. Victims need to tell their story, their "truth," perhaps over and over, to people who matter in order to redefine their identities. This includes the opportunity to vent their feelings of anger, betrayal, and grief — natural parts of the healing journey.

Finally, victims need to feel empowered. Power has been taken away from them. They need activities and experiences that encourage involvement and empowerment.

DOING JUSTICE:
OPPORTUNITIES FOR THE CHURCH

A number of restorative justice processes are emerging throughout the world that attempt to address these needs.[17] In most cases, they involve forms of victim-offender "conferencing" that work parallel to and in cooperation with the established legal system. Some — such as those in Canada and New Zealand — draw upon indigenous justice traditions but adapt them to the realities of the modern world, including the Western legal system. New Zealand is unique so far in that it has reshaped its entire juvenile justice system — according to F. W. M. McElrea, one of its judges — into the first restorative-justice system institutionalized within a Western legal system.[18] The process has been successful at meeting victims' needs while holding offenders accountable and is now being piloted on the adult level as well.

These approaches first emerged in North America in the form of Victim-Offender Reconciliation Programs (VORP). Victim-offender reconciliation or mediation programs work in cooperation with the

---

17. Recent sourcebooks on the practical approaches discussed here include *Satisfying Justice: Safe Community Options* (Ottawa, Canada: Church Council of Canada, 1996); *Restorative Justice: International Perspectives*, ed. Burt Galaway and Joe Hudson (Monsey, N.Y.: Criminal Justice Press, 1996); and *Family Group Conferences: Perspectives on Policy and Practice*, ed. Burt Galaway et al. (Monsey, N.Y.: Criminal Justice Press, 1995).

18. See, for example, F. W. M. McElrea, "The New Zealand Youth Courts," in *Restorative Justice*, pp. 69-83.

existing legal system, receiving referrals from prosecutors, judges, and probation officers. Victims and offenders who agree to participate are brought together with a trained mediator or facilitator. In that meeting, victims are provided an opportunity to express their feelings, to tell their stories, to ask their questions, and to arrange for restitution for the wrong. Offenders are encouraged to develop empathy for their victims, to take responsibility, and to try to make things as right as possible — in effect, to be accountable for their actions. A restitution agreement is signed, often with the understanding that restitution is to be completed while the offender is on probation or while prosecution is deferred. Studies find that victims feel empowered and vindicated by these processes: satisfaction rates are high, fears are reduced, questions are answered, and healing is facilitated.[19]

More recent developments include forms of victim-offender conferencing that enlarge the circle to include families of victims and offenders, community members, and representatives of the justice process, such as police officers and prosecutors. Typically these approaches not only work toward a restitution agreement but also develop an overall plan for resolution of the entire case. For instance, Family Group Conferences — sometimes called community resolution conferences — emerged first in New Zealand and have been adapted in Australia, Europe, and here in North America. Sentencing Circles took shape in Native Canadian communities, and they too are being adapted elsewhere. These forms of victim-offender conferencing are today influencing existing victim-offender mediation programs to enlarge the circle of inclusion and the scope of the resolution.

Here is a natural opportunity for the Church. Indeed, the Church is essential to restorative justice. This is very much the Church's business. Christians are called to be ministers of reconciliation, to help create *shalom*. Victim-offender reconciliation is one of the best opportunities available for the Church to carry out this essential mission in our world today. Moreover, only if the Church acts will the essential

---

19. See Harry Mika, ed., *Victim Offender Mediation*, special issue of *Medallion Quarterly* 12 (Spring 1995); and Mark Umbreit, *Victim Meets Offender* (Monsey, N.Y.: Criminal Justice Press, 1994).

values of healing and reconciliation be maintained. The Church must not only support but also initiate these parallel justice processes. In doing this work, the Church will be meeting victims' needs for justice in a concrete way. Such work is central to our mission, as it was for the mission of Jesus, who began His ministry with these words: "The Spirit of the Lord is upon me because he has anointed me . . . to let the broken victim go free" (Luke 4:18, NEB).

We are working toward restorative justice when we . . .

focus on the harms of wrongdoing more than the rules that have been broken,

show equal concern and commitment to victims and offenders, involving both in the process of justice,

work toward the restoration of victims, empowering them and responding to their needs as they see them,

support offenders while encouraging them to understand, accept, and carry out their obligations,

recognize that while obligations may be difficult for offenders, they should not be intended as harms and they must be achievable,

provide opportunities for dialogue, direct or indirect, between victims and offenders as appropriate,

involve and empower the affected community through the justice process, and increase its capacity to recognize and respond to community bases of crime,

encourage collaboration and reintegration rather than coercion and isolation,

give attention to the unintended consequences of our actions and programs, and

show respect to all parties, including victims, offenders, and justice colleagues.

Howard Zehr and Harry Mika, "Restorative Justice Signposts" (Akron, Pa.: Mennonite Central Committee, 1997)

THE WRONG RESPONSE

Far too often we as members of the Christian community fail to respect victims' needs and as a result magnify their pain and isolation.

Charlotte Hullinger, co-founder of Parents of Murdered Children, has pointed out that the book of Job provides a textbook on what not to do. Listen to these friends of Job:

Think now, who that was innocent ever perished?
Translation: You must be guilty of something or this would not have happened. The victim is blamed.

Happy is the one whom God reproves.
Translation: You are being punished for your own good, to teach you a lesson. Again, you must deserve this; you are ultimately responsible. Your children died for your good. Guilt is again heaped upon the victim.

Know then that God exacts less of you than your guilt deserves.
Translation: You are being punished and you deserved it; be glad it isn't worse!

Like the rest of us, Job's friends did not want to hear his story because it made them experience his pain; this is called "secondary victimization." When he did get through to them, they were uncomfortable with his anger and told him that he needed to move on. They gave unhelpful explanations, most of which blamed him in some way. They tried to provide answers rather than establish a context in which he could find his own. Hullinger has pointed out that Job's friends did well for the first seven days, until they quit listening and opened their mouths![20]

Like most victims, Job was trying to find answers.[21] The journey

---

20. Charlotte Hullinger, unpublished materials.
21. Adapted from Charles Finley and Hamilton I. McCubbin, *Stress and the Family*, vol. 2 (New York: Brunner/Mazel, 1983).

to healing often involves finding answers to six fundamental questions:

What happened?
Why did it happen to me?
Why did I act as I did at the time?
Why have I acted as I have since that time?
What will I do if it happens again?
What does this mean for my self-image and my worldview?

Some of these questions are factual. Others are interpretive, and the answers cannot or should not be provided by others. Rather, our task is to support victims in a way that facilitates their search for meaning.

The question of responsibility looms large in these questions; as Herman has explained, judgment is very important in recovery. Victims do not want to be blamed for what happened, but neither do they necessarily expect blind affirmation. Victims are trying to find a balance between unrealistic guilt and complete denial of moral responsibility, between harsh criticism and blind acceptance. What they certainly do not need is the kind of blame implied when we ask, "Why were you carrying money? Why were you out alone? What did you do to deserve this?"

Listen to these words from a survivor of incest:

> I feel very trapped and afraid I won't make it sometimes. Is there hope for people like me? The Church hasn't been much help to me. I have felt that I am an outcast with a deadly disease, and people want to stay away from me. They didn't want to hear how I was doing; they just said that God would take care of it. But I am often angry with God and still have a problem relating to God. But nobody wants to hear that either.[22]

The Church should be a place of refuge, but often we have not known how to listen, how to be present to victims. We have told

22. Source unknown.

them that their anger is wrong, that they need to move on, to for-give, to forget. We have denied their right to mourn and instead have laid new burdens on them. All this is understandable — as part of our effort to distance ourselves from pain and vulnerability — but not at all helpful.

THE RIGHT RESPONSE

Fortunately, the Scriptures provide positive as well as negative les-sons about responding to victims. The Psalms in particular hold some important keys. As Walter Brueggemann has observed in *The Message of the Psalms,* we usually focus on psalms of joy and reassur-ance.[23] Actually, the Psalms hold many expressions of grief and an-ger, of lament. Brueggemann says that they form a pattern that rec-ognizes the reality of human experience. They recognize that lives involve pain, and that pain in turn evokes rage, depression, and guilt. These reactions are natural and necessary, but they do not have to grip one forever: life also holds times of surprise and bless-ing and recovery, of new coherence when we thought all was lost. The Psalms recognize that life is a movement among these states — organization, disorganization, and reorganization.

According to the Psalms, the key to that movement toward reorga-nization and recovery is this: Everything must be brought to speech and to God. There is no emotion and no experience that is not a proper subject for discussion with God. As we see in Job, that includes anger, even at God. Everything, says Brueggemann, must be brought to God, even if it is scandalous. God is a God of sorrow, "acquainted with grief," who does not will evil and who suffers with us. This is the ultimate meaning of the cross: God suffers with us, and from this suf-fering can come new life. After the cross is resurrection; after dark Fri-day comes the light of Easter. We cannot have one without the other.

In Schreiter's terms, we must tell the narrative of pain in order to ease the trauma and to create a new, victorious narrative. In doing

23. The discussion of lament draws heavily upon Walter Brueggemann's *The Message of the Psalms: A Theological Commentary* (Minneapolis: Augsburg, 1984.)

so, we embrace a new story that is not about shame and humiliation but, as Richard Mollica has noted, about dignity and triumph.[24]

Many of the Psalms help us get to that point; Brueggemann calls them "lament psalms." Look, for example, at Psalm 109, which was quoted earlier. It expresses vindictiveness toward the offender, a yearning for retaliation. Like many victims, the psalmist wants the offender to experience the suffering he himself has endured. He gives voice to these feelings without guilt, then sees that hope and deliverance can come only from God. By expressing his rage, the psalmist has handed it over to God. The lament is complete.[25] Ultimately, then, Psalm 109 is an act of liberation, moving the speaker to freedom.

This suggests that coming alongside those who need to lament is a crucial task of the Church, not only to help crime victims but to help those who are ill, who are dealing with divorce, who are suffering the pains that life inevitably delivers. This lament may be expressed through a variety of rituals within settings of worship and support. Such lament within the community of believers has at least four functions:

1. It gives victims an opportunity to tell their "truth," to give their sorrow words — an important step in healing, as we have seen. (Note that in Mark 5:33, Jesus asks "Who touched me?" after the woman who touched his cloak is healed from her bleeding. With this question, Jesus encourages her to tell him "the whole truth" as part of her healing.)
2. It recognizes that the wrong should not have happened. It acknowledges and denounces the wrong without placing blame.
3. It provides scope for questions without imposing answers; answers are important, but they must be found, not given.
4. It frees others to talk and share with those who have been hurt. It breaks the ice so that friends no longer have to be afraid to broach the subject and victims no longer have to feel like outcasts because people are afraid to talk to them.

24. Cited in Herman, *Trauma and Recovery*, p. 181.
25. See also Mort MacCullum-Patterson, *Toward a Justice that Heals* (United Church Publishing Co., 1988).

Lament is a precondition for healing. To remind those who suffer that God suffers with us is to help them connect their stories to a larger narrative of meaning, the larger story of the Gospel and the Church. This can and should happen in public as well as private settings within the life of the Church community.

AND FORGIVENESS?

This article appeared in the *Lancaster New Era* newspaper in Pennsylvania:

> Dr. R. Clair Weaver and his family spent Sunday doing what they enjoyed — they attended church in the morning and joined other relatives for a meal and get-together in the afternoon.
>
> There was no indication that anything was amiss with the well-known area doctor, his wife, Anna May, or two of their children. There was no argument, no conflict, nothing at all to indicate what would happen next.
>
> Later Sunday evening, the Weavers' 14-year-old son, Keith, told police he stabbed and killed his parents and sister, Kimberly, 15, and raped and assaulted another teen-age relative at the Weavers' East Hempfield Township home.
>
> The Rev. Samuel Thomas, pastor of Landisville Mennonite Church, which the family attended, said the Weavers "have had the normal parent-teen struggles that families had. I don't think there were any indicators leading up to this."[26]

This was a horrendous crime, unfathomable, that rocked the community and the church to its core. In the days and months that followed, the surviving family and the Landisville Mennonite Church struggled to respond. The way was often unclear, and they will tell you that there are things they should have done differently, but they did many things well. Here are some of the things they did:

26. *Lancaster New Era*, 18 January 1991.

On the Sunday following, a hospital chaplain directly addressed the tragedy in a sermon, and resource people trained in grief counseling were provided for each Sunday school class. This initial response was followed by a series of sermons on grief, forgiveness, and other related topics.

Church members helped to clean up the house and came to see this as an important part of the grief process.

An ongoing organization, the Bereavement Resource Group, was established.

The church established a legal support committee to look out for the needs of Keith, the offender. In this way, the surviving brother and sister would not need to feel responsible and could work on their own needs.

Eight months later, Charlotte Hullinger, formerly with Parents of Murdered Children, was brought in to spend time with the family and the church.

A year later, a memorial was held at the church as a time of remembrance of the lives lost. Lament was central in this process, and it did not mean that the question of forgiveness was ignored. In fact, the surviving family members had made a public commitment to forgiveness at the funeral, but they recognized that this was not simple. Rather, they acknowledged that they did not necessarily feel forgiving, and often would not feel forgiving, but that it was a journey to which they were committed.

To make that concrete, the church and family established a "seventy times seven" fund to collect money for Keith's expenses, recognizing that forgiveness was a decision that would need to be made over and over, "seventy times seven."[27]

The difficulty of this undertaking was captured by reporter Mark Beach in the Lancaster *Sunday News:* "Inside Janice Horning, Keith's aunt, was a tug-of-war. One side, full of pain and anger, wanted to pull away from him. The other side, filled with unrelent-

---

27. For an account, see Andrea Schrock Wenger, "How Does a Congregation Deal with a Triple Murder?" *Gospel Herald,* 9 February 1993, pp. 6-8.

ing anguish, called her to forgive the teen. . . . Forgiveness? It is not an easy task, Horning admitted, but in the same breath, she said forgiveness is what she chooses."[28]

Pastor Sam Thomas put it like this: "My own personal, human sense of justice is to get even. But forgiveness is an act of God's grace. You don't forgive and forget; you forgive again and again and again."

A precondition for that journey of forgiveness is the space to lament. Listen, for example, to Wilma Derksen,[29] a journalist for the *Canadian Mennonite Reporter*, whose daughter was abducted and murdered:

> Soon after the funeral, when I was still raw with grief, a friend came over. The tea was good, the room warm and quiet, and she said, "Wilma, I know that you have forgiven. I sense no vengeance. But knowing that, if you could let yourself go, what would satisfy justice for you? Would it be an execution?"
>
> Till that point I had never allowed myself [to ask} the question. But I felt safe with her, and her question was a fair one, so I decided to explore my inner feelings.
>
> My first reaction was no, it wouldn't be enough. If the offender were executed, he would be dying for something he had done and deserved. Candace died in the prime of her youth for no fault of her own. I groped for some kind of equality.
>
> I was shocked when my answer was, "Ten child murderers would have to die . . . and I would have to pull the trigger."
>
> In my mind's eye, I saw ten hooded figures lined up against a brick wall, and I pulled the trigger ten times. The feeling was delicious.
>
> But the camera of my imagination continued to roll, and I saw the ten hooded figures fall. I saw the blood and desecration. I saw the hoods fall loose and their faces vulnerable in death. I looked up and saw the mothers mourning the losses of their

28. Lancaster *Sunday News,* 27 October 1991.

29. Wilma Derksen attended the theological forum as a participant. For more of her story, see the sidebar on p. 192.

sons. And being so close to my own grief, I could identify fully and felt their losses as keenly as I felt my own. Coming back to reality, I was devastated.

But I was grateful for the friend who gave me the security to explore my anger and who recognized the need to clarify justice for myself. I felt I was one step closer to wholeness.[30]

JUSTICE IN TERMS OF PEACE AND RESPECT

Let us conclude by returning to the question of justice and beginning to reframe justice in new terms: instead of using the language of war and violence, using the language of peacemaking and respect.

Criminologists Richard Quinney and John Wildeman note that since its origin in the late eighteenth century, criminology has focused on retribution and punishment. The historical drift in criminological theory has been that if crime is violent and wreaks violence on our fellows and our social relations, then the effort to understand and control crime must be violent and repressive.

The alternative, they argue, is a criminology of peace, justice, and liberation. They go on to observe that such a peacemaking school of criminology is beginning to develop. I urge that we continue to develop this school, redefining justice so that the goal becomes that of making peace. True justice is not achieved by waging a "war on crime" but rather by building just and peaceful relationships.[31]

When we offer university classes on crime, they are often framed as studies in "delinquency" — that is, rule-breaking. We might look instead at an alternate perspective: What is fundamental about crime is less delinquency than disrespect.[32]

---

30. Derksen, "Capital Punishment: A Murder Victim's Mother Searches for a Response," *Mennonite Reporter*, 11 May 1987, p. 5.

31. Richard Quinney and John Wildeman, *The Problem of Crime: A Peace and Social Justice Perspective* (Mountain View, Calif.: Mayfield Publishing Co., 1991), pp. 40-41.

32. For the relationship between violence and disrespect, I am indebted to Harold E. Pepinsky, *The Geometry of Violence and Democracy* (Bloomington: Indiana University Press, 1991).

We have seen that victims certainly experience crime as that: a fundamental disrespect for their space, their property, and their person. Too often, however, that is also how they experience justice: as disrespect for their person and for their needs. What many victims resent most fundamentally is not that the law was broken but that their privacy, autonomy, and worth were disrespected. What they want most from justice — and so rarely get — is an experience of respect.

Many of us believe the old maxim "violence begets violence." Violence is essentially the ultimate form of disrespect, so disrespect can be said to lead to disrespect. This is definitely true for victims, who find it almost impossible to respect offenders. Consequently, they are inclined to objectify offenders, seeing them as stereotypes, which in turn increases suspicions, fears, even racism.

But victims may also pass on the disrespect they have felt as victims to others, who then become victims. For example, children who are abused often grow up to abuse others. This phenomenon may be more prevalent than we think. Victimologist Ezzat Fattah argues that much violence is motivated by the experience (or perception) of having been victimized — the transformation of victim into victimizer, as he calls it.[33] Disrespect begets disrespect.

I suspect that much of the crime and violence we experience in our societies is rooted in or motivated by issues of respect and disrespect. At minimum, crime represents a lack of respect and empathy for others, but then also for oneself. How can one respect others if one cannot respect oneself? Much crime, much violence, is actually an effort to assert one's worth and power, to attain a sense of self-respect, albeit in unhealthy ways.

We live in a society that judges people's worth by their wealth and their access to power. We are constantly bombarded with images of affluence and status, with a single-minded emphasis on material success, yet opportunities for attaining these goals are limited. When denied legitimate avenues to these crucial sources of respect, some individuals may resort to illegitimate means to obtain them.

---

33. Ezzat Fattah, "Doing unto Others: The Revolving Roles of Victim and Victimizer," *Simon Fraser University Alumni Journal,* vol. 1, no. 1 (Spring 1993). See also *Accord* (Mennonite Central Committee, Canada), January 1994.

When denied the acceptance and the respect of society as a whole, they seek the acceptance and the respect of deviant subcultures. When denied legitimate means for gaining the acceptance and respect that we all require, they may strike out in anger.

One example of the role of respect is the "code of the streets" that is coming to dominate America's inner cities. In these places, where individuals are cut off from legitimate jobs and futures, a sense of nihilism has set in. Cornel West has described it as an eclipse of hope and the absence of love of self and others, "the lived experience of coping with a life of horrifying meaninglessness, hopelessness, and (most important) lovelessness."[34]

In this situation, the "code of the streets" reflects the values of an oppositional culture, says sociologist Elijah Anderson.[35] Respect or "juice" is hard-won and easily lost, and quantities are limited: getting it means putting someone else down, then trying hard to keep others from taking it away. The code involves presenting oneself as violent, unpredictable, risk-taking. Illegal possessions symbolize the ability to violate another, a positive value. Hard drugs are "cool" precisely because they are dangerous. Prison time is valuable because it proves one is tough. The code, then, is basically a framework for negotiating respect in a world turned upside down.

To address this condition, West calls for a politics of conversion. Listen to his prescription:

> Nihilism is not overcome by arguments or analyses; love and care tame it. A turning of one's soul must conquer any disease of the soul. This turning is done through one's own affirmation of one's worth — an affirmation fueled by the concern of others. A love ethic must be at the center of a politics of conversion.

He concludes that we have two choices: "Either we learn a new language of empathy and compassion, or the fire this time will consume us all."[36]

34. Cornel West, *Race Matters* (Boston: Beacon Press, 1993), p. 14.

35. Elijah Anderson, "The Code of the Streets," *The Atlantic Monthly*, May 1994, pp. 81-94.

36. West, *Race Matters*, p. 19.

If crime is rooted in issues of respect, the justice-as-war strategy is doomed to fail. Only a policy that addresses those underlying causes which deprive men and women of self-respect can hope to be successful. Only a justice that treats each actor as a full participant, that encourages communication and empathy, that addresses the needs of victims as well as offenders — only this kind of justice can provide a way out of the mess in which the Western world finds itself.

The only true justice is one where peace and justice embrace. This is the Church's business.

CHAPTER NINE

Behold, I Make All Things New

L. GREGORY JONES

Sometimes life's experiences are difficult to understand. During those times that seem cloaked in sin and evil, we either remember our pain in order to condemn others, or we try to forget in order to free ourselves. But Jesus has set a different example for us, the example of forgiveness, a concept that must reshape our thinking and living. The challenge becomes one of making God's reconciling love more of a reality in our lives and world. As we help victims of crime — as well as ourselves — learn the steps to the "dance of forgiveness," the way is opened for us to see our lives in the grace of the crucified and risen Christ.

Victims of crime can generally count on hearing two standard clichés: "Forgive and forget" and "Time heals all wounds." There is a certain measure of folk wisdom in each of these sayings, wisdom that ensures their survival from generation to generation. We recognize, for instance, that there is danger in claiming to forgive someone for an offense, only to plan on remembering it for use against the person in the future. We know of situations and relationships in which we need to let the past stay in the past, for otherwise the past would burden us and block our growth. Further, we know that some cuts and wounds simply take time to heal. Given such time, our bodies and our spirits exhibit a wondrous restorative power; often we forget that the wounds were even there.

Yet we also know the limits of these sayings, particularly the latter one. Time alone does *not* heal all wounds; if it did, we would not need physicians, surgeons, counselors, or psychiatrists. On the contrary, many untreated wounds will fester, become infected, and perhaps spread poison throughout our bodies. A more accurate saying would be, "Time heals some wounds, but time also causes some untreated wounds to fester and spread." But then, that is not nearly so pithy.

We are less attentive to the limits of "forgive and forget." One problem, which I will mention only briefly, is that it presumes our power to judge and forgive others in our day-to-day lives but ignores the fact that we too face judgment and need forgiveness. It is at least as important for us to learn to be forgiven; that is the logic of Matthew 7:1-5.

A deeper problem with this phrase is that we have so closely linked the logic of the two ideas — "forgiving" and "forgetting" — that we rarely subject them to scrutiny to see if they really belong together in the ways we typically expect. What about the time it takes, for instance, to come to a place of forgiveness? C. S. Lewis reported in one of his "letters to Malcolm" that he had finally forgiven someone after thirty years of trying and praying that he might do so. If it can take a very long time to discover forgiveness, how much more difficult might be the burden of forgetting, when the memory has been nurtured that long as well?

Ironically, in some sense the concept of time healing all wounds helps to minimize the potential danger of equating forgiveness with forgetting. Perhaps if we take a long enough view of the time necessary for healing, then we can have confidence that eventually — perhaps only after this life — we will be able to link our forgiveness of others and self to an ability to forget.

But other problems arise. Christian thinking about and living of forgiveness have too often been distorted; as a result, these things seem either cheap or impossible. And is it really in our best interests to forget? Should we remove from our hearts and minds those sins that we or others committed, sins that exemplified our separation from God and from one another? Could it be that the injunction to "forgive and forget" actually inhibits our ability to exhibit God's forgiveness as holy people? Put most starkly, linking forgiveness with forgetting tempts us to worship an uncrucified Christ, rather than Christ crucified and risen.

Hence, there are important psychological, moral, and theological issues involved in the dynamics of remembering and forgetting in relation to forgiveness. *Psychologically,* the crucial question is this: Even if we want to, can we find ways to forget things that happened — exclusive, of course, of unhealthy repression? *Morally,* the crucial question is this: Should we try to forget, or does that involve a betrayal of those who have been sinned against? *Theologically,* the crucial question is this: What would it mean for us to learn to "remember well" — a term that expresses the desire to view the past from a place of wholeness?

Such questions are pressed upon us in particularly poignant ways when we reflect on the experiences of victims of crime. Their experiences haunt us and burden our memories in ways that make it difficult truly to believe that God's Holy Spirit is indeed "making all things new."

This chapter will approach these difficult questions of forgiveness for crime victims in three steps. First, we will identify some crucial ways in which we need to re-envision our thinking and living of forgiveness. Second, we will explore how we might assist victims of crime in the healing of their memories through ministries of forgiveness. Third, we will look at the power of forgiveness in the life of a fictional character, Mr. Edward Ives, as he struggles with the burdens of his son's murder and, over time, locates his wounds in the healing wounds of the crucified and risen Christ.

PART ONE: FORGIVENESS AS A WAY OF LIFE

For Christians, forgiveness is the means by which God's love moves us toward reconciliation and restoration, even in the midst of the sin and evil that mar God's good creation. This forgiveness is costly, for it involves acknowledging and experiencing the truth of human sin — from our loveless indifference to our most horrifyingly evil behavior. In fact, the surest way to evade the importance of forgiveness is to deny that we ever need it. When someone responds to an offense by insisting that "I never forgive," a most appropriate response would be "Then, my friend, I hope you never sin."

The tragedy is that all human beings are complicit in sin. It is because of God's forgiveness in the midst of such brokenness — embodied most fully in the life, death, and resurrection of Jesus of Nazareth — that lives can be healed and communion re-created. This healing also involves us in practices that witness to God's forgiving, re-creating work. As such, forgiveness includes the imagination and enactment of a future that is not bound by the past or condemned to repeat it.

Misunderstanding Christian Forgiveness

So how do we misunderstand the implications of Christian forgiveness? One way is by separating the God of the Old Testament — a so-called "God of Wrath" — from the God of the New Testament — a so-called "God of Love." We forget that Scripture testifies to God's forgiveness in both the Old and the New Testaments. Israel knows a gracious, forgiving God even in the midst of its sinful betrayals of the covenant with God and of the Israelites' sins against one another. Moses appeals to God's character as a forgiving God (Exod. 33-34); the psalmists sing powerful penitential songs (Ps. 51); God reaches out to wayward Israel (Hos. 11); and the people offer sacri-

163

fices to God to forgive both intentional and unintentional sin (Lev. 4:22-31; 16:29-34). Further, this forgiveness is enacted in specific practices of the Jewish people, such as the observation of Yom Kippur, during which prayers of repentance are offered, and the process of seeking out those whom one has offended to request forgiveness and make reparation.

We also misunderstand the implications of forgiveness when we separate Jesus' ministry from His cross and resurrection. In the Incarnation, Jesus becomes vulnerable to the world of human beings. He becomes vulnerable not only to our capacity for forgiveness and love and joy but also to the manifold ways in which people diminish, betray, oppress, abandon, and kill one another. But though He is vulnerable to them, He does not allow Himself or us to be defined by them. Rather, He breaks our cycles of destruction by offering us new and renewed ways of living together.

So Jesus teaches His disciples to embody forgiveness as a way of life. He seeks to draw others into communion with God and with one another. As His ministry progresses, however, He is attacked in ways that are both more persistent and more threatening, leading ultimately to His death. Yet even in our unjust judgment, Jesus absorbs our sin and evil without passing them on. And in the resurrection, God vindicates the ministry of Jesus, showing that God's forgiving and reconciling love, His desire for communion, overcomes human sin and evil even at its worst. The risen Christ returns with a judgment that does not condemn but offers forgiveness and new life.

Just as Jesus in His ministry embodies forgiveness and calls us to imitate Him in this way of life, so His cross and resurrection provide the context for us to receive God's forgiveness and to forgive others in God's name. When Christians gather together for worship, we recall the significance of God's giving and forgiving love in Jesus Christ. All are invited to participate in that new life by hearing Jesus' judgment as a message of grace that can transform our way of living together.

Our worship of the risen Christ also sets the context for us to find new ways of coping with the conflicts and tragedies that can all too easily destroy others and ourselves. It can help us move in ways that embody forgiveness with one another, as the following true story suggests.

John, a twelve-year-old boy, and Marie, a nine-year-old girl who lived next door, were playing together one day. Unfortunately, they found a loaded pistol in a dresser drawer, and before long their make-believe game turned into a tragic nightmare: little Marie was dead. Everyone in town attended the funeral of the little girl — everyone except John, who refused to talk to anyone.

The morning after the funeral, Marie's older brother went next door to talk to John. "John, come with me," he said. "I want to take you to school." John refused, saying that he never wanted to see anyone again. "I wish it was me who was dead," he said. But the brother insisted and finally persuaded John to go with him.

Then this brother talked with the school principal and asked him to call a special assembly; soon 580 students filled the gymnasium. Marie's brother stood before them and said, "A terrible thing has happened; my little sister was accidentally shot by one of your fellow classmates. This is one of those tragedies that mar lives. Now I want you all to know that my family and John's family have been to church together this morning, and we shared in Holy Communion." Then he called John to come stand next to him, put his arm around his shoulders, and continued, "This boy's future depends much on us. My family has forgiven John because we love him. Marie would want that. And I ask you to love and forgive him, too." Then he hugged John, and they wept together.

To be sure, this is as much the beginning as it is the end of the story. Marie's family would need to continue to struggle to embody that love and forgiveness each and every day of their lives. And John would undoubtedly continue to struggle to accept that love and forgiveness. Yet Marie's brother had sought John out when he most needed it, had risked his own feelings of grief to offer a judgment of grace to John. Beyond that, he had also offered public witness to others, calling the whole community to practice forgiveness. The pattern of Christ's own ministry, death, and resurrection provides a context whereby Marie's brother could offer specific words, gestures, and actions that transformed the possibilities for a community to deal with its painful brokenness.

Christian Forgiveness at Work

Where, then, does God's forgiveness occur in our own lives? British theologian Nicholas Lash suggests that it occurs in "our transformed behavior as the outcome, in the Spirit, of God's utterance in the life and death of Christ." That is, we need the ongoing presence of the Holy Spirit as consoler and critic, as comforter, judge, and guide to empower us as we discern how to embody Christ's forgiveness in the world. This includes stimulating our imaginations with stories like the one about John and Marie as well as those from our own lives and communities. It also involves communicating and living with one another in ways that invite innovative gestures of forgiving love.

Christian forgiveness is not confined to churches; indeed, God's forgiveness also appears as the Holy Spirit works in the world. Whenever we see people who refuse to submit to sin and evil, we see glimpses of the Spirit's work of forgiving and making new. So, for example, in post-apartheid South Africa, the national commission on "truth and reconciliation" has been established as a means of avoiding the repetition of violence, vengeance, and conflict while nonetheless taking seriously people's responsibilities for their actions. There are also less dramatic — but no less profound — examples of ordinary people who glimpse the possibilities of reconciliation and new life. The Church needs to see where God's forgiveness may already be found in the world through the working of God's Spirit, recognizing and encouraging such healing and reconciliation as parables of God's forgiveness in Christ.

We understand the world and our own lives better as we come to understand the nature and purpose of God's forgiving and reconciling love. But how do we embody that understanding and make it more of a reality in our world? That is, how can we go about practicing forgiveness in our lives together? How do we help people — specifically, victims of crime — cope with their searing memories through forgiveness? In fact, can we?

A woman enrolled in one of my classes while she was in the midst of a trial as the victim of a rapist. I suggested that she might want to wait to take the course, as discussions on sin and forgiveness would undoubtedly open wounds for her, but she wanted to stay.

One time after we came to the session in class on loving enemies, she came to my office and said, "You know, that sounds good, and I know that Jesus said it, but I want the guy to rot in hell." I told her that I understood that. She then asked, "You talked about people praying. What did you mean?"

I answered by asking, "Would you be willing to let me pray for him for you?" There was a long silence. Then she said, "Well, I suppose."

A couple of months went by. She stopped me one day on campus and said, "Are you praying for him?" I said yes. She said, "O.K."

Six more months went by, and she came by my office. She asked, "Are you still praying for him?" I said yes, and she said, "Yes, I am, too." I asked her what she was praying, and she said, "I don't know. I just call out his name."

Two years later she wrote me a letter and said that she still could only call out his name. "But," she added, "I hope you are still praying for him."

Forgiveness can take a long time. A very long time.

The Dance of Forgiveness

We need to begin to learn the steps of a beautiful — if sometimes awkward — "dance of forgiveness." In what follows I briefly outline six steps that can help us in rehearsal but that are integrally interrelated in the actual performance.[1]

1. This list can be found in a modified form in my essay on forgiveness in *Practicing Our Faith*, ed. Dorothy C. Bass (San Francisco: Jossey-Bass, 1977), pp. 138-39.

My son died in a mountain-climbing accident. He was twenty-five. While this was not an instance of crime, we went through many of the same painful experiences that crime victims do. The response from well-meaning friends was especially difficult.

The most painful thing was the silence of friends. I will never forget one friend, a month later, asking my wife and me to go out for dinner with him and his wife. He laughed throughout the dinner and said not a word about the accident. He had never said anything before. We had ridden to the restaurant with him, and when we got back to his house he invited us in. I said, "No, I'm not feeling well." I am sure that he interpreted that as physical. Well, it was physical. There is nothing more painful than this kind of silence.

Part of the reason that people don't say anything about a crime or a death is that they think that wise words are expected, and they can't think of wise words. No one needs wise words to help people. All you have to say is, "I'd like to sit with you."

Another painful thing in these situations is that people think that they have to bring you consolation. Consolation takes the form of saying, "It's not so bad. You still have two children, etc." But that is not what the grieving, wounded person wants to hear. It is better to say, "This is bad" or "What happened to you was evil."

And, finally, there are the comments to this effect: "Put it behind you. Get over it. Get on with your life." It takes time to incorporate such a tragedy into the narrative of who we are. With victims of crime, this is even more difficult because of the shame and such things often connected with it.

Don't tell someone to "get over it." Don't give them a schedule. Don't read books on seven stages and say, "You are probably in the three-and-a-half stage now, right?" Oh, no! Sit beside them and give them all the time they need.

Dr. Nicholas Wolterstorff

1. We become willing to speak truthfully and patiently about the conflicts that have arisen. This is not easy, and there may not even be agreement about what has happened. Therefore, we need not only truthfulness but also patience, the virtue that the ancient theologian Tertullian called "the mother of mercy." When we try to be patient and truthful, we can more clearly discern what is going on.

2. We acknowledge both the existence of anger and bitterness and a desire to overcome them. Whether these emotions are our own or belong to the other party, it does no good to deny them. Besides, anger can be a sign of life, of passion; we should be more troubled by those whose passion is hidden or, worse, extinguished. Even so, we can learn to overcome and let go of anger and bitterness as we begin to live differently through practices that transform hatred into love. This is important, for otherwise anger can destroy. As Frederick Buechner puts it, "Of the seven deadly sins, anger is possibly the most fun. To lick your wounds, to smack your lips over grievances long past, to roll over your tongue the prospect of bitter confrontations still to come, to savor to the last toothsome morsel both the pain you are given and the pain you are giving back — in many ways it is a feast fit for a king. The chief drawback is that what you are wolfing down is yourself. The skeleton at the feast is you."[2]

3. We summon a concern for the well-being of the other as a child of God. Sometimes our partner in the dance of forgiveness is a total stranger; at other times, he or she is an intimate from whom we have become estranged. Either way, seeing those on whom we focus our bitterness as children of God challenges our tendency to perceive them simply as enemies, rivals, or threats. Now they are potential friends in God.

4. We recognize our own complicity in conflicts, remember that we have been forgiven in the past, and take the step of repentance. This does not mean ignoring differences between victims and victimizers; people need to be held accountable for their actions, and some people need to repent and ask forgiveness while those who have been victimized struggle to forgive. Even so, in all

2. Frederick Buechner, *World,* January/February 1996.

but the most extreme cases, we also need to recognize and resist our temptation to blame others while exonerating ourselves as wholly innocent victims. All too often, we see the specks in other people's eyes while not noticing the log in our own (Matt. 7:1-5). This is why it is important for us to remember our own forgiven-ness.

5. We make a commitment to work to change whatever caused and continues to perpetuate conflicts and crimes. Forgiveness does not merely refer backward to the absolution of guilt; it also looks forward to the restoration of community. Forgiveness ought to usher in repentance and change; it ought to inspire prophetic protest wherever people's lives are being diminished or destroyed. Many important changes have emerged as the result of people's willingness to embody forgiveness through struggles for change.

6. We confess our yearning for the possibility of reconciliation. Sometimes a situation is so painful that reconciliation may seem impossible. At such times, prayer and struggle may be the only imaginable options. However, continuing to maintain reconciliation as the goal — even if this is "hoping against hope" for reconciliation in this life — is important as a way of reminding us of the ministry of reconciliation that has been entrusted to us by God (2 Cor. 5:16-21).

As we learn to perform the dance of forgiveness in creative and innovative ways, we can more faithfully testify to Christ's reconciliation. We can do this in our ordinary lives as we learn — albeit slowly and often painfully — the habits and practices that shape a forgiven and forgiving people. They can begin with a refusal to accept the lack of love that has, over time, created a chill in our relationships. Or with a commitment to abandon the verbal and emotional abuse through which we diminish other people. Or with a steadfast commitment to pray for those who persecute others and us. Or perhaps by deciding to re-establish contact with someone from whom we became estranged a long time ago.

Those of us who have, over time, cultivated habits and virtues of holiness of heart, mind, and life will be better equipped to respond to those who face extreme crisis in ways that testify to the God who is making all things new.

PART TWO: FACING THE MEMORIES OF CRIME

We have seen from the outset that it is dangerous to link forgiving with forgetting, as forgiveness is bound up with learning to remember well. In fact, to suggest to many victims that they forget is to present them with a seemingly impossible task. Rather, they face the horrifying presence of memories with the power to paralyze them from even envisioning a better future. How does one cope with those realities where a degree of forgetfulness might help in the healing of the psyche?

Here is a suggestion made with particular poignancy in Amos Elon's 1993 essay entitled "The Politics of Memory":

> I have lived in Israel most of my life and have come to the conclusion that where there is so much traumatic memory, so much pain, so much memory innocently or deliberately mobilized for political purposes, a little forgetfulness might finally be in order. This should not be seen as a banal plea to "forgive and forget." Forgiveness has nothing to do with it. While remembrance is often a form of vengeance, it is also, paradoxically, the basis of reconciliation. What is needed, in my view, is a shift in emphasis and proportion, and a new equilibrium in Israeli political life between memory and hope.[3]

Elon addresses a difficult political issue in his recognition of remembrance as a form of vengeance and, perhaps, the basis of reconciliation. What would it mean for us to discover that "a little forgetfulness might finally be in order" and to suggest that, contra Elon, forgiveness does have something to do with it?

The Dynamics of Traumatic Memory

In order to begin dealing with this issue, we need to disentangle several different dynamics involved in traumatic memory, dynamics

3. Amos Elon, "The Politics of Memory," *The New York Review of Books,* 7 October 1993, p. 5.

that all too often converge in our most difficult social and political dilemmas — of victims of horrifying crime here and around the world, of the Middle East, of Bosnia, of Rwanda, of racial divisions in the United States, just to name a few. Disentangling them will help us understand the different yet overlapping issues involved in coping with searing memories.

First, there is the difficulty in coming to terms with a single individual episode whose horrifying effects are imprinted on our memories: the murder or suicide of a child, a rape or other sexual assault, a devastating betrayal, a bomb that destroys one's home and surroundings. Lloyd LeBlanc, a father whose son was brutally murdered and whose story is told in Helen Prejean's *Dead Man Walking*, has to struggle with memories each and every day of his life as he prays for the strength to embody forgiveness.

Second, there is the horror that grows out of repeated abuse, violence, or torture, the effect of which endures in the soul long after the beatings or the emotional assaults or the violence stop (if, in fact, they do stop).[4] This is particularly painful when there are permanent marks or wounds left on the body, but it is no less painful — and perhaps more difficult to identify and treat — when the wounds are imprinted only on the soul.[5]

Third, there is the horror that has not only assaulted individuals in isolated acts or in repeated abuse and violence, but whose effects have so pervaded a culture, a people, that they are passed on from generation to generation. A particular person may not have experienced anything directly, but the traumatic memories are searing precisely because of the ways in which the legacies of *prior* horrors continue to haunt the present.

Finally, there is the horror that mars people's memories not because the devastation happened to them but because they perpetrated it. An apt example of this is Albert Speer, the Nazi architect and Minister of Armaments who, after the end of World War II, genuinely

---

4. See the discussion in G. Simon Harak, "Child Abuse and Embodiment from a Thomistic Perspective," *Modern Theology* 11 (July 1995): 315-40.

5. For a particularly powerful discussion of these issues, see Elaine Scarry, *The Body in Pain* (New York: Oxford University Press, 1985).

sought to repent for his complicity in the Nazi regime. Even so, he was unable ever to acknowledge the full force of what he did — most specifically, his knowledge of the Final Solution — perhaps because he feared that he would have been unable to do so and continue to live.[6]

People may suffer from one or more of these diverse forms of haunting memories. They present different yet overlapping challenges, depending on the degree to which the memories reside in one's mind (even if they can't be controlled there, for both physiological and psychological reasons), or are found in social and political traditions, or, more generally, in some amorphous place "out there."

Remembering Well: Starting with the Return of Memories

In the midst of these struggles with memories, is it true, as Elon states, that forgiveness has nothing to do with it? Are there situations and relations where forgiveness and reconciliation are at best a matter of hoping against hope? Or is it perhaps the case that forgiveness has everything to do with it, understood in the eschatological work of the crucified and risen Christ?

At the heart of our learning to remember well is learning to be forgiven by God. As Rowan Williams has noted, "God is the agency that gives us back our memories, because God is the 'presence' to which all reality is present." Yet Williams does not shrink from the harder questions. He asks, "What if the past that is returned or recovered is a record of guilt, hurt, and diminution? The memory I have to recover is that of my particular, unalterable past; and if that is a memory whose recollection is unbearably painful, the record of a moral and spiritual 'shrinkage' or deprivation, how is it liberating? What of the destructive power of 'the bitterness which in human life so often succeeds what at least in memory seems fraught with promise,' the 'seeds of corruption' sown unseen?"[7]

6. See my analysis of Gitta Sereny's *Albert Speer: His Battle with Truth,* in "Becoming a Different Man: Inside Albert Speer," *Christian Century,* 8 May 1996, pp. 516-19.

7. Rowan Williams, *Resurrection* (New York: Pilgrim Press, 1982). p. 32. The internal quotation is from D. M. MacKinnon, "Some Notes on the Irreversibility of Time," in *Explorations in Theology,* vol. 5 (London: SCM, 1979), pp. 96-97.

Here we confront the complexities of memory: the tendency to forget, to indulge in vast self-deception, to wallow in bitterness and anger over hurts suffered, grievances unheard, offenses unforgiven or unforgiving. We struggle with the willingness to accept the diminution of ourselves through our refusal to remember well, whether it is the memory of abandonment, as it was for Mary at the tomb; or of betrayal, as it was for Peter by the fire; or of a refusal to repent, as it was for Cain, who was unable to master the sin lurking at the door; or of hostility because our enemies *do* repent, as it was for Jonah, who pouted outside the city. Whatever the situation and history of our sin, God engages with our particular pasts, seeking to redeem them for renewed life in the future.

Remembering Well: Finding Completion in Forgiveness

In this sense, forgiveness has everything to do with it. For, as Williams suggests, "If forgiveness is liberation, it is also a recovery of the past in hope, a return of memory, in which what is potentially threatening, destructive, despair-inducing in the past is transfigured into the ground of hope."[8] This occurs as the risen Christ returns to those who crucified Him with a judgment that does not condemn but instead offers the hope found in new life. But it is a hope that comes through the return of memory, not its erasure or its denial. Christ redeems the past; He does not undo it. Because of the offer of new life in Christ, the past — whatever it is — can be borne.

Our life in Christ is ritually signified in our dying and rising with Christ in baptism. We die to the old self, to be raised in newness of life. As forgiven sinners, we can learn to tell the story of our life differently — presumably, more truthfully — because we are freed of the burdens of telling forgetful or deceptive stories. We need not hide the truth about ourselves — both in praise and in penitence — for we find ourselves enveloped in God's grace. Further, as we live into our baptism, perhaps signified from time to time through services of

8. Williams, *Resurrection*, p. 32.

baptismal renewal, we locate our lives, our memories, and our forgiveness in the grace of the crucified and risen Christ.

Moreover, the Eucharist is the sign of a reconciled fellowship broken by human sin and infidelity. Note Williams's comments about John's and Luke's descriptions of the resurrection meals: in both, the meals "echo specific occasions of crisis, misunderstanding, illusion, and disaster. They 'recover' not only the memory of table-fellowship, but the memory of false hope, betrayal, and desertion, of a past in which ignorance and pride and the rejection of *Jesus'* account of His destiny in favor of power-fantasies of their own led the disciples into their most tragic failure, their indirect but real share in the ruin of their Lord. Yet Jesus, even as He sees their rejection taking shape, nonetheless gives Himself to His betrayers in the breaking of bread. The resurrection meals restore precisely that poignant juxtaposition of His unfailing grace and their rejection, distortion, and betrayal of it."[9]

So also the practice of reading Scripture can help to school us as people of forgiveness and holiness, as people whose memories are nurtured and conformed by the Spirit's uniquely particular grace regarding the crucified and risen Christ. For ancient and medieval Christians, there was nothing so important as memory, understood to be shaped by the habits and practices of attention to God and God's Word.

> What is at the heart of the issue of forgiveness is coming to a place where remembering is no longer a resource to be drawn upon for the possibility of vengeance.

In all of these ways, I am suggesting that forgiveness be linked far more closely to remembering well than to forgetting. Even so, what do we do about those situations in which Elon suggests "a little forgetfulness might be in order"? In part, this has to do with whether

9. Williams, *Resurrection*, pp. 39-40.

we really want our remembering to be the ground of reconciliation, or whether we prefer to completely absorb ourselves in our own wounds, licking them, savoring them, even allowing them to fester for the sake, in some cases, of moral and political mobilization. And if we are struggling for reconciliation, for healing, how do we learn to remember well if the day's task seems to be keeping the past from intruding into the present?

Memory: A Shield against Sin

In his recent book *Exclusion and Embrace,* Miroslav Volf offers a rich and complex set of suggestions about "the affliction of memory" and the potential significance of forgetting — or, as he (to my mind more accurately) also calls it, the significance of a "divine gift of non-remembering." Volf describes well the dangers of forgetting and the importance of learning to remember well as a sign of our forgiveness and reconciliation with God and others. The "certain kind of forgetting" that he advocates assumes that the matters of "truth" and "justice" have been taken care of, that perpetrators have been named, judged, and (hopefully) transformed, that victims are safe and their wounds healed, so that the forgetting can ultimately take place *only together with* the creation of "all things new."

He goes on to suggest that "if we must remember wrongdoing to be safe in an unsafe world, we must also let go of [its] memory in order to be finally redeemed, or so I want to argue here, and suggest that only those who are willing ultimately to forget will be able to remember rightly."[10]

Volf's analysis is profound, though — as I will suggest more fully below — I think his use of "the grace of nonremembering" is a preferable description to "forgetting." In this life we must be guided by the memory of sin as a shield against sin, by the memory of Christ's wounds that are healing in solidarity with all victims who have suffered and those who continue to suffer; and, as Volf insists, we must

10. Miroslav Volf, *Exclusion and Embrace: A Theological Exploration of Identity, Otherness, and Reconciliation* (Nashville: Abingdon Press, 1966), pp. 131-32.

remember their suffering, and we must allow that memory to be spoken out loud for all to hear.

Volf believes that this "indispensable remembering" should be guided by "the vision of that same redemption that will one day make us lose the memory of hurts suffered and offenses committed against us. For ultimately, forgetting the suffering is better than remembering it, because wholeness is better than brokenness, the communion of love better than the distance of suspicion, harmony better than disharmony. We remember now in order that we may forget then; and we will forget then in order that we may love without reservation. Though we would be unwise to drop the shield of memory from our hands before the dawn of the new age, we may be able to move it cautiously to the side by opening our arms to embrace the other, even the former enemy."[11]

Volf's proposal has the virtue of helping us to see a way clear to envisioning how to understand Elon's plea for "a little forgetfulness." Further, his analysis helps us understand the significance of key biblical passages that refer to God's forgetting sin, blotting out Israel's transgressions (Jer. 31:34; Isa. 43:25) and to God's imploring people not to remember "the former things" because He is doing "a new thing" (Isa. 43:18-19; 65:17).

Volf's suggestion that the task means being sure that the memories are "fully healed" is more fruitful than language about forgetting or erasing memories. There are two reasons why this is so. First, we need to be able to maintain some measure of continuity in the stories of our lives. Features of our lives and our relationships that are central to defining our identities include the horrors, the shattered brokenness that we experience. The only way in which we can still be identifiably ourselves and have even reconstituted identities and relationships is if our memories are healed rather than erased or forgotten.

The second reason is that, as I read the biblical passages dealing with these issues, including the book of Revelation, the vision of the Kingdom is a vision of wounds and brokenness fully healed rather than erased. Indeed, erasing memories would seem to be much

---

11. Volf, *Exclusion and Embrace*, p. 139.

closer to "uncrucifying" Christ than would healing those memories fully — eschatologically — through the healing wounds of the crucified and risen Christ.

Remembering Well: Healed Histories

How, then, do we understand the language about God "blotting out transgressions," "remembering their sin no more," and even the reference in Revelation's vision of the "first things passing away" with the new heaven and the new earth?

In brief, I believe that these refer to a transformation in which we will learn to remember our histories, even in their ugliness, in such a way that *we need not remember them as sin* because they will have been fully healed. We might use as an analogy the way that, in this life, time does heal many minor wounds so well that we don't remember them. So also in God's Kingdom, even the most horrifying memories of this life will be healed by the wounds of Christ — whose unjust suffering and death is, fundamentally, the most horrifying thing imaginable. This, I take it, is the force of Paul's statement in Romans 8:18 (NRSV): "I consider that the sufferings of this present time are not worth comparing with the glory about to be revealed to us."[12] In this sense, we will discover the passing of the first things, because our joy will be complete.

Ultimately, then, my description is slightly different from Volf's. Given the reality of sin and evil, there is nothing so whole as a broken and healed heart, nothing so complete as a new creation whose fractures have been fully healed, nothing so hopeful as the promise of the passing of forgiveness through the perfected holiness of disciples washed in the blood of the Lamb. We are given the eschatological divine gift of nonremembrance precisely through being "remembered" as the Body of Christ.

---

12. Compare Volf's assessment of the same verse on page 138 of *Exclusion and Embrace:* "If something is not worth comparing, then it will not be compared, and if it will not be compared, then it will not have been remembered." In my terms, it will not *need* to be remembered because it will have been fully healed and reconciled.

In this way, I join with Volf in suggesting the importance of vigilance in this life, standing in solidarity with the memory of those who have suffered and continue to suffer, while nonetheless opening our arms to begin to learn to embrace the other, even the former enemy. A little nonremembrance is in order, but only because that nonremembrance has — contra Elon — everything to do with the forgiveness wrought by Jesus Christ.

PART THREE: MR. IVES' HEALING

In this third and final section, I turn from these theological and speculative heights to a fictionalized account of an ordinary Christian man — a victim of crime — who suffered the trauma of memory and came dangerously close to the abyss of believing that the only hope of getting through the day was to keep the past at bay. However, because habits and practices of Christian living shaped his life — because his life was located in the drama of the God of Jesus Christ — he was enabled to pass on forgiveness. Ultimately, he began to envision the possibility of his own life being fully healed, even — or perhaps especially — in its brokenness.

This man is Mr. Edward Ives, the fictional character whose story is told in Oscar Hijuelos's *Mr. Ives' Christmas*.[13]

Mr. Ives had been abandoned at birth and adopted as a young child by a kindly man. He was nurtured in the Roman Catholic Church; the people and practices offered him a community that enabled him to tell the story of his life.

In many ways, Mr. Ives was just an ordinary New Yorker: he married, had two children, and worked as an executive in an advertising agency. But he was shaping a faithful Christian life through his ordinary habits and practices of Christian living.

But then, just before Christmas 1967, Ives' world was shattered. His teenage son Robert, who was preparing to enter the priesthood

---

13. Oscar Hijuelos, *Mr. Ives' Christmas* (New York: HarperCollins, 1995). My retelling here is adapted from my review of the book called "A World Shaped by Christmas," *Christian Century*, 22-29 May 1996, pp. 581-86.

the next year, was randomly murdered by a teenager, Danny Gomez, a Hispanic like Mr. Ives, who thought Robert had slighted him. When Ives saw his son's slain body, he thought of Jesus on the cross, trembling, as Ives imagined his son had trembled in his last moments. Then he remembered that Jesus had risen, and he wanted his son to rise up and the world to be right again.

They buried his son on Christmas Eve morning. Ives went to church to pray for guidance, begging God to bring forgiveness into his heart. Day after day, he knelt before the crèche and the crucifix and wondered how such tragedy could happen. But there was no clear answer; he felt an aching numbness descend upon him. He began to despair about the supernatural, yet waited every night for a supernatural event.

When Father Jimenez, a priest, asked him to visit the Gomez family, Ives went. At the family's apartment, he was met by the boy's grandmother. She begged for his forgiveness, and Ives embraced her. But the boy's mother insisted on her son's innocence, and in her scornful expression Ives read the story of her son's life.

Despite his own darkening spirit and his doubts about God's goodness, Ives began writing to Danny Gomez in prison. He also sent magazines and books to help him learn to read. Ives was not simply being altruistic; he thought his bitterness toward Danny was poisoning him inside, and he had to do something to get the poison out of himself.

Ives was haunted by his inability to forgive Danny. Danny had repeatedly invited Ives to visit him at the prison, but Ives had ignored the invitations. When Father Jimenez called Ives one Christmas to tell him that Danny was being released from prison, the very mention of Gomez's name had the effect of "spilling a poisonous gas into the room."

Ives' internal pain was manifested by the way he dug at his own skin while he was asleep. Welts and deep scratches began to form, and his body felt as raw as his heart. Half asleep, Ives associated his own wounds with those of the crucified Christ. He mistakenly thought that, as Christ's wounds were necessary to the resurrection, so his wounds were necessary — he needed to dig deeper into himself.

Then Ives had a dream in which he encountered his son as a man of forty-three, wading waist-high in a stream. His son asked him, "Pop, why do you keep doing this to yourself?" The narrator continues: "Then, bending, his hands cupped, his son scooped out a handful of water, and this he poured over his father's head, and then he brought up some more and washed his limbs with water; and then he was gone." When Ives awakened, the marks on his body had disappeared. He had been healed by a baptismal renewal at the hands of his deceased son. He had been digging into his own body in a morbid attempt to identify with Christ; his baptismal renewal identified him with Christ's healing power.

The following Christmas, when Father Jimenez called again, saying that Danny had changed and that "a little forgiveness and goodwill would go a long way," Ives agreed. When Danny met Ives, he saw a face filled with compassion. For his part, Ives "found himself trembling — with rage, joy, forgiveness?" But he controlled himself and put his arms around Danny, who "had started to cry, over the very goodness he had glimpsed so briefly just then in Ives' gaze." In those moments, Ives knew that his son was somewhere in the room, approving of what he beheld.

What enabled Ives finally to embrace his son's murderer, to offer and receive the gift of forgiveness, even in the midst of his own struggles and doubts? In part, he was sustained by his own disciplined practices. He refused to abandon Danny, just as he also refused the false consolations of repressing painful memories of his son. He continued his habits and practices of trusting in God and clinging to the path of righteousness, even in the midst of doubts and struggles about whether such things really mattered. In so doing, he had traveled much farther down the path of forgiveness than he had recognized. His final decision to meet Danny and to show him compassion and forgiveness had been forged by the habits of thinking, feeling, and acting that he had cultivated. Over time, such practices, as well as friendships, create habits of ordinary goodness that provide an extraordinary witness in times of crisis.

Most centrally, Ives was sustained by Christmas — or, more specifically, by the One at the center of Christmas. Ives was nurtured so profoundly in Christian living that he recognized that the won-

181

drous goodness of God's incarnate presence in the world couldn't be separated from God's confrontation with sin and death in the crucified and risen Christ. As at the beginning of the story, Ives discovered on the far side of his reconciliation with Danny the intimate connection between the first and the second advent of Christ: the coming of the babe in the manger and the coming again of the crucified and risen Christ.

Ives finally discovered that his experience of the world's goodness as well as his own could be found only in the midst of the world's wounds, focused in Christ's unjust death. Yet that goodness does prevail, because the redeeming light of Easter pierces the darkness of Good Friday, providing a renewed glimpse of the creating light of Christmas.

Ives came to this discovery painfully, as he had to learn that will and discipline alone are not enough for cultivating goodness and forgiveness. Even good people like Ives can destroy themselves if they fail to embody the practices of giving and forgiving love, which envelop us as recipients of the gift of God's grace. Ives' disciplined goodness enabled him to recognize the importance of such grace through his dream of baptismal renewal. The story of Mr. Ives eloquently shows us that the Jesus we encounter at Christmas, the expression of God's goodness and generosity, is none other than the crucified and risen Lord.

Ives' baptismal and Eucharistic practices enabled him to embody the reconciling power of Christian forgiveness. In so doing, he also offered a powerful witness to the ways in which we can respond to crime victimization with Christian forgiveness. People's lives, whether those of the criminal offenders or the victims themselves, can be changed by the grace of God in Jesus Christ. Mr. Ives was tormented by his memories of the harrowing murder of his son, but by living in Christ, he was enabled to keep the vision of God's eschatological reconciliation — and God's gift of divine nonremembrance — ever before him.

As we discover over and over again, forgiveness has everything to do with the ways in which, by the power of God's Holy Spirit, all things are being made new.

CHAPTER TEN

Every Knee Shall Bow

MARY WHITE

Generally in life we enjoy a balance of many plans and dreams, emotions, needs, and desires. One day flows into the next with the promise of familiarity and normalcy. But when crime attacks the safe boundaries of normal living, nothing is ever the same. Joys are shattered; pain is intensified to the point of being unbearable. Questions go unanswered. And Christians grapple not only with their own pain but with the command to reach out with the compassionate act of forgiveness to the one who caused the destruction of their happiness. Is this possible? Are there consequences for not forgiving? Here is the story of one woman's remarkable struggle to restore the balance of her own life. She offers help for those who need to find peace once again.

Forgiveness is never easy. It is difficult even with mild offenses. In the case of criminal attack, forgiving the offender comes at great cost. My interest in the topic of forgiveness comes from the impact of crime on my own life. That experience has more firmly rooted my belief that practicing forgiveness is a foundational need in every Christian's — every person's — life and growth.

Forgiveness demonstrates the aspect of God's character that we find most difficult to practice. The magnitude of God's forgiveness of humankind, shown most fully in the exchange of His Son's life for our redemption, staggers the mind. It also sets the example for human forgiveness.

We find it much easier, though, to extend grace and mercy and love. We can feel the impact of this goodness bettering the world we live in. Forgiveness, on the other hand, requires attitudes and behavior in direct opposition to our human inclinations. When we are deeply hurt, we resist offering absolution to the offender. This is especially true when we feel the impact of crime. Then we respond instinctively with rage.

Crime had never been a consideration in my life. Although I had observed crime through the media and felt an abstract pity for the victims, no one in my family had ever experienced crime firsthand. Its devastation remained remote to me.

All of that changed in 1990, when our thirty-year-old son, our only son, was brutally murdered on his job. Steve was a radio announcer for a National Public Radio affiliate and also owned and drove his own taxi in his off-hours. It was in that cab that a fare pulled a gun from his pocket and shot Steve three times in the back of the head, severing his spinal cord and killing him instantly.

This horrifying event plunged us into the sorrowful world of crime victims. Someone most precious was stolen from us. We were drawn immediately into the complex quagmire that all victims are forced to make their way through after a crime.

Crime is never isolated in its impact. Although Steve was the primary victim, our family and others who loved him were victims as well. In fact, for every victim there are dozens of family members and friends who feel the impact as well. They not only struggle with their own grief but endeavor to offer advice and guidance and support through the difficult days that follow.

UNENDING QUESTIONS

Initially I didn't want to think about the murderer. I knew I couldn't grieve fully or share comfort with my family if I gave my emotional energy and attention to the person who had ended my son's life.

However, as I began to heal and slowly began to think rationally again, I recognized my need to grapple with forgiveness. When the murderer was apprehended two weeks following the homicide, his photo appeared in the newspaper. It was then that the reality of the profound evil one person could do to another hit home.

> Could I truthfully and completely forgive the man who placed a pistol at the base of my son's head and destroyed him, destroying as well the peace and joy of his family?

I have learned that all crime victims face the same questions: *Why? Why me? What did I do to deserve this? Where does the criminal think he gets the right to hurt me?* The answers remain hidden because there is no rational explanation for the viciousness and injustice of crime.

And yet the questions do not end. A year following Steve's death, long after I first confronted the need to forgive, I sat in the courtroom and heard the murderer confess to the crime, saying, "I shot Steve White three times in the back of the head." Once again those impossible questions flooded my mind: *Why? Why Steve? What did he ever do to this man?*

We were not allowed then and have not been allowed since to speak with the killer because of his erratic and often violent behavior. But this lack of communication in no way diminishes God's call to us to forgive. Direct confrontation is not required for forgiveness.

We may never speak with the murderer, yet God asks us to maintain a forgiving attitude toward him. This challenge has remained with us since Steve's death, for a day never passes without our remembering him, and consequently, his murderer.

NO OTHER ROUTE

My pathway through grief and to forgiveness has been long and arduous. The love and care of good friends has helped immensely. Undertaking a renewed study of the topic of forgiveness in Scripture helped me fashion a stronger foundation for my personal forgiveness of the murderer. The process moves from level to deeper level. Perhaps I will always be finding new areas of loss in my life for which to forgive the man who murdered Steve. But forgiveness must be as complete as possible given the present knowledge of the situation and the uncompromising admonitions of Scripture.

A familiar Bible verse that many of us learned in the early days of Sunday school came to mind frequently as I struggled with the concept of forgiveness. "Be kind and compassionate to one another, forgiving each other, just as in Christ God forgave you" (Eph. 4:32).[1] The clarity of this injunction didn't leave much room for doubt about the forgiving process.

Can forgiveness be an essential part of dealing with the criminal and the crime? Should someone who so clearly defies the laws of God and the tenets of common decency be granted the luxury of forgiveness?

We know the answer. Even when a criminal doesn't deserve forgiveness, God calls us to offer it. The way of forgiveness provides the perfect path toward a deeper life of faith in God and normalcy of life once again. In fact, forgiveness actually benefits the forgiver as much as the forgiven. The forgiver finds peace and power and release through the act of forgiving. He or she breaks the chains of angry thoughts toward the perpetrator and walks into healing and

1. Unless otherwise indicated, all Scripture quotations are taken from the New International Version.

freedom. Difficult though it may be, God commands forgiveness for the benefit of all.

GOD IS IN CONTROL

Following a crime, a Christian victim must re-examine trusted beliefs. Hard questions must be asked and answered:

Where was God when this dreadful act took place?
Is He truly sovereign?
Does He really care?
Are grace and mercy part of His nature?
How strong is evil in the world? Stronger than God's goodness?

Platitudes and clichés offer nothing. Only a renewed awareness and conviction that God is in control stabilize and guide a victim, like a sturdy rudder, through the rough waters of doubt and fear.

Although the justice system labels every crime with a few terse words, the reality for the victim is incredibly complex. A man may be charged with domestic abuse, but his wife bears the physical scars and suffers from inward fear, a sense of betrayal, and depression. Murder takes a victim's life but robs that person's family and friends for a lifetime. The crimes of slander and libel bring a loss of reputation and theft of peace of mind. Burglary and theft dispossess the victim of property but, more significantly, breed distrust and fear. Child abuse steals a childhood and may be reflected in loss of security, self-respect, and love. Even if the destruction is never reflected in the legal criminal charges, the crime kills the victim's security and destroys his or her trust in people.

Every crime is multidimensional. Jesus verified this when He said, "The thief comes only to steal and kill and destroy" (John 10:10). A thief will employ any means to accomplish his objective — even stealing, murdering, and destroying.

While every Christian affected by crime must confront the question of forgiveness, it helps to remember that it is a question of *biblical* forgiveness. In other words, we are not talking about a weak de-

Crime is incredibly complex and sudden. Victims have no preparation for the offense, no practice in dealing with the horror and lasting imprint of crime. No one anticipates or plans to be robbed or assaulted or raped. Life changes to turmoil and trauma. Normal existence disappears.

Neither is one prepared for the emotional reactions, which are immediate and powerful: fear, anger, despair, depression, confusion, bewilderment, and an overwhelming sense of grievance and injustice.

For a time, life is reduced to dealing with the traumatic consequences of the crime. Horror and shock engulf the victims. They are plunged into a frightening mass of conflicting emotions, confusing legal proceedings, and the complicated reconstruction of life after the crime.

nial of the wreckage left by the destroyer. Forgiveness goes to the essence of the God we love and serve. True biblical forgiveness recognizes the offense, recognizes the inhumanity of the offender, and chooses to forgive in spite of the hurt. The apostle Paul wrote, "Bear with each other and forgive whatever grievances you may have against one another. Forgive as the Lord forgave you" (Col. 3:13).

JUSTICE WILL BE SERVED

Many crime victims want to forget the offense ever happened. The memories are so horrible, so personally disabling, that suppressing the memories and consequences seems the only way to handle the hurt. But actually the reverse is true: recognizing the depth of harm provides a vital foundation for healing and complete forgiveness.

One helpful thing to know is that biblical forgiveness never eliminates justice. When Steve died, one of my most powerful fears was that he would be forgotten, and I feared that that would make his life seem meaningless. Finding justice for Steve seemed to ease that irrational fear. But a deeper truth penetrated my thinking: God is the pre-eminent judge. God's sense of fair play supersedes anything we might imagine. Justice meted out for the crime in human terms may not coincide with what the victim wants. Perhaps the criminal is never found or, if apprehended, is given a meager punishment for the crime. That doesn't change the fact that we are still called to forgive. But we can find great comfort in the fact that ultimate justice rests with God alone.

In America we have a system of law. That system attempts to protect both the accused and the victim. The proceedings may or may not result in adequate punishment. Law and justice do not always co-exist harmoniously. As the system strives for fairness and equity, the victim may encounter more abuse. Even when the assigned punishment is commensurate with the crime, the victim has still been unjustly harmed.

Thus, any crime victim who seeks consolation in equitable penalties for the crimes committed will be doomed to disappointment. True and impartial justice can be found only in God. Ultimate justice will be served by the supreme Judge of the universe. Waiting for justice before forgiving leads only to disappointment and frustration.

> God's command to forgive is a call to obey Him rather than our sense of human justice. It is a call to trust in His commands rather than focus on the severity of the offense. The command to forgive is clearly based on God's desire for what is best for us, because forgiveness brings with it a sense of release and peace.

Forgiveness presents a formidable dilemma for every crime victim. Crime inevitably alters life. Never again is life as simple and innocent as it was before the victim felt the blows of another's misdeeds. The powerful calamities that result from crime require direct confrontation by the victim. Chief among those confrontations is the essential obligation to forgive. Every crime brings loss. It is in order to heal that loss, that hurt, that we must forgive.

It is startling for a Christian to realize that a life of faith and trust in God does not exempt believers from the evil in the world. Job recognized this. Following the theft of his herds, the murder of his employees, the death of all his children, and the loss of his health, he posed a question to his bitter wife: "Shall we accept good from God, and not trouble?" (Job 2:10).

As part of the human family, we are subject to the frailties and tragedies that beset everyone. The difference lies in the strength and power that come from God to help us cope with the difficult challenges of life. Forgiving offenders ranks high among those challenges. Yet God never asks difficult things from us unless He gives us adequate strength and capacity to follow through.

THE HARD REQUIREMENT OF FORGIVING

Forgiveness, this very difficult assignment in our journey of faith, is presented with a frightening addendum. The record in the Gospel of Matthew clearly states that Jesus said, "Your heavenly Father will forgive you if you forgive those who sin against you; but if *you* refuse to forgive *them*, he will not forgive *you*" (Matt. 6:14-15, LB). These are very difficult words. The crime victim is innocent of wrongdoing. Why should he or she have to forgive? Because God commands it and because He wants us to experience the ultimate outcome of a forgiving nature: peace of mind and release from anger and hurt.

The threat of loss of relationship with God should be motivation enough for crime victims living the life of faith to forgive. God gives us warnings only when dire consequences will overtake us if we do not obey. Painful as it is to forgive, it is more painful to realize that God does not forgive our sin if we fail to forgive others.

But surely there are sins too horrifying, too hideous, too hurtful to forgive? Scripture lists no exceptions. Our forgiveness acknowledges and demonstrates the forgiveness we have received from God. Forgiveness is not optional in God's Kingdom. It is the bedrock of

God's relationship with us. Forgiveness is a crucial test of a Christian's obedience to God in the painful issues of life.

Forgiveness is a process. Rather than waiting for all feelings to fall into line, the victim can step out in faith and start the journey of forgiveness. Following the crime, some time may pass before the victim recognizes the need to forgive the perpetrator. But if the victim waits to fully understand the crime, forgiveness can be delayed. There is no human comprehension of the evil one person can inflict on another. Jeremiah 17:9 confirms this: "The heart is deceitful above all things and beyond cure. Who can understand it?"

An initial commitment to forgiveness is made by an act of will with God's help. The feelings will eventually follow.

Is this a hard requirement? Without question. Forgiveness is more difficult than suffering, sometimes more painful than the consequences of the crime itself. According to biblical injunction, there are no choices. No matter what the offense, God requires forgiveness. It is vitally important to Him because forgiving cost Him His son. Forgiveness of the deep hurts of life demonstrates the very nature of God.[2]

Forgiveness brings personal freedom, a sense of peace, inner strength, and the ability to live in the future, not in the past. There is a special kind of power in forgiveness. That power comes from God. That power takes us beyond our common selves and elevates us to a plane where we find control over our feelings and actions.

Forgiveness initiates release from the offender and enhances a vital relationship with God. It brings a renewed sense of dignity and internal tranquility. Forgiveness conveys power to the person who grants it.

---

2. Editor's note: Mary White shows us the grace of God in her attitude toward the forgiveness of transgressors. Some readers may have questions about when forgiveness should be extended, or whether we are responsible for forgiving even those who admit no guilt, demonstrate no repentance, and seek no forgiveness. The discussion of forgiveness is receiving a great deal of attention from scholars. Readers are encouraged to consult additional literature on the subject.

Thirteen years ago my daughter was killed. The city had helped us look for her for six-and-a-half weeks and, we wanted to thank everyone, so we held a news conference.

During the news conference we were asked, "What would your reaction be to the murderer if he were found?" Both my husband and I come from a Mennonite background, and we grabbed the only word that we thought would help us through. We said that we would forgive, not knowing what that word really meant.

Well, as we tried to forgive, I discovered that it did not spare us from the journey that we had to walk with our hearts. The rage was unreal.

It has been a long, long journey.

But I also realize that God takes His time. Only in this last year have I felt that I have some concept of forgiveness. And that came about because God designed something for me that was really unique. After talking about it for years and recounting the story of how I would want to kill ten child murderers to feel that justice had been done [see story, page 155], I was able to face ten violent men who were serving life sentences in prison. It wasn't designed intentionally that way; it just happened. I was alone with them and could ask them questions, and we had a wonderful two-and-a-half hours of exchange. I think that at that point I felt a kind of completion, especially since the person who murdered my daughter has never been found.

God is a part of this journey, and we have to allow victims to walk it. God has a plan, a way He wants to heal us. I had wanted to rush the process. I had wanted to be spared the journey, and now I realize that the journey is the richness of light. Maybe we have to drop forgiveness and forgetting at the door and just start walking.

Wilma Derksen

192

THE HIGH COST OF NOT FORGIVING

An unwillingness to forgive can lock victims in the past and enslave them to the offender. Rather than finding release, they remain linked to the past by unrelenting rage.

I have met many victims of crime who, years after the offense, still speak bitterly of the perpetrator. Their mental focus and emotional energy remain tied to the offender. What a sad waste of their lives.

In my association with the organization called Parents of Murdered Children, I have observed the despair and devastation of unforgiveness. One mother has announced, "I will never, never, never forgive the man who murdered my son. I hate him with every ounce of my being. He doesn't deserve forgiveness, and he will never get it from me." She rarely converses on any other topic. Her health is unsteady and fragile. Her friends are disappearing. Her life is consumed by her vehement fervor for revenge.

Another victim was a grandfather whose baby grandson had been shaken to death by the mother's boyfriend. He once told my husband and me in all seriousness, "I walked the streets today, looking for a hit man." We talked with him about a saner path toward healing. Although we have not maintained a personal relationship with him, we have since read in our local paper that his family has turned the tragedy to commemoration by establishing parenting clinics for at-risk young parents.

Forgiveness releases the victim to rise above the devastation of crime.

HELP FROM THE CHURCH

All this having been said, how can the Church participate in encouraging victims of crime to forgive?

Forgiveness can present the greatest challenge for the Church in aiding victims of crime. Practical aid and assistance following the crime give immediate relief and provide the Church with obvious ways to serve hurting people. The example of the Good Samaritan recorded in Luke 10 may be the most famous illustration of goodness in action. In our own century we had the vibrant model of Mother Teresa, who lived her life for the benefit of others in the direst of circumstances.

And all around us are selfless individuals who live out their lives in service to others. When the church encourages and mobilizes such people, the help given the hurting, the desperate, and the lost will bring about remarkable healing.

The Church will face immediate roadblocks when attempting to help crime victims face the implications and task of forgiving offenders. As we have seen, the average victim, even the solid Christian, naturally resists the idea of forgiving one who has inflicted such pain. The very notion that forgiveness is in order offends a victim's sense of justice and fair play. It is into that resistant environment that loving Christians can bring practical help and suggest the healing power of forgiveness.

What about people who lack faith and have no knowledge of a forgiving God? Should the Church guide them toward forgiveness as well? God has established a number of institutions and precepts that benefit all humanity. Take, for example, the institution of marriage. Marriage is not a "Christian" institution; it is a human institution. The Ten Commandments benefit humanity through their wisdom and orderly instructions. So it is with forgiveness. When practiced, forgiveness brings peace on a personal, societal, and global level.

> The Church has an important role in sharing the goodness of God in every situation of life. It is the task of the Body of Christ to foster stability in and offer spiritual guidance to those who are hurting, believers and nonbelievers alike. The opportunities for practical help and spiritual guidance abound among those who have been wounded by crime.

Although an appeal on the basis of biblical conviction cannot be made to someone who has no confidence in the Bible, the concept of forgiving for the sake of personal release and serenity bears repeating. Forgiveness will operate the same way for Christian and non-Christian alike. It usually proves more of a struggle for someone who does not rely on God's power for help. A caring Christian can offer such an individual the support and counsel to move toward forgiveness.

It is a daunting task for a loving member of the Body of Christ to help a crime victim understand and practice forgiveness. A personal friendship provides the most effective way to counsel crime victims toward forgiveness. Certainly teaching from the pulpit will aid in this process, but a relationship in which a victim is personally accountable to a concerned and tender mentor offers the most persuasive help. This need not be a relationship of long standing; it can develop after the crime takes place. The important thing is to offer the victim a haven for processing the grim aftermath of criminal offense.

Professional counseling may be useful, especially if the situation is particularly complicated or long-standing. But many situations need only the loving concern of a friend or mentor to help create an environment in which trust can be rebuilt and forgiveness can find a place.

Here are some specific suggestions that the Church can follow:

1. Help the victim face the offense. Many victims choose to ignore the pain of their victimization and bury it beneath an avalanche of rage and bitterness. Encourage the victim to feel the pain and move through it. If the victim doesn't go through this process, the effects of the crime linger within, waiting for acknowledgment, sometimes for years. Deft and gentle questions can aid in this painful procedure. Anticipate the anger and hurt of the victim during this process. Every victim rightly feels these emotions and needs a secure place to express them before moving to the next logical level of forgiveness.

2. Help the victim acknowledge the severity of the hurt. A loving friend can give a wounded victim the right to rehearse the offense and define the grievousness of the hurt. A quick and flippant dismissal of the pain will only deepen the harm. On the other hand, thoughtful confirmation of the distress will help the victim express the extent of the wounding.

3. Help the victim recognize that God's personal forgiveness is available for every human being. The crucial message of the Gospel is wrapped up in God's love and forgiveness. That fact remains foundational even when we are victimized by crime. Being a victim doesn't elevate one to a place where the personal practice of forgiveness is unnecessary. Rather, it provides a context in which the victim can recognize God's forgiveness and the command to practice it toward others.

4. Help the victim seek God's strength in order to obey God's command to forgive. Sensitively and prayerfully encourage the victim to forgive the offender as quickly as possible following a crime. This involves releasing the offender to the mercy and justice of God and refusing to live in anger and bitterness or be consumed by a desire for revenge. This step in healing presents a huge hurdle for many crime victims because, as mentioned before, the injustice seems overwhelming. The recognition that forgiveness is essential may take some time.

5. Do not make the victim feel "guilty" if he or she struggles with forgiveness. Reassure the victim that forgiving does not mean forgetting. The devastation of the crime will remain forever in the mind. Forgetting is impossible, but the crime can be put in perspective by forgiveness.

6. Help the victim practice repeated forgiveness when necessary. An inquiring Peter smugly asked Jesus, "'Lord, how many times shall I forgive my brother when he sins against me? Up to seven times?'" Jesus answered, "'I tell you, not seven times, but seventy-seven times'" (Matt. 18:21-22).

Jesus decreed repeated forgiveness. Knowing the frailty of the human condition, Jesus devised a plan of forgiveness that goes far beyond anything we would require of ourselves.

Some in the Christian community might suggest that forgiveness be deferred until the victim gains an understanding and grasp of the offense. But a victim may never fully comprehend the deadly evil behind crime. A victim needs to practice forgiveness to the fullest extent possible. Forgiveness is essential to peace of mind and healing.

7. Help the victim focus on hope for the future. Hope resides in a personal relationship with Christ and God's promises to us that He has our best interests at heart. In Jeremiah we read, "'For I know the plans I have for you,' declares the Lord, 'plans to prosper you and not to harm you, plans to give you hope and a future'" (Jer. 29:11). Through loving Christian relationships, crime victims can move toward a new future and renewed hope. Life may never be the same, but because of God's loving power, it can be even better than before the crime.

As the prophet tells us in Isaiah 61:2-3, God is a redemptive God who comes "to comfort all who mourn," to bestow on those who grieve "a crown of beauty instead of ashes" and "a garment of praise instead of a spirit of despair."

8. Summon prayer support for those struggling to offer forgiveness. Many church members feel inadequate and awkward in offering direct help to those who are in pain and hurting, but they can pray and want to pray. Mobilize them to undertake this important support task for victims. Just knowing that others are praying brings comfort and energy to those who need to be restored and to forgive.

9. Develop support groups as a resource for encouragement. Support groups are important, but keep in mind that some victims may be reluctant to share the details of their experience in a larger setting. Approaching a support group for additional help is something that a crime victim has to feel ready to do; the timing is different for everyone.

10. Avoid pushing for victim/offender reconciliation too quickly. Legal considerations often prevent contact between victim and offender. If the possibility arises for a confrontation leading to reconciliation, the victim needs support and guidance through this process. The victim should always be accompanied by an impartial person when in the presence of the offender.

All victims need a safe place to go and a caring person with whom to share their anger, fear, and outrage. When they find it in a Christian context, they can be encouraged to face the hurt and the offense against them. Then forgiveness is the next logical step toward healing. With forgiveness comes release, a changed mental focus, personal freedom, and, finally, recognition that ultimate justice is in God's hands.

When I consider the damage inflicted on our family by the murder of our son, I can only place it in relationship to the comfort and healing God has given us. Can God forgive our son's murderer? Without question — if he chooses to seek forgiveness. Without personal contact, we have no way of knowing if the murderer has requested forgiveness from God. We have forgiven him. We know that forgiveness from God is available to him.

And when, in eternity, "every knee shall bow . . . and every tongue shall confess that Jesus Christ is Lord" (Phil. 2:10-11, LB), Steve and his murderer can kneel together, forgiven, before the throne of God. The loving, merciful, powerful forgiveness of God is offered to everyone. He asks for that same forgiving spirit in each one of us.

CHAPTER ELEVEN

"Forgive and Forget" and Other Myths of Forgiveness

DAN B. ALLENDER

Forgive and forget. Isn't that the "Christian" way to deal with the pain and rage of assaults against us? No, says Dr. Allender, we miss the mark when we misunderstand the biblical aspects of forgiveness and reconciliation. By dismantling this and other "myths" of forgiveness and then addressing what forgiveness really means, Dr. Allender fills us with the hope that true forgiveness is within reach after all. It is a reality that we can embrace, in every hurtful and devastating circumstance, with whole and peaceful hearts.

The woman sitting in my office seethed with a growing anger. I could see her pulse quicken and her face redden with rage. The father who had sexually abused her when she was a child had called recently, after years of neglect, to invite her to dinner. Finally her anger erupted. "How dare he walk into my life and expect me to take him back with open arms! I want him dead!"

Almost as suddenly as she said this, she began to wither. Her skin took on a lifeless pallor. She spoke in a drab, wooden fashion. "I know I need to forgive him. I just can't seem to break free of the hurt and anger."

As a counselor, I felt stuck. We both agreed that she was unforgiving, but I knew that her shift from hatred to guilt had nothing to do with a true understanding of what it means to forgive. She feared that forgiving would lead to a deep inner deadness, not a taste of life. She believed that forgiving her father would invite him to further abuse her and crush her heart.

I probed further. "You say you would like to see him dead. Is it even more accurate to say you would like to kill him?" She sat back in her chair. The color returned to her face, and she admitted hesitantly, "I'd love to shoot him. I want him to pay for what he did to me and to the other people I know he abused."

"What a shame," I replied.

She lowered her head, and the shroud of guilt again descended. "I know, I know," she lamented. "I shouldn't want to hurt him, but I do." Her anger and her desire for revenge proved to her that she was unforgiving.

"I think you've misunderstood my remark," I continued. "The shame is not in wanting to see him pay, but in the method of revenge you've chosen. What would you think about the prospect of his lying face down in a pool of excrement, inhaling dung until he drowned?"

Her head popped up.

"You are sick!" she blurted out, incredulous. "That is the most awful thing I've ever heard in my life. Are you a Christian?"

I assured her I was. And I attributed the idea of drowning an unrepentant sinner in dung to its proper source. It was not my idea of revenge. It was God's (Isa. 25:10-12).

Like my client, many believers have an understanding of forgiveness — and all of its aspects, including the concept of vengeance by God's own merciful hand — that is clouded by a haze of error. Forgiveness is too often seen as merely an exercise in releasing bad feelings and ignoring past harm, pretending all is well. Yet nothing could be further from the truth. True forgiveness often deepens internal passion and sorrow. Yet it is a powerful agent in a process that can transform both the forgiver and the forgiven. It is a gift that pierces a hardened, defensive heart with rays of redemptive kindness.

PART ONE: MYTHS ABOUT FORGIVENESS

Let's look first at the misunderstandings of forgiveness that rob Christians of perspective, passion, and purpose. In Part Two we'll explore what it means to forgive.

The Myth of Forgetting the Harm

A central misunderstanding that fuels many other myths about forgiveness is the notion that we are to "forgive and forget." The concept comes from two major passages of Scripture: Psalm 25 and Jeremiah 31. In Psalm 25:6-7, the psalmist asks God not to remember the sins of his youth but instead to remember His mercy and love. In Jeremiah 31:34, God says, "I will forgive their wickedness and will remember their sins no more."[1] Christians are told to be like God, who does not remember sin but forgives wickedness.

This would be a good principle to follow were it not for one fact: God does remember sin. We are told that one day we will all appear before God and receive our rewards based on "the things done while in the body, whether good or bad" (2 Cor. 5:10). God remembers sin and righteousness, and He uses the data to determine our due.

When the writers of Scripture say God has taken away our sins

1. All Scripture quotations are taken from the New International Version.

"as far as the east is from the west" (Ps. 103:12) and will "hurl all our iniquities into the depths of the sea" (Mic. 7:19), they are using metaphors, not making statements of fact about God's loss of memory. A metaphor is like an impressionistic painting. It is overstated and dramatic, full of life, but not intended to be taken as a precise, literal representation of the scene painted. Imagine how absurd it would be if someone wanted to discover the actual place where the east is divided from the west. In the same way, it is absurd to take the metaphor of God's forgetfulness and make it into a tangible requirement of forgiveness.

When we try to forget the wrongs we have suffered, we lose our perspective on our personal history. In many cases, we are trying to create a less distressing and disappointing past. Because we are terrified that we cannot face the past without being overwhelmed by pain, we never taste the wonder of God's forgiveness — both of our own sin and of the sins of those who have harmed us.

The effort to erase the past fuels a spirit of independence and denial. I spoke to one man who seemed enormously proud of the fact that he had risen above his alcoholic father and promiscuous mother. I asked him if he ever felt overwhelmed by the sadness of his family history. He responded, "I've forgiven them. I don't look behind me. I just press on like Paul to the goal of godliness."

For him, forgiveness meant cutting his losses, ignoring the pain of the past, and keeping busy enough to outpace the sadness. Yet this kind of detachment dulls the senses and distorts perspective. His zeal to forget blinded him to the baggage he carried from the past and strengthened his determination to remain emotionally distant, rigid, and dogmatic. His family paid a terrible price for his "forgetting."

The Myth of Releasing Anger

For most believers, the proof of forgiveness is the absence of anger. It is assumed that if you still feel a stab of betrayal when you see the friend who told lies about you, then you haven't forgiven him. If you still seethe when you remember how someone used you for his own wicked pleasure, then you haven't forgiven him. The proof, so it seems, is in the emotional pudding — strong emotions are evidence that you have failed to forgive.

Christian thinking about and living of forgiveness have too often been distorted; as a result they seem either cheap or impossible.

L. Gregory Jones

Many attempt to put their injuries behind them through a dramatic, climactic, once-and-for-all deliverance from anger. They assume that forgiving involves a sudden, marked change from being filled with bitterness and hatred to feeling untroubled peace. Those who hold this view refer to forgiveness as a finished event ("It took years before I forgave my father") rather than an ongoing work of the Spirit of God.

Some people do experience one climactic moment when a transition from bitterness to forgiveness takes place. The problem comes when they assume that the struggle to forgive is then over and the tumultuous feelings resolved.

It is naïve to believe that forgiving another, whether for a single failure or for a lifetime of harm, is ever entirely finished. In truth, the more fully we face the harm we have suffered, the more deeply we must forgive. Forgiving another is an ongoing process, rather than a once-and-for-all event.

The "once forgiven, always forgiven" approach often leads to enormous pressure to keep bad feelings at bay. One woman told me that she held a grudge against her husband for nearly a year after she discovered he was having an affair. During an emotional church service, she responded to the pastor's invitation to come forward and leave any anger or bitterness at the altar. In a moment of cleansing absolution, she poured her heart out before the Lord, asking for forgiveness for her hardened heart. She wept. She felt released.

A week later, she told me that she no longer felt angry with her husband. Nor did she experience pangs of hurt when he approached her sexually. I rejoiced with her, but I felt a tinge of doubt when she claimed to be entirely free of anger. Sure enough, several weeks after the release of her bitterness, she saw her husband talking to another woman at church. The woman stood close to him and stroked his arm with an intimate familiarity. The wife was furious, but she handled her anger by chastising herself for being so suspicious. She questioned how she could forgive and then succumb to anger so quickly. "What have I failed to do?" she asked.

Are feelings of anger or hurt contrary to forgiveness? Listen to the heart of God: "Is not Ephraim my dear son, the child in whom I delight? Though I often speak against him, I still remember him. Therefore my heart yearns for him; I have great compassion for him" (Jer. 31:20).

Sin hurts God, and it draws a passionate response from Him. God speaks of His hurt and anger over the sin of His children in deeply personal terms. Our natural response to deep personal pain may be to deaden our hearts to the sorrow. God's way is different. God says He will remember the one who hurt Him, no matter how deep the anguish.

God is active in His expression of holy anger. Hurt and anger are not the final proof of a lack of forgiveness. In fact, an absence of strong feelings implies a lack of the heart's involvement.

When bitterness is released, there seems to be a propensity to toss holy anger out with it. True, anger can be full of sinful demands. But anger can also be a loving response to someone who has violated the beauty of God's glory and the humanness of others. Anger can reflect a passion that desires to destroy the cancerous arrogance that will eventually sap beauty and life from the offender's soul.

If we forsake holy anger — the passionate desire to destroy that which compromises what God intended — we are apt to detach ourselves from the battle on the grounds that we are exhibiting an unforgiving spirit. We will be less likely to deal with the "plank" in our own eyes or "the speck of sawdust" in the eye of the one who hurt us (Matt. 7:3).

We must retain a zeal for righteousness and a hatred for sin while we live in a world that tears at our integrity and wearies the strongest of pilgrims.

The Myth of Not Desiring Revenge

Most people assume that revenge is bad, that the desire for revenge is a base, primitive emotion that has no place in Christian society. This is why the client I mentioned at the beginning of this chapter viewed her desire to make her father pay as proof of her unforgiving spirit.

Unfortunately, we are all apt to dress the concept of forgiveness in garments that are too refined and delicate to handle the battle of life. When I suggested to this client that she allow herself to savor the thought that God would ultimately punish her father, she was stunned and aghast. Many Christians view the desire for revenge as incompatible with love and forgiveness. Revenge seems to come from an ugly, bitter heart. But is that necessarily the case?

Revenge involves a desire for justice. It is the intense wish to see ugliness destroyed, wrongs righted, and God's glory restored. Anyone who strays outside the parameters of love and acts to destroy God's order is a weed that might diminish the beauty or destroy the fruitfulness of His "garden." Consequently, vengeance is merely the pulling of the weed to keep the garden lovely and fruitful. A commitment to God's glory is the heart of true biblical revenge.

A true and deep hunger for vengeance energizes our commitment to destroy sin — both in ourselves and in others. Godly vengeance is not vindictive punishment taken out of season; it is energized love that does good in order to overcome evil.

Though we are not to seek vengeance on our own, we can joyfully anticipate the Day of the Lord, when vengeance will be righteously unleashed. We will look at specific ways of conquering evil without seeking revenge in Part Two.

The Myth of Peace at Any Price

Let's return once more to the client I described at the beginning of this chapter. When she told her father that she was not willing to restore the relationship quickly, nor would she help him with some financial problems, he responded, "What kind of Christian are you? I thought you were supposed to forgive! I'm sorry for what I did, but you don't seem to be very forgiving." She was put on the defensive, and she began alternately to blame herself for her failure to forgive and to attack him mentally for his failure to be involved in her life. Soon she was exhausted. She caved in and agreed to loan him several hundred dollars. She knew full well that she would never see the money again. Nor would she hear from him again until he needed more help.

Many people believe that the person with the forgiving heart turns the other cheek. He accepts emotional and even physical harm without complaint or confrontation. This view is often encouraged by manipulative people, who take great delight in using this grave misunderstanding of forgiveness to shame, attack, and control the naïve.

This approach to forgiveness assumes that the offender will ultimately be won over by unconditional love, which is defined as a patient, nondemanding acceptance of the other. It does not hold the other accountable for his behavior. The argument is offered that we are to carry the load one more mile, and give up not only our shirts but offer our coats as well.

We are to "turn the other cheek," but radical sacrifice is not the same as fear-based service offered to avoid guilt or attack. Forgiving does involve costly sacrifice, but it is not a weak, look-the-other-way pretense that all is well. Forgiveness involves a courageous commitment to "overcome evil with good" (Rom. 12:21). And the good that is done is an assault against the inner cancer of arrogance and independence that, left unchecked, will eat away at the offender's soul.

Overlooking harm in order to achieve a sentimental but nonsubstantive peace actually encourages sin. When we put the best face on sinful behavior ("Dad has never been very emotional" or "What do you expect of someone who grew up in a dysfunctional family?"), we deny the full extent of the harm, and we neglect our part in dealing with the offender's sin.

Overlooking harm also destroys one of the purposes of our relationships. Am I simply to love you? Am I to accept you as you are and let the Holy Spirit change you? Or do I offer a taste of the Spirit's kindness and strength by disrupting your sin and enticing your soul with a taste of a better life? I believe forgiveness is a weapon of wisdom that is designed to disrupt and entice.

In that light, the key to turning the other cheek and offering our cloaks is the principle of shrewd sacrifice. Shrewd sacrifice exposes the heart of the one doing harm. If any enemy demands that you carry his bag one mile, then carry it two miles. The enemy expects that intimidation and shame will get him what he wants. He will not anticipate receiving kindness and generosity.

But let me be very clear: this is generosity with a redemptive bite. Voluntarily turning the other cheek removes the pressure of the blow. The abuser enjoys inflicting the harm, to some degree, because it gives him power and control. Turning one's cheek to the enemy's assault demonstrates that the first blow was impotent and worthy of shame. What was meant to enslave is foiled. Like a boomerang, the harm swoops around and smacks the one who meant harm in the back of the head. When the Holy Spirit is at work, someone with a sore head may ask himself, "Why did I strike that person?" and eventually may ask the one he hit, "Why didn't you retaliate?"

I think it would have been wiser and more loving for my client to say to her father, "Dad, I would love to give you some money, but I know you would feel more honorable if you earned it rather than having me lend it to you. I have some work that needs to be done around the house that I'll have to hire out. Would you like to do it?" We are not to seek easy, peace-at-any-price relationships, but honorable, integrity-based, and beauty-enhancing relationships that give glory to the purposes of God.

We have seen that forgiveness does not mean trying to forget the offense against us, being free from anger, giving up the idea of revenge, or accepting peace at any price. What, then, is true forgiveness? As we will see, it means hungering for restoration, revoking revenge, and pursuing goodness.

PART TWO: WHAT TRUE FORGIVENESS MEANS

Two unforgiving people sat in my office, defiant and afraid. Their lives had just been shattered. Janet had discovered a few days before that her husband, Gary, was involved in an affair with his secretary. The painful revelation had magnified their differences and deepened the chasm between them. Now it seemed the only thing they had in common was the inability to forgive.

Janet admitted with clipped irritation, "I know I should forgive him, but I can't do it." Gary quietly murmured, "I just can't forgive myself for the pain I've caused my family." The relationship seemed doomed.

Every day we face both transgressions that cry out for forgiveness and God's unrelenting demand to forgive. Most of us struggle to forgive those who harm us. And the greater the damage, the more difficult it is to forgive.

And as we saw in Part One of our study, we often feel confused about what it means to forgive: "Should I just ignore the harm and somehow live as if it didn't happen?" At other times we feel helpless to forgive those who have exacted a pound of flesh at our expense: "I've tried, but I just can't get rid of my bitterness."

Our confusion is natural. God's relentless demand to forgive, to turn the other cheek, to offer one's coat to an enemy is at times infuriating, at other times seemingly illogical, and always costly. No wonder the requirement to forgive is often seen as noble but impractical, or, just as tragically, is applied without wisdom or understanding.

Forgiving others is not an easy concept to understand, let alone to apply. But there is not a more important subject in the Christian life. Let us then explore (I wish I could say answer) the question. What does it mean to "love my enemy" — the person who sexually abused me, my angry and insensitive spouse, my friend who gossiped behind my back and damaged my reputation, or even my child who snarls at my offer to go for a walk?

What is forgiveness? Perhaps the best place to start in understanding what forgiveness is all about is to look at the way God forgives. God's forgiveness of us is a passionate movement of strength and mercy toward us, the offenders.

His bold strength is the force of His holiness, which will not rest until all sin is destroyed and His glory shines like the sun. His bold mercy constantly beckons us to return to His embrace, a place of rest and joy. He forgives our sin but strongly moves to destroy the cancer within us that limits our joy and vitality; simultaneously, He extends His arms in mercy to receive us as we turn back to Him. He fully faces the damage we have done while offering us a taste of kindness intended to lead us to repentance and reconciliation.

In the Parable of the Unmerciful Servant, Jesus uses a dramatic picture to portray this kind of forgiveness. A master mercifully cancels an incomprehensible debt, freeing the debtor from imprisonment, shame, and destitution. The only debt that remains for the debtor is to offer others a taste of redemptive love (Matt. 6:12-15; 18:21-35).

Given this scriptural picture of God's forgiveness, we might define forgiveness this way: To forgive another means to cancel a debt in order to open a door of opportunity for both repentance and restoration of the broken relationship.

But understanding what forgiveness means and finding the strength within ourselves to offer it are two different matters. How can we get beyond an intellectual understanding and learn to forgive in the way God does? Here are four facets of forgiveness, beginning with the need to get a glimpse of the frightening, surprising wonder of having been forgiven.

Facet One: A Forgiving Heart Knows How Much It Has Been Forgiven

After Janet discovered her husband's affair, she became cold and indifferent toward him. She put all her energy into survival. She couldn't bear (or so it seemed) to allow herself to feel the passion and tenderness required to forgive because her heart ached so deeply. But although she intended to remain aloof and superior, her occasional outbursts of punitive rage mocked her efforts.

The only prospect of forgiving Gary came when she realized that divorce was the only other option. She was trapped between rage and reality. Rage allowed her to detach and survive; reality called her to the awareness that she didn't want to raise her children, support herself, or face life alone. Forgiveness seemed like the only way back to a normal life, but it also seemed like a door that would open her heart to death.

209

> I don't think that there is ultimate forgiveness unless I come to the place where I am willing to give away a piece of myself on behalf of the other.
>
> Bill O'Brien, forum participant

Janet's desire for a return to normalcy wasn't strong enough to give her the energy to forgive. Assume for the moment that she is a Christian and knows something about God's forgiveness. What would it take for her to offer true forgiveness to Gary, a forgiveness that goes beyond pragmatic concerns?

When Jesus told His disciples that He expected them to forgive someone who hurt them time and time again, they knew instinctively that they didn't have the strength to obey. "Increase our faith!" was their reply to His admonition to forgive an offender numerous times. He then promised this: "If you have faith as small as a mustard seed, you can say to this mulberry tree, 'Be uprooted and planted in the sea,' and it will obey you" (Luke 17:3-6). What does faith have to do with forgiveness? What did the Lord mean when He said that even puny faith is sufficient to forgive again and again and again? Let me add one more thought before we tackle this question.

A forgiving heart offers others a glimpse of the mysterious wonder of God's character. The taste of God we have to offer others will be no greater than our own taste of God's forgiveness. Jesus said to Simon, the arrogant, legalistic Pharisee, "He who has been forgiven little loves little" (Luke 7:47). Jesus seems to be saying that the energy to forgive is directly related to our awareness of how much we have been forgiven, or how deeply we deserve God's condemnation. Simon was impressed with his own command of godliness; consequently, he was not drawn to the One who can forgive sin. The same is essentially true for us. What, then, energizes our ability both to receive and to offer forgiveness?

A true view of ourselves. Faith, even if it is as small as a mustard seed, makes us "certain of what we do not see" (Heb. 11:1). The truth is that we are far worse than we appear; we are far worse than we even know. We need faith to see our own sin because our deceit makes us compare our sin with that of others and blinds us to our own need for forgiveness. Faith occasionally enables us to glimpse the depths of why we need God's ongoing mercy.

A true view of God. We also need faith to face the most incomprehensible fact: God's glory moves toward us when we are in the depths of our greatest rage against Him. He moves toward us with searing kindness and strong, open arms, with eyes that weep with delight at our return. Through faith we see beyond the veil of our presumption of innocence and into the heart of the Father who forgives sin.

Once we have experienced God's mercy and forgiveness, we will find the energy to cancel others' debts. A taste of His mercy enables us to offer others a taste of it. And we will not stop with offering forgiveness; following God's example, we will pursue the one who hurt us for the purpose of reconciliation.

Facet Two: A Forgiving Heart Yearns for Reconciliation

The driving passion of a forgiving heart is to see, touch, taste, feel, and smell reconciliation. Most of us have experienced moments of tension with a friend. Though nothing is said, the air is heavy with an unstated offense. A forgiving heart seeks the kind of rest and joy we experience when the air is finally cleared and hearts are reconnected. Reconciliation is restored peace, true shalom, wholeness and health returned to something that was broken and diseased.

Reconciliation is costly for both the one offended and the offender. The offended forgives (cancels) the debt by not terminating the relationship, as might be reasonable and expected, given the offense.[2] Instead, he offers mercy and strength in order to restore the

---

2. Editor's note: Sometimes reconciliation with the offender is not a possibility. For example, in Mary White's case (see chapter 10), opportunities for possible reconciliation have been blocked by the criminal justice system. Also, there may be times when there is no prior relationship between the offender and the victim to restore and forgiveness may be the only resolution possible.

relationship. The cost for the offended comes in withholding judgment and instead offering the possibility of restoration.

The cost for the offender is repentance. Reconciliation is never one-sided; it is not "forgiveness" that allows the offender to go scot-free, enabled to do harm again and again without any consequence. Instead, forgiveness *offers* reconciliation but does not grant it.

Jesus said, "If your brother sins, rebuke him, and if he repents, forgive him. If he sins against you seven times in a day, and seven times comes back to you and says, 'I repent,' forgive him" (Luke 17:3-4). Is Jesus saying that forgiveness is conditional? That we are not to forgive unless the offender repents?

If that were His meaning, it would contradict His other teaching on forgiveness (Matt. 6:12, 14-15; Mark 11:25; Luke 6:37). Clearly, we are to forgive, irrespective of the other person's response. What I believe He meant in the Luke 17 passage was that we are not to grant *reconciliation* until the person repents.

We see this principle in action in Jesus' cry from the cross: "Father, forgive them." When the Lord forgave those who crucified Him, did He grant to each of them, at that moment, a place of eternal intimacy with His Father? I don't think so. I believe He was freeing them from the immediate consequences of killing Him. They deserved the kind of judgment that occurred in the Old Testament when Israelites touched the Ark of the Covenant: instant death. Jesus forestalled their punishment by asking for them to be forgiven. But they would have had to respond in repentance and faith, as did the thief who was crucified beside Jesus, in order for God to grant reconciliation.

What can we learn here? We must always offer reconciliation when, in the face of rebuke, the offender demonstrates repentance — deep, heart-changing acknowledgment of sin and a radical redirection of life. But we need not extend restoration and peace to someone who has not repented.

A forgiving heart cancels the debt but does not lend new money until repentance occurs. A forgiving heart opens the door to any who knock. But entry into the home — that is, the heart — does not occur until the muddy shoes and dirty coat have been taken off. The offender must repent if true intimacy and reconciliation are ever to

> There is often confusion about the terms *forgiveness* and *reconciliation*. Reconciliation is the restoration of the relationship between the parties, whereas forgiveness can happen independently. Forgiveness is available to us spiritually because of what Christ did on the cross. But the promise of reconciliation is still in the future. Forgiveness is a precondition for reconciliation, just as justice is a precondition for Shalom. When all the different relationships in the Kingdom are righted, we will have that reconciliation, and that is the enjoyment of Shalom.
>
> Joan Orgon Coolidge, forum participant

take place.[3] That means that cheap forgiveness — peace at any price — is not true forgiveness.

It is the passionate desire for reconciliation that enables us to offer true forgiveness. Forgiveness that is offered without the deep desire for the offender to be restored to God and to the one who was harmed is at best antiseptic and mechanical. At worst, it is pharisaical self-righteousness. Forgiveness is far, far more than a business transaction: it is the sacrifice of a heartbroken father who weeps over the loss of his child and longs to see the child restored to life and love and goodness.

Further, a forgiving heart does not wait passively for repentance to occur. Instead, it offers the offender a taste of mercy and strength intended to expose and destroy sin.

3. Editor's note: Discerning whether true repentance has taken place, particularly with an offender who has committed violent acts, requires prayer, discernment, and wise counsel from others who have intimate knowledge of the offender's attitude and behavior. Forgiveness of the offending act does not relieve the offender from consequences, nor does it necessitate a re-establishment of trust on the part of the victim.

Facet Three: A Forgiving Heart Works to Destroy Sin

A forgiving heart hates sin and longs for reconciliation. It works to destroy sin and offers strong incentives to repent and return to relationship. It exposes the sinner's emptiness and tantalizes him to return to the Father's fold.

Paul tells us to offer food and drink to our enemy: "'In doing this, you will heap burning coals on his head.' Do not be overcome by evil, but overcome evil with good" (Rom. 12:20-21). Heaping burning coals on someone's head is an image that seems to symbolize God's hot, smoldering justice (Ps. 140:9-10). And it is a metaphor of shame — coals on one's head turn the face red. Yet it is also a symbol of mercy. As a sign of favor, Bedouins gave hot coals to someone who was without fire.

What is the point of this complex image? I understand it to mean that offering goodness has two effects: it conquers evil by surprising and shaming the sinner, and it invites the evildoer to pursue life.

Surprise disrupts the enemy's expectations. The enemy usually has an idea, even if it's vague and unconscious, about how his victim will respond to his sin. Having his attack greeted with kindness and strength frustrates his expectations and foils his plans. The more radical the kindness, the more likely that his response will crumble in uncertainty.

Shame is the gift of exposure — it gives the enemy an opportunity to look deep inside to see what rules his heart. The curtain lifts, and he sees himself as the wizard of a sham kingdom. In that sense, shame is a severe mercy.

Every time we give our enemy a gift of "good food," we expose his sin in the light of God's goodness. What does it mean to offer our enemy good food? Good food is any gift that simultaneously reveals both God's mercy and strength. What will that look like in practice? The answer will likely be different in every situation. Let me give a few examples.

You might handle an angry, shaming attack directed against you by flight ("I'm sorry; I'll try to do better") or fight ("How dare you question my motives! What is your problem?"). In either case, the shaming attack worked — it unnerved you and gained control over your heart. In contrast, a gift of "good food" would involve neither the flight nor the fight response. One woman said to her angry, shaming husband, "Honey, when you speak to me so angrily, it reminds me of how strong I know you can be. But when you try to bully me, it makes you appear weak." Her response pierced his rage and invited him to interact in a strong, passionate, and tender manner. Her words were both strong (she exposed his hideous rage) and tender (with passion and grace she invited him to move toward her). Good food is neither bitter — strong without mercy — nor saccharine — tender without strength.

I know a woman who struggles with her negative next-door neighbor. Every time her neighbor visits, she finds fault with something. For months my friend quietly endured the assaults. Finally, after much thought and prayer, she respectfully and kindly asked her, "Jane, you always seem to be struggling with some injustice. How do you deal with all the inner pain you must feel?" My friend's good food was redemptive curiosity that highlighted both the neighbor's negativism and her inner struggle.

An enemy faced with the surprise and shame that result from being offered good food will respond with either fury or stunned disbelief. In either case, change will occur — either repentance or greater evil. The repentant heart comes out of the woods, declares defeat, and asks for honorable terms of surrender. The hardened heart comes out of the woods and brandishes a sword, declaring battle. Evil can then be addressed and fought directly.

We are to offer others an understanding of the gift of God's wrath and mercy. It is both a warning (God hates sin) and an invitation (embrace God's goodness and come under the blood of protection). To offer forgiveness, we must have the tenderness to show mercy and the strength to confront the enemy's arrogance.

Facet Four: A Forgiving Heart Offers the Gift of Forgiveness

Forgiveness involves more than merely releasing bitterness or saying, "I forgive you." It requires us to deeply ponder certain questions: "What does it mean to give this person a taste of both the strength and the mercy of God's character?" "How can I give him a taste of goodness that will surprise and shame his wickedness?" Let me conclude with an example of forgiveness in action by briefly describing what happened with Gary and Janet.

Janet was furious. Gary wallowed in self-contempt. The marriage was a mess. Yet over time the Spirit of God opened Janet's eyes to see how often she subtly betrayed Gary by undercutting his strength and putting down his ideas. Gary began to see how often he set Janet up to make a decision and then hated her for being knowledgeable and strong.

Before the affair, their relationship looked good on the outside, but it was riddled with hidden sin. The affair was a turbulent earthquake that brought the deceitful, decaying remains to the surface. It compelled them to face sin that would eventually have robbed their lives of joy and the energy to love.

Janet was able to forgive Gary when she realized that her sin was just as grievous as his. She was not the cause of the affair, but her attitude had invited Gary to look elsewhere for involvement. Janet's heart was softened and also strengthened. She began to notice when Gary tried to put her in charge. She continued to forgive him — to offer him good food — by gently turning decisions back to him.

Gary came to see his inability to forgive himself as a subtle excuse to justify his self-serving insecurities. As long as he was self-pitying and weak, Janet would never expect him to take the initiative. He saw God's forgiveness as sufficient and chose to see that his angry wife had been injured by his cowardice. He began to show kindness to her when she treated him with contempt. The growing strength he demonstrated by getting close to her sin in order to hear her hurt stunned her and elicited her quiet gratitude.

Gary's gentle yet strong intrusion was a gift of forgiveness. Janet's openness to his involvement was a gift of forgiveness. The couple changed when they came to grips with the darkness of their own sin, the passion of the Father's eyes and the strength of His arms, and the offensive, intrusive, disruptive goodness of offering bold love.

CHAPTER TWELVE

Assisting Crime Victims: A Continuum of Care

MARLENE A. YOUNG

A unified effort to assist victims of crime is a relatively new concept, one that arose from a growing awareness of the devastation caused by criminal attacks. With this effort has come understanding of the mental and emotional reactions of victims, outlined here, as well as the physical and spiritual trauma suffered. The overview of victim-assistance services offered in this chapter is designed to help us understand the great need that exists. Professionals can't do it all — community leaders and volunteers must work alongside professionals to provide the support and care that victims need. May our response be one of compassion, so that as individuals and communities we can join the continuum of care and help heal the pain of the victim's world.

The modern study of victims and the effects of their victimization arose after World War II, compelled in part by the recognition of the evils of genocide perpetrated in Nazi Germany.
"Traumatology" had its precursors in the study of the effects of
World War I and World War II on soldiers confronting the horrors
of war. State financial compensation of crime victims was first initi-
ated in the 1960s as part of social welfare programs. And the 1968
Presidential Commission on Violence helped to inspire the study of
the scope and breadth of victimization.

But the gestation of these seeds of concern for victims into growing social action focusing on victims' needs and resulting in a victims' movement was the result of a confluence of disparate forces.
In the early 1970s there was the impact of the women who banded
together in consciousness-raising groups, protesting the degrading
horrors of violence committed against women. There was the parallel awakening of young prosecutors who recognized that victims
and witnesses needed to be treated with fairness — indeed, kindness
— if they were to cooperate in the criminal justice system. And perhaps most important, there were the victims themselves, who
sought support from each other as they rallied to define appropriate treatment for traumatized victims and to protest what they considered abuses in the criminal justice system.

Over the last twenty-five years these forces have converged to create a revolutionary era of legal and social change. They have given us
a new body of knowledge leading to ever clearer standards for quality services for crime victims, from the time of their victimization
onward — even, when necessary, throughout their lives. Today the
challenge is to ensure that people who interact and work with crime
victims have a more complete understanding of their reactions and
how to respond with informed compassion.

THE TRAUMA OF VICTIMIZATION

Most individuals function on a day-to-day basis by maintaining a
physical, emotional, mental, social, and spiritual equilibrium by
which they balance their lives. When they face a crisis such as

crime victimization, their ordinary equilibrium is upset with such force that they often feel powerless and out of control. At the outset, they react viscerally: they are in a state of physical shock, disoriented and numb. Their bodies mobilize to either fight or flee from the danger confronting them. Their senses become extremely acute, gathering in all available information to help them determine what to do.

At the same time, their minds try to comprehend what has happened. Typically the initial reaction is disbelief and denial. This reaction may subside for a while but re-emerge over time. Burglary victims, for example, often experience ongoing shock as they discover just how many possessions are missing from their homes. As one individual remarked, "It wasn't until Christmas that I realized that the burglar had taken all of the Christmas tree ornaments. I sat down and wept. Many of those ornaments had been saved and treasured for twenty-five years. I remember wondering what a burglar would have done with them. They couldn't have been valuable to him."[1]

Sometimes victims regress to a childlike state. They reach out for someone who can assume a parenting role to guide them through the tragedy that has befallen them. That person may be a law enforcement officer who responds to the call for help, a clergy member who is asked to help, or a victim-assistance professional who is on the scene at the time. A rape victim recalls her regression with chilling clarity:

> All I wanted was my mommy to take care of me. I huddled in a corner after I was raped in my home. My mommy was not alive, and I knew that, but I wanted her to take care of me. I kept praying that she would come. When someone finally found me and told me I was safe, I looked up at a face and said, "Mommy, help me." I knew it wasn't rational because the face wasn't Mommy's, but somehow I also knew that this person would take care of me.[2]

1. National Organization for Victim Assistance, Case Notes, October 1986.
2. National Organization for Victim Assistance, Case Notes, March 1988.

Victims' sense of helplessness is compounded by the turmoil of emotions that tend to dominate their reactions. Even after the immediate victimization or threat of victimization is over, the strength of seemingly disorganized emotions may overwhelm victims. They may feel as though they are going crazy or having a nervous breakdown. This morass of emotional responses can continue to be deeply disturbing for days, months, or years, particularly when victims or their loved ones lack an understanding of what has happened and is happening to them.

THE RANGE OF EMOTIONAL REACTIONS

Current research suggests that while the experience of victimization is chaotic and often random, the experience of emotional reactions has a certain logical pattern. Those who work with victims should be aware of these emotions, described below, in order to better provide comfort and reassurance.

Fear

Fear seems to be a primal reaction. Fear may be inspired by the loss of autonomy, which is the ability to control impulses and to address situations through planning, a uniquely human characteristic. It is also related to the state of regression. Fear is the most commonly seen reaction in children. When they are faced with a fight-or-flight situation, instinct warns them that they lack the power to fight, and so fear becomes the impetus for fleeing.

Fear grows into terror when victims internalize the knowledge that they or their loved ones may not survive the threatening situation. The following report after a murderous attack in Florida illustrates the terror of the expectation of death:

Numerous calls on the 911 tape illustrated the victims' terror. . . . "There's a man in our office with a gun," a man's voice rasped on the 911 tape. "He has fired at several people." Asked

220

for details, the man dropped his voice, whispering, "It's a semi-automatic, definitely. He's still shooting. Yes . . . We're being killed . . . and he's killing everybody."[3]

Interestingly, there is some evidence that in chronic victimization, such as ongoing child abuse, the threat to inflict pain can trigger fears that are more damaging than the actual sensation of pain after injury. In these situations, the threat of death is something of a useless weapon for the aggressor, since it may confirm for the victim the hopelessness of the situation and offer surcease from pain. In sudden random crisis, however, the threat of death or the knowledge that a loved one has been killed is often paralyzing. Terror becomes transformed into horror when victims realize that their lives have been brutally and purposely violated by criminal attack.

Anger

Anger is closely related to fear. Its force derives from the need to respond aggressively to a threat through the physical "fight" reaction. Anger caused by the crisis of criminal attack is often directed at an offender or a person held responsible for a tragic event, although it may be displaced onto God, family members, or social institutions, or turned inward on oneself.

A teenage boy told a focus group on victimization about some of his reactions after his home was burglarized. The burglar had entered the house through his bedroom and stolen his computer, his tape deck, a number of travel souvenirs, general household items, and money. At first he said that he just wanted to kill the burglar, but that wasn't possible because no one had been identified as the offender. Next he talked about how it was really his parents' fault, because they should have made the house more secure. Then he explained how upset he was with the police, who hadn't done anything. As he talked, he got angrier and angrier, until he finally said

3. L. Parker, "Jacksonville Gunman Shot Four Others before Rampage at Finance Company," *The Washington Post,* 20 June 1990.

with quiet fury, "I don't care. I don't care about anything or anyone, because it just doesn't make any difference to care." Such rage can lead to depression and withdrawal from healthy relationships and activities.

Anger may be associated with the desire for revenge. This common desire subsides for many, even though they may still feel overwhelming rage toward the situation. Anger may also be associated with hatred, which has been called "calcified anger." It leaves people feeling empty, bitter, morally conflicted, and painfully out of synch with the normal feelings of humanity. The intensity of anger and its antisocial aspects are often new to victims and survivors of crime. Victims who express this anger may evoke the disapproval and disgust of loved ones, friends, and community members, which may complicate the expression of their feelings.

Confusion and Frustration

Victims are commonly confused by the fact that they do not have a clear picture of what happened to them. Often they remember only scattered impressions of a traumatic event. Many of these impressions are sensory perceptions or fragmented feelings about what happened; they do not form a coherent whole.

The confusion becomes frustration when victims think they should remember or could remember if only they tried. The fact is that most traumatic memories are disjointed and disorganized and may not be recalled in chronological or contextual order. This confusion is evident during the criminal justice process. The story that a victim relates to a law enforcement officer at the scene of a crime may differ from the story he or she tells a few weeks later, when an investigative interview is conducted, and may change again if the victim testifies at trial.

These changes mark various stages in memory processing. Victims may remember only fragments of what happened at first, but as they review the event in their minds over and over again, more and more pieces start to come together to create a coherent narrative of the event.

> Victims are often confused and frustrated by their inability to define or control their emotions, and the sense that others do not understand them.

As victims attempt to piece together the story of what happened, their confusion may be compounded because they do not understand why it happened. If those around them are unresponsive, their frustration is exacerbated. The need to explain and understand a crime event is central to regaining control in life.

Guilt and Self-Blame

Guilt and self-blame are cognitive emotions that arise from the effort to identify why something happened. As victims seek to discover why they were victimized and find no rational explanations, they come to the conclusion that they were at fault for something they did or didn't do. Their thoughts might follow these lines: "If I hadn't been walking down the street after dark, I wouldn't have been robbed"; "It was my fault that I was burglarized because I didn't have deadbolt locks on my doors." Sometimes victims conclude that they are to blame because of who they are. They accept the blame because "bad things only happen to bad people." They fault themselves for being victimized because they were incompetent, stupid, ignorant, too trusting, or too cowardly.

Sometimes victims experience what is known as "survivor guilt." These individuals are plagued with internal questions about why they survived a tragedy, or were minimally injured, while others were seriously injured or died. Survivors may also feel guilty because they have been hurt or harmed, but friends and family keep telling them that they are "lucky" because they're alive. The guilt-producing conflict arises from the fact that they are certainly glad to have survived, but they are not grateful for having been victimized.

Survivor guilt seems to manifest itself particularly in crimes that affect whole communities — for example, those in which violence is directed toward groups of people. In those cases, the inevitable assessments of self and community lead to an exercise in comparisons — "comparative trauma" — and produce additional survivor guilt.

Shame and Humiliation

Shame and humiliation are associated with guilt and self-blame. They reflect, in part, victims' internalizing their belief that they are responsible for their own tragedies. They also arise out of the sense of vulnerability and degradation that victims suffer, having been diminished by their losses. Sometimes a criminal may contribute intentionally to an individual's shame. A burglary victim's home may not only be vandalized but also smeared with feces or profane graffiti. A rape victim may be taunted or forced to perform unspeakable acts.

The shame is made more unbearable, of course, when community or family members stigmatize victims, and they suffer a loss of status as a result of their victimization. Stigmatization of victims is common in most societies. Victims are seen as weak and vulnerable, and their presence is an unwanted reminder to others of their own weaknesses and vulnerabilities. Many people do not want to hear stories of pain and misfortune because those stories can cause them to become more worried, anxious, and distressed about what might happen to them.

One young victim was stalked for months by an obsessed man who, after she rebuffed him several times, attacked her by throwing kerosene on her in the middle of a street and setting her on fire. She was burned severely and left with a scarred and mutilated face. While the physical pain was agonizing, she said that her emotional wounds were deeper than her physical injuries. When she was out in public, people often averted their eyes or turned away. One day she was in a grocery store where a mother and daughter were shopping. She was mortified to hear the mother tell her daughter that if she wasn't a good girl, she would grow up to look like the victim.

Grief

Grief may be the most intense, long-term emotional reaction to traumatic loss. Traumatic grief is not ordinary grief. The emotions that are caused by crime complicate the grieving process. Ordinary grief is painful enough. But when grief is accompanied by the anger and fear evoked by a sudden criminal violation, the grief can be so debilitating that the victim or survivor is unable to acknowledge or mourn the depth of his or her loss.

Traumatic grief after crime is made more complex by the fact that there are multifaceted losses. There are the practical and physical losses — the loss of property, money, physical integrity. And there are obvious emotional losses, such as the loss of a loved one. But there are also intangible losses, such as the loss of trust in others, the loss of a sense of identity, the loss of confidence, the loss of meaning in life, the loss of hope, and, for some, the loss of faith in God. It is not unusual for traumatized victims of crime to feel as though the victimization was a concrete manifestation of evil in their lives, and they may not know how to cope with this perception. Those who have believed that all people are inherently good may find it difficult to reconcile human brutality and cruelty with that faith.

With good support systems and effective interventions, victims can get off the emotional roller coaster caused by crime and can reconstruct their lives. Their lives will be different; for many, they will continue to be punctuated by traumatic memories or spasms of grief. But most individuals can learn to cope with this, particularly if they have appropriate assistance. Such assistance involves more than a kindly response by the criminal justice system or by sympathetic family members and/or friends. It involves treating victims with compassionate and knowledgeable understanding of the victimization experience, giving victims practical aid by helping them replace property or get the medical care they need, and guiding them through the social and justice institutions mandated to offer resources or respond to crime.

The following section summarizes some of the kinds of assistance that should be available to all victims of crime in communities that offer victims a continuum of care.

225

VICTIM ASSISTANCE SERVICES

Victim assistance services should be provided by every community. They include six basic components, ranging from crisis intervention to the prevention of victimization. Each component can be provided by professionals or trained volunteers and should address victims' needs for emotional support, for other forms of direct assistance, and for information. The victims' movement across the world has identified the minimum level of services that should be available to victims, as well as what kinds of services might be offered in an ideal situation. It is important to emphasize that all services should be proactive, meaning reaching out actively to victims, and that particular attention should be paid to providing for special needs, including multilingual services, services for the disabled, and culturally appropriate services.

While, ideally, communities should be prepared to assist all victims, it is often necessary, due to limited resources, to set priorities concerning which victims receive which services. These decisions take into account the severity of the victimizing event and its impact on the victim. Since many communities have long-standing programs that serve certain types of victims, such as sexual assault victims or child victims and their families, new or expanding programs may want to focus on other kinds of victims for service, such as victims of burglary, robbery, or fraud. Programs and service networks are encouraged to identify gaps in services through community partnerships. They are further encouraged to identify who should address these gaps and to develop strong referral systems in order to avoid duplication.

Crisis Intervention

Immediate crisis intervention is a primary service component. This means that crisis services are available twenty-four hours a day via telephone, on-scene response, home visits, or walk-in clinics. Trained counselors should be able to respond within fifteen minutes of a victim call or referral. This contact with a victim could

226

come immediately after a criminal attack, but in many cases it comes much later. Some victims who have received assistance earlier may go back into a crisis state when "trigger events" occur in their lives, such as the anniversary of the crime itself or their participation as witnesses in the criminal justice system.

Crisis intervention involves three main factors: the provision of safety and security, the opportunity for victims to express their feelings and be validated, and knowledgeable prediction of and preparation for future events related to the crime.

Safety and Security. Crisis counselors can help create an environment that feels safe for victims. Counselors can begin to engender feelings of safety by telling victims that they are sorry the crime happened and that the victims are safe now, if that is in fact the case. Simple, common-sense activities can help victims begin to regain control of their surroundings. Such activities include letting victims decide where they want to talk, giving them a glass of water, assuring them of the confidentiality of what they say, and preventing other people from intruding on their privacy. Safety measures should also be taken, such as repairing a door or window broken in a burglary or robbery, finding the victim a place to stay if his or her home does not provide the safety needed at that time, and so on.

Counselors can also foster a sense of security by reassuring victims that they are not to blame for their plight. Bad things do happen to good people, and no matter what they did or did not do, they are not responsible for the criminal attack that left them bereft.

Validating Feelings. Crisis counselors should understand that victims need to tell their stories in their own words and in their own time — to vent. As they tell their stories, they will express a variety of emotional reactions. These should be validated no matter what they are. Trained crisis counselors know the difference between the expected expressions of anger and outrage and statements that reflect a conscious determination to do harm to oneself or another. Counselors may want to take precautions to ensure that no actual harm will be done, but at the same time they should reassure victims that their reactions are normal and that the verbal expression of those reactions is okay. The process of telling a story over and over again allows victims to begin to comprehend what happened and to regain a sense of control in their lives.

Prediction and Preparation. Using as much concrete, factual information as is available, crisis counselors should be prepared to predict for victims what will happen next in their lives as a result of the crime. Burglary victims need to be told what happens when law enforcement officers dust for fingerprints in their homes, and why their own fingerprints will be taken. Rape victims need to be given information about what will happen during a forensic examination. Survivors of homicide victims need to know what steps law enforcement will take to find the offenders, or, if suspects are in custody, what the next steps will be in the investigation or prosecution of the case.

Crisis counselors should also be knowledgeable about available practical resources that may be able to help the victims with their immediate needs for alternative shelter, clothing, food, protection, transportation, and/or property repair or replacement. Such knowledge should include an understanding of state victim-compensation guidelines as well as charitable funds that may help victims with emergency or long-term financial needs. Sometimes counselors are called upon to provide practical assistance themselves. It is often a shock to both victims and new counselors to learn that in many communities there is no agency to designate the cleanup of a crime after it occurs in someone's home or place of business.

Crisis counselors should also know how to safely and compassionately notify family members about the death or serious physical injury of victims. These are difficult tasks, and it is essential that counselors are well trained and skilled. This is a time when the spiritual needs of victims are often the most pronounced, and the involvement of clergy may be crucial to the mental and emotional health of victims and survivors.

Counseling

Ongoing supportive professional, pastoral, and/or trained lay counseling services should be available for individuals and groups. Most victims do not need mental health therapy, but they may need to talk about the crime for a long time. This helps them sort out the issues that confronted them at the time they were victimized as well as develop a more complete story in their minds about what happened.

Counselors are a source of reassurance for victims as they process the past and face new challenges in the future. When appropriately trained, counselors can help victims mentally visualize and "rehearse" what happened to them in order to deepen their understanding of their stories. A number of therapeutic interventions have been developed in the last decade that may help victims to better control or cope with intrusive memories of the event, nightmares, flashbacks, hyper-arousal, feelings of estrangement from others, and other traumatic responses. Victim counselors should be prepared to work closely with mental health professionals when necessary to help victims explore these options for trauma relief.

> Peer support groups can provide opportunities for victims and survivors to tell their stories and to hear how others who have faced a similar victimization have coped in the aftermath.

Many victims also need the time and support a concerned counselor can offer as they reconstruct some basic values. The systems of meaning in their lives may have been challenged by the victimization, and they need time to rethink those values and to reassert them in a new context.

Some rape victims, for example, feel that their values of chastity have been violated or their marriage vows broken even though they recognize that they were assaulted against their will. Some parents of injured or murdered children feel that they failed in their parental responsibility to protect their children from harm. Individual counselors can be good sounding boards for survivors as they face such concerns.

Supportive counseling is more than simply listening to the stories of victims. Trained counselors help to educate victims about what they are going through, various options available to them, and useful coping skills. It is important to provide victims with opportunities to learn about crisis and trauma reactions, crisis intervention techniques, and coping skills; opportunities to get information about grief and loss; and, if they are involved in the criminal justice system, opportunities to learn about their rights and responsibilities in the justice process.

Counselors should also be prepared to help victims with practical concerns such as long-term child or adult care if victims are unable to provide such care for their children or parents. They should aid in the process of document replacement if items like a driver's license, medical records, or identification papers were stolen in a burglary or robbery. Sometimes counselors can help by engaging in cooperative problem-solving with victims, sometimes by finding resources to solve problems, sometimes by undertaking certain tasks themselves.

Counseling may also include providing essential information on prevention of victimization in the future, substance abuse treatment, and referrals for social, health, or legal services.

Advocacy

An overlooked service in some communities is the need for victim advocacy. Victim service providers should be prepared to reassure and support those victims who want to become involved in active efforts to change the system or to speak publicly about their victimization. More and more mental health research suggests that activism is very helpful to many victims in reconstructing their lives and their sense of purpose in the world.

In their tragedy, some victims find motivation to help others facing similar plights. After their daughter was brutally murdered, Charlotte and Robert Hullinger founded Parents of Murdered Children to foster the creation of support groups for such parents throughout the nation. After her daughter was killed by a drunk driver, Candy Leitner founded Mothers Against Drunk Driving to spearhead efforts to pass legislation to reduce drunk-driving crashes and fatalities. After her daughter was murdered, Roberta Roper founded the Stephanie Roper Committee and Foundation to pass victim rights legislation in the state of Maryland. She now is co-chair of the National Victim Constitutional Amendment Network seeking passage of a federal constitutional amendment on victims' rights.

Other victims might not create organizations but find consolation in becoming trained victim advocates, counselors, or program directors themselves. They should take time to process their own reactions and grief after victimization. But if they have worked through the unique issues and concerns emanating from their experiences, these often serve as excellent resources for other victims. Still other victims give public testimony about their experiences. Their stories of survival and growth can inspire others to begin to hope again. All of these are examples of the efficacy of victim activism.

> Victim advocates are responsible for identifying the individual needs of victims and finding the resources necessary to meet them.

Advocacy also involves directly assisting victims as they struggle with the ongoing ramifications of the crime. They may need help in preparing victim compensation claims or private insurance claims. They may also need intervention and advocacy to ensure the continuity of their credit or employment. Sometimes in domestic violence cases, landlords seek to evict victims because they fear that their property may be damaged if the abuse becomes more violent. If a crime has attracted media attention, victims may seek an advocate to represent them to, or be a buffer against, the media. In this situation, advocates need to be knowledgeable about how the media operates, how it might intrude on victims' lives, and what kinds of privacy victims can demand.

231

Advocates are also important representatives for victims facing the criminal justice process, as outlined below. They can help ensure that victims' concerns are considered at every stage of the criminal justice process.

Support Services during the Criminal Justice Process

Victims commonly need ongoing crisis intervention, counseling, and advocacy services if they become involved in the criminal justice system. Being asked to identify an accused individual as the assailant or to testify at a trial can trigger tumultuous emotional reactions. Even when they voluntarily take part in attending court hearings, trials, sentencing proceedings, or parole hearings, victims find comfort in having someone with them for support and encouragement.

An intermediary can help obtain prompt return of recovered property or ensure that victims receive timely and accurate information about the status of a case. (Accurate information is particularly important when it concerns issues such as detention of a suspect, bail or bond conditions, the release of a suspect or an offender, and appeals and appellate procedures.)

Victims may also need representation or assistance in the process of obtaining restitution, participating in hearings on bail or plea agreements, or preparing victim-impact statements for sentencing or parole hearings. It is often assumed that criminal justice professionals will ensure that a victim's rights are honored, but there are times when prosecutors or judges are not aware of the rights of victims or do not understand their importance or relevance.

Practical needs are also paramount during criminal justice processes. Victims may need transportation to and from interviews, hearings, or trials. They may need assistance in finding available and accessible parking during the time they are attending proceedings. They may need child care while they participate in the proceedings. Sometimes it is very helpful to find inexpensive meals for victims or witnesses as they wait to attend a hearing or to testify in a proceeding.

232

Logistics are of particular concern for victims who have disabilities. It is estimated that there are about 43 million individuals with disabilities in the United States — these include people with seeing or hearing impairments, developmental disabilities, mental illnesses, physical impairments, and so on. Still, many courthouses are not accessible to people with disabilities. Often there are no interpreters available for the deaf or hearing impaired. Advocates help to ensure that rights or services are not denied because of lack of accessibility.

Support Services after Case Disposition

In the early years of the victims' movement, the prevailing perspective held that victim services were completed when a criminal case had been closed or a final disposition given. Experience in dealing with the long-term effects of trauma as well as ongoing events after case disposition has changed that view. Victims often need continuing emotional support for years and, as mentioned earlier, may need serious crisis intervention when trigger events occur. Thus, emotional support should also be available during all appeals, motions for retrials, and hearings on probation revocation, parole, or clemency.

In recent times, victim assistance providers have become even more aware of how the consequences of sentencing can affect victims. A final sentence may well be a source of relief to victims. On the other hand, it may also throw them into a new state of crisis because they realize that the case is closed in the justice system, but they have not yet dealt with their grief or losses. If the sentence is not perceived as just, victims may once again confront issues of fairness and equity. Death-penalty cases and the execution of offenders can be particularly troubling. Many victims are deeply concerned by the concept of the death penalty, even when they are still angry with the offenders or feel that a sentence of death is deserved. They struggle with moral and spiritual issues and may need ongoing support in resolving these issues or coming to grips with the reality of the sentence and its execution.

Victimization Prevention Services

The ultimate service that can be provided to victims and the communities in which they live is the prevention of victimization. While it is improbable that crime and violence will be eradicated in the near future, victim service programs can take active steps in prevention efforts. Alliances with other community groups that are working to develop and promote educational programs aimed at violence prevention are critical. Also important are the many victim assistance providers who work with correctional agencies to develop victim education programs or intervention programs for offenders.

CONCLUSION

The trauma of victimization and its aftermath is not limited to the direct victims of a crime or crisis. Victimization affects not only the individual violated but also family members, friends, and the community as a whole. There is often a ripple effect as each person with whom a victim comes into contact absorbs some of his or her pain and in turn passes it on to others.

This ripple effect is one reason why it is so important that victims receive a continuum of care through community-wide services and community-wide involvement. Neighbor-to-neighbor compassion can spread quickly, helping stanch the pain of victimization, if neighbors and friends know how to respond and where to find help.

CHAPTER THIRTEEN

The Spiritual Problem of Crime: A Pastor's Call

LEE A. EARL

Rarely is a pastor more challenged than when crime rocks a community and, thus, his church. Many pastors work tirelessly to show that the Church has something relevant to say in a devastating situation, but much depends on the parishioners. Will the Church respond actively and in practical ways to tragedy, or will the members merely stay in the pews, meditating on right beliefs and theology? It is during these times that the ultimate questions of life are blazoned on the hearts of the hurting. Can the theology of the Church stand before such a confrontation? As Pastor Lee Earl discovered, crime is more than a social problem; it is a spiritual problem, and as such the Church is called to respond. If it does, miracles can happen.

I told the Johnson family that I would return in the morning to check on them and their mother, even though the doctors said it was unlikely she would survive the night. As a minister, I felt compelled to remind the family that the doctors spoke from "medical opinion" and that God was able to do things that science could not predict or understand. Polite and respectful, the children looked at me and said simply, "Thanks, Reverend." Underneath, we all feared the harsh reality — that a piece of our hearts would be lost before another Sabbath.

These children were not typical "church children," who understood the religious jargon often repeated in these situations. On the contrary, these children were growing up on Detroit's notorious Twelfth Street. Though a few of them had recently started coming to church, life on the street was still their main point of reference. They understood better than most what the doctors meant by the difference between being shot with a small-caliber weapon and a large one.

That Saturday evening had seemed so full of promise a few short hours earlier as we left Twelfth Street Baptist Church. The male chorus had just finished a spirited rehearsal and was anticipating a "high time" in church the following morning. As a number of us lingered, chatting on the sidewalk, we could hear children enjoying their play; young men were polishing their spotless automobiles. The church lawn had been cut and trimmed, and the sermon was ready. It was at that time that Alice Johnson and her children were returning from a walk to the store.

Suddenly gunshots rang through the heavy summer air. The fellowship that had been taking place on the sidewalk in front of the church stopped abruptly. Some folks said good-bye quickly; others just disappeared. A few of us, after a moment of stunned silence, ran across the street to a group huddled over a figure lying on the ground. There, in a pool of blood, lay Alice. Her children stood over her, weeping, confronting a reality they could not escape. Every year more than a million women are the victims of violent crimes.[1] Now, one of these victims lay just across the street from my church.

---

1. U.S. Department of Justice, "Violence against Women: Estimates from the Redesigned Survey" (Washington, D.C.: Bureau of Justice Statistics, 1995).

The police arrived soon and apprehended the perpetrator — a man whose family lived nearby — and the EMS Squad took Alice to Henry Ford Hospital. I went with the children to the hospital. It was vital that they experience the love of Christ at that moment. I sensed that words were inadequate for those streetwise kids; only action would be meaningful.

I had only recently had success in reaching out to two of the children. Just a few weeks earlier, Alice's daughter Terri had appeared suddenly in the sanctuary of the church, intending to beat up some of the other children. I don't remember what the issue was, but I was fascinated by the boldness of this fourteen-year-old, stomping into the church with war in her eyes. After resolving the immediate crisis, I spent some time talking with Terri. I invited her and her sister, Debbie, to join us for the rest of Vacation Bible School and the Summer Youth Program. They accepted my invitation and became regular attendees at the summer youth events.

Now their mother had been gunned down in front of them. What would become of their willingness to stay involved with the church and learn about Christ? How would the other children in the neighborhood feel about Christianity? Would they judge Christianity by the church's response to this tragedy? What could be done to keep this small flame alive in these youngsters amidst such a violent storm? How could I get my church to minister in practical ways to this family without looking for anything in return? And in the larger picture, how could I, as pastor, navigate the place where the waters of a somewhat self-indulgent congregation and a deteriorating neighborhood met?

I left the hospital late, asking the family to call me if anything changed. Early the next morning, before sunrise, I received the call informing me that Alice had died. I remained awake as the sun rose and the new day began, wondering about Alice's children, who had watched their mother lie dying in the street; wondering about the man who had shot her and his family; wondering about the church I had to preach to. Would we still have the "high time" of worship we had planned as a testimony to our faith in God? Would the church be shocked by the events of the previous evening? Or, more disturbing, would the morning be business as usual? Surely the death of any human being should alter the usual behavior of a church and a community. If it does not, we are in more danger than we realize.

Streams of light from the early morning sun also brought a dawning of understanding: Alice's murder was not to be taken lightly. The ultimate questions of life were being asked, and the value of the Church was being weighed in the balance of practicality and relevance. Did my church have a theology that would lead to action? We were about to find out.

CRIME: A NATIONAL EPIDEMIC

Americans are faced with a crime wave of epidemic proportions. One murder takes place every 24 minutes; one forcible rape every five minutes; one robbery every 54 seconds; one aggravated assault every 18 seconds.[2] In 1995, more than 35 million Americans became victims of crime. More than 20 percent of U.S. families are victimized each year. Studies show that there is a 99 percent chance that every American, at some point in life, will be a victim of a crime.[3]

Children and young people are even more susceptible to crime, both as victims and as perpetrators. A young person today is 20 times more likely to become a victim of violent crime than an elderly person. Twenty-nine percent of all rape victims are under the age of eleven. Homicide is one of the five leading causes of child mortality. And it is getting worse. Since 1976, childhood victimization has more than tripled.

This is the statement issued by the National Victim Academy of the Office of Victims of Crime: "Every day in America, children are victimized. They are beaten, sexually abused, murdered, and neglected by family members. Children not targeted for physical acts of victimization are often victimized by emotional neglect or abuse or by witnessing the murder, rape, or robbery of family members and friends. Their childhood is stolen from them as they are forced

2. U.S. Department of Justice, *Crime in the United States: Uniform Crime Reports, 1995* (Washington, D.C.: Federal Bureau of Investigation, 1996).
3. U.S. Department of Justice, Bureau of Statistics, 1988.

to deal with emotions, fears, and losses that adults often find hard to face."

Unfortunately, juvenile delinquency is rising at just as alarming a rate. In 1991, juveniles committed 28 percent of all rapes, thefts, assaults, and robberies. In addition, juveniles committed one out of every five violent crimes. According to the National Institute for Justice, "Childhood victimization represents a widespread serious social problem that increases the likelihood of delinquency, adult criminality, and violent criminal behavior . . . overall by 40 percent."

In addition, our urban areas are experiencing crime at a rate significantly higher than that of the rest of the country. In 1995, 715 violent crimes per 100,000 residents occurred in America's largest urban areas. This compares to 482 violent crimes per 100,000 residents in cities not large enough to be considered major urban areas, and 233 violent crimes per 100,000 residents in rural areas. The same is true for property-related crimes. In 1995, 4,986 property crimes per 100,000 residents took place in urban areas. In comparison, 4,832 took place in non-urban cities and 1,849 per 100,000 residents in rural areas.[4]

THE CHURCH AND CRIME-RELATED MINISTRY

With crime and victimization at such alarmingly high rates, the Church cannot afford to ignore its impact on our congregations and communities. In 1997, Neighbors Who Care commissioned the Barna Research Group, Ltd., to conduct a nationwide survey of evangelical, mainline, and Catholic pastors. The purpose of the survey was to determine churches' current levels of awareness of and interest and involvement in crime-related efforts and ministry.

The Barna survey results revealed that less than half (46 percent) of churches around the country offer some type of crime-related ministry. The majority of churches involved in crime-related ministry are located in larger urban areas, with large congregations made

4. Bureau of Justice Statistics Sourcebook, 1996. U.S. Department of Justice, Office of Justice Programs, Washington, D.C.

up primarily of African-American and Latino members, and the churches often have counseling services and other outreach programs to assist the homeless and the poor.

The churches involved in crime-related ministry are the churches that are witnessing the impact of crime and violence all around them and have decided to respond to the communities' need for help. Still, all churches, whether located in urban, high-crime areas or suburban and rural communities, are feeling the impact of crime. The Church must realize the need to respond through raising awareness of crime's impact, channeling that awareness, and incorporating that awareness into missions.

> I have discovered more and more in my work with victims throughout the world that the issue of meaning in one's life is probably the issue that is going to control whether or not one survives well and continues to live well. That meaning stems from issues of, certainly, justice, but equally important, the spiritual life.
>
> Marlene Young

THE WORK BEGINS

As a result of Alice's death, I realized that the Church and the community face an enemy much more subtle and dangerous than even Alice's killer: apathy. Only apathy is more dangerous than crime itself. Apathy says, "It's someone else's problem — let him worry about it." Apathy refuses to see the wounds of those who have been victimized and to offer help. After much prayer, I decided that our church had to act, and that I, as the pastor, had to lead the way to ensure an appropriate response. Words would not be enough. We had to show the community the value of caring. And this might be costly.

The immediate need was a proper burial for Alice. While I knew that the idea would receive some strong opposition, I proposed that we hold the funeral in the sanctuary and pay for the cost of the coffin if the family could not afford it. It was clear that the consequences of taking this stance — spending church funds on "someone like Alice" — could cost me my position. I was pleased, therefore, that a number of the members of the church were excited about the idea and welcomed the opportunity to minister to this family and the community in the name of Christ. Some of the members never saw the importance of ministry to the poor; they never caught the vision for reaching out to "the least of these." As the church cautiously approved the action, the skeptics adopted a "wait-and-see" attitude. The opposition was silent — yet clearly appalled that we would hold the funeral in the sanctuary and invite all the members of the community. Since Alice was not a "churchwoman," most of her friends would be from the "hood."

But the momentum had begun. For instance, our church did most of its funeral business with the Barksdale Funeral Home. The owner had always been a staunch supporter of the pastors of Twelfth Street. She gave the family an extremely fair price and used her influence in our church to help the skeptics realize the importance of this action. She embraced the children and shared her faith in Christ with them when the arrangements were made. In addition, many members of the church leaped into compassionate action. They called the family to express their condolences and offered to serve meals or give money.

The community was surprised by the church's show of concern. When the Friday evening service began, the church was filled with both church folk and street folk. My sermon was short and simple: "If we didn't care, we wouldn't be here." My point was clear and concise: "If we can care about Alice in death, we can care about each other in life. If we can demonstrate our care for each member of this community, we can turn it around." The spirit of the Lord was at work that night in the community surrounding Twelfth Street, Detroit.

MIRACLES IN MINISTRY

Even though Alice's murderer had been apprehended and sent to prison, the ordeal was far from over. The community still had to heal. Dr. Carl Henry states that "the community assuredly becomes a crime victim whenever criminality compromises its reputation for safety and respect for law and order." In the case of our community, there was very little safety left — the police had even stopped sending squad cars after a certain time at night. Our community needed to take action, and the church led the charge.

The funeral for Alice was just the beginning. The church became more than a member of the community with a stake in its future and welfare; it became a neighbor. The church lived out the love of Christ; it let its light shine and its salt be sprinkled. We watched as miracles happened. With the church's support, the families of the murderer and the victim were reconciled. Alice's son, Vernon, did not retaliate against the killer's mother or brother. Both young men became supportive of the church. We even saw Vernon come to the Lord and be baptized.

The church became the cornerstone of an effort to revive the community and stem the devastating crime wave. Eventually a community development corporation, R.E.A.C.H., Inc., was born out of the church. Many ministries were started, including a child development center, a food program, a small business development center, and a housing development ministry. The activity of the church attracted national attention, and Harvard University conducted an evaluation of the impact of the church's programs. The Harvard study results indicated a 37 percent reduction in crime in the R.E.A.C.H. service area.[5]

I believe that the church's outreach was successful because the church recognized that the community's problems were not just social problems. Crime and community deterioration were viewed for

5. *REACH: Fighting Crack and Crime in Pilgrim Village, Detroit*, written by Nancy D. Kates under the direction of Mark Moore and Francis X. Hartmann for use at the John F. Kennedy School of Government, Harvard University. Copyright 1990 by the President and Fellows of Harvard College. C16-90-936.0.

what they really are — spiritual problems. The church came to see itself as the primary institution in the community that was equipped, authorized, and specifically called by Christ to meet this challenge. Once I, as pastor, decided to act and accept the risk, the church followed. Once the church started to live out the teachings of Christ, the quality of life around Twelfth Street changed for the better.

I believe that this kind of outreach can and must be repeated many times over in this country. The Church is the key to reducing the menace of crime that is robbing our society of the freedoms and pursuits we cherish. The Church has incredible power within communities and is in a position to make a difference in stemming the tide of crime.

COMMUNITY DEVELOPMENT
VERSUS COMMUNITY RESTORATION

The vast majority of pastors in urban America recognize that the Church ought to be involved in community and economic development. Many churches that have community outreach programs are involved in housing, business development, food distribution centers, or private and Christians schools. What we have learned over the last decade is that all these efforts, while worthy, are greatly hindered if they do not start by addressing the problem of crime. A group may be able to provide housing, but if the crime problem in the area is not addressed, no one will want to live in the houses. Or if they do, they will be robbed and terrorized and will live in a state of perpetual fear.

Crime is a foundational social and spiritual problem that must be addressed before community development can take place. Until the issue of crime is addressed, community development efforts are like the house built on sand — unstable and sure to fall.

As time went on, Twelfth Street Baptist Church and R.E.A.C.H., Inc., became the examples of what community and economic development were all about. We were featured in almost every major media format and market in the country. The leaders of the work received honors from every kind of body on the local, state, and national levels. In our minds, however, the reduction in crime was our greatest achievement because it allowed people to enjoy the community in peace.

It is my strong belief that to invest large sums of capital and time in community development projects without a serious commitment to reduce crime is to build on sand. In the Sermon on the Mount, Jesus talked about how unwise it would be to build a house on sand because it would be unable to withstand the storms and trials of life. Likewise, to spend millions on the physical development of a neighborhood and neglect its spiritual need is foolish. Sincere community developers can no more avoid the reality of crime and its devastation than they can deteriorating houses or abandoned businesses. We can't focus on Matthew 25 and neglect Luke 4. Let me show you what I mean.

In Matthew 25, a familiar passage in Scripture, the Lord judges the Church. Part of the criteria for that judgment is given in verses 35-36. In the passage the Lord says, "For I was hungry and you gave me something to eat, I was thirsty and you gave me something to drink, I was a stranger and you invited me in, I needed clothes and you clothed me, I was sick and you looked after me, I was in prison and you came to visit me" (NIV). This passage is often used to exhort the Church to provide practical ministries that meet the basic needs of humankind. This is good, and we must continue this vital work; however, not to meet the interior needs of the individual who has been broken and torn by personal tragedy is to leave the job half-done.

In Luke 4:18, at the very outset of His ministry, Jesus says, "The Spirit of the Lord is on me, because he has anointed me to preach good news to the poor. He has sent me to proclaim freedom for the prisoners and recovery of sight for the blind, to release the oppressed" (NIV). It appears that before Jesus began to minister to the physical needs of people, His primary mission was to address the spiritual, emotional, and psychological needs of humankind. This could be due to the fact that unless people are healed internally, making their external environment healthy does little long-lasting or permanent good.

Without an intentional effort to rid our communities of crime and its destructive forces, all other efforts are like building houses on sand. People who are scared and intimidated will never be able to enjoy a decent and affordable house; people who have been assaulted, raped, and robbed will never be made to feel safe because we organize a neighborhood watch; the families that survive homicide can't be healed by longer jail sentences for the offenders. These are social and well-meaning secular efforts. The Church has a stronger and more effective weapon to use in this warfare — the Gospel of Christ.

CHURCH AND STATE

How is the Church to address the issue of crime? The Church can learn a lesson about how *not* to address the issue of crime by looking at the way the state deals with it. Historically and biblically, the community has always been heavily involved in dealing with crime. In earlier days, persons who had committed crimes were considered to have offended the persons harmed. As a result, they were expected not only to suffer punishment for the crime but also to provide restitution and recompense to the individuals wronged. The entire community held offenders accountable in this process.

Only recently has crime been defined as an offense not against the individual wronged but against the state. The state makes and enforces laws. Thus, the reasoning goes, a person who commits a crime has violated the laws of the state. As a result, the wronged individual is no longer viewed as the primary victim. The offender is punished by the state and is often not required to make any kind of restitution or recompense to the victim. In addition, the community no longer has a role to play in holding the offender accountable.

This is where I believe the Church comes in. The Church must be about the business of community restoration prior to community development. The Church must focus on raising community awareness about the issue of crime, fighting apathy, and developing the community's sense of power to act, so that people start holding one another accountable. Communities can have a significant impact on crime, and the Church has the power to be a key player and motivator behind the community. It all begins with the Church's theology.

THE THEOLOGY

When Twelfth Street Baptist Church began to reach out to the community after Alice's death, we did not set out to reduce crime. That was not our original mission. We hoped to establish, maintain, and demonstrate the presence of God in the midst of that community and to do what the Lord had called us to do. What we discovered in the process is that in doing ministry the way that Jesus commanded, we had an impact on crime. The church that lives out the teaching of Jesus Christ has the ability to have a concrete, quantifiable, measurable impact on improving quality of life in the community.

The supreme lesson of the Gospel is that God so loved the world in its brokenness that He gave His only begotten and beloved Son for the restoration of the community He created. Christ's chief goal in His ministry was to have people experience the redemptive grace of the Kingdom of God. This grace is the result of the love of God. Through the gospel proclaimed by Christ, people could be redeemed, restored, or reborn into right relationship with God. The evidence of this conversion is love for our neighbor.

> I have a one-sentence definition for *forgiveness* that has worked for me as a victim of crime: Look beyond the faults and see the needs of the offender. Also, I see myself as an offender and needing forgiveness, something that Jesus gives me every day.
> Charlene Turner Johnson, forum participant

There can be no true definition of love for God without love for one's neighbor. Just knowing who God is will not suffice; we must act as He would. We must be willing to love our neighbors as ourselves; we must be willing to act in loving ways toward others. The rituals of the Church are meaningless if they reach only up and not out. Everyday in this country in every type of community, sin and crime are striking at the very roots of our civilization. They stand in

246

the valley of despair and violation as a Goliath, challenging and defying the Church of God. The current plague of crime gives the Church an unprecedented opportunity to demonstrate the immensity of God in the affairs of humankind.

Interestingly, according to the *Preacher's Outline and Sermon Bible,* this has eternal consequences. If a man wishes eternal life, he has to love his *neighbor.* The first commandment, "Love God," is abstract; it cannot be seen or understood standing by itself. There has to be a *demonstration, an act, something done* for love to be seen and understood. A profession of love without demonstration is empty. It is profession only. Love is not known if it is not shown.[6]

If we live out the theology of the Church and realize that crime is the product of sin and evil, then we can release the weapons of the Kingdom of God against the enemy. We can do this by living out the meaning of "Neighbors Who Care."

THE ROLE OF PREACHER AND PASTOR

More than twenty-five years of preaching and pastoring, thirty-seven years of church membership, and a lifetime of church affiliation have taught me a few things about the nature of the local church. I'm also aware of the need for accountability and responsibility for the proper use of authority. It pleased God to save the world by "the foolishness of preaching," according to the Scriptures, and if the Church is going to make a strong and proper response to any challenge, preaching and pastoral authority will be the point of departure.

Alice was not the first person murdered in our community. However, her death marked the first time the church had taken such a bold step. The church had been in the community for more than fifty years, and many had been the lives lost in street violence, but this was the first time the matter had made it onto the preaching agenda as an action item. I believe my proclamation, given with the

---

6. *Preacher's Outline and Sermon Bible,* vol. 4 (Florence, S.C.: Christian Publications and Ministries, 1991), p. 206.

intent to persuade the church to act in certain ways toward the victims in this matter, made the difference. Without this proclamation, "How shall they hear?"

Clergy serve at the calling of God and, in many cases, the people. This makes the role of the preacher a key factor in the church's decision to take action. The people understand the preacher to represent the mind of God and to give God's view of the affairs of this life. Ministers play a tremendous role in determining the dialogue of the Church. Therefore, it is imperative that the need for the Church to minister to the victims of crime in the name of Christ be proclaimed from the pulpit.

Not only must preachers bring and keep the need before the people; they must monitor the extent of its penetration into the life and heart of the church. As I listened to the prayers of the members and heard them lifting up Alice's family in prayer in corporate settings, I knew the Spirit was working in the hearts and minds of the church. It was time to move from preacher to pastor.

As preacher, I had hammered home the "what" to do; now it was time to show the people "how" to do it. Their prayers said they were ready to act; what they needed now was leadership. Without a plan of action, the likelihood of frustration was great. It is one thing to point out the problem; it is quite another to act in ways that solve it. Many are those who major in problem identification but have not the slightest idea how to address them. We must be prepared to take action when the Spirit has moved the need from the preaching agenda to the church's prayer life.

The Church can act in a number of ways to respond to crime victims. Certainly preaching and praying are ways of acting; however, if we only say to people, in effect, "Be warmed and filled," and do not put our faith into acts, we are guilty of possessing dead faith. Providing for the practical needs of the person is a way of acting. Being present in the immediate circumstances of the violation can be of tremendous value; simple acts of kindness, such as bringing food or cleaning a house, bring comfort to the victim. The type of action that is required is the kind born of corporate commitment. Preaching and pastoral leadership are directed to the whole body as well as its individual members.

Corporate responses have the potential to allow the effort to become part of the culture of caring in the local church. It is good for members to give personally to those hurt by crime, but the whole can give more and validate the actions of the one. When the effort becomes a budget item or has its own time of recognition in the annual program or plan of the church life cycle, it has the potential to endure and be self-perpetuating. The pastor is key and needs to model the way.

Several months after Alice's death, our immediate family was still deeply committed to her youngest daughter, Terri. We moved her into our home and encouraged her to finish high school. She shared a bedroom with our daughter, Veronica. She became part of our family in every way. She was just as active in church as any of the children, and we were convinced that she had survived the homicide of her mother. It felt good to see her happy and so full of life and believing in the good of humanity and knowing Christ was the reason for her blessing.

So it was very hard when we learned that she had been shot to death right in front of the restaurant our nonprofit branch was renovating and planning to open later that same year. Terri would have worked there; she would have gone to the community college at night, lived in one of the apartments we were renovating, and attended our computer lab. But crime stole Terri just as it had Alice, and just as it does many every year.

By reaching out to Alice's children and the community, my church and I began a difficult yet rewarding and effective ministry in our neighborhood. My family gained a daughter, Terri, through those tragic events. Unfortunately, the cycle of violence is a vicious one. When Terri was murdered, we as a family became the homicide survivors in need of the care and support of our congregation and community.

I don't know all of the answers, but I have seen what the Church can do, both as pastor and as one hurt by violence. I have personally experienced the power of caring. May the Church continue to minister to those hurt and broken by crime.

Study Guide

written by
Gregory Strong

Introduction

NEIGHBORS WHO CARE

If you have read Charles Colson's introduction to this book, you know that Neighbors Who Care (NWC) is a Christian ministry assisting churches that serve victims of crime in their congregations and communities. Victims are offered various kinds of help, including spiritual, emotional, and practical support. NWC specifically assists churches by providing advisory consultation, resource materials, and training. Affiliated with Prison Fellowship Ministries (founded by Charles Colson in 1976), NWC is a vital part of a "full circle" approach to understanding and responding to those involved in and affected by crime.

Seeing a need for serious theological and biblical reflection on issues of crime victimization and the Christian Church, NWC sponsored the Theological Forum on Crime Victims and the Church on October 10-11, 1997. NWC invited a number of religious scholars, pastors, and victim service-providers to present papers on and discuss key issues facing crime victims. From these materials, NWC developed this book, *God and the Victim*.

PURPOSE OF THE STUDY

The purpose of this study is to help you and/or the members of your group to better understand and respond to many of the key spiritual and emotional issues that crime victims face. Topics for study include the spiritual needs of crime victims, evil, victimization, justice, forgiveness, assisting crime victims, and the role of the clergy in victim ministry. By studying and discussing the topic addressed in each chapter, you can deepen your understanding of that topic and how it affects crime victims. As you examine the reality of the impact of crime on individual lives, you will also identify ways in which you can assist victims of crime facing critical spiritual and emotional issues.

RESULTS OF THE STUDY

By the end of the study, you and/or the members of your group will have accomplished several things:

- You will have examined major theological and biblical themes on the spiritual and emotional issues that crime victims face, including victimization, justice, evil, and forgiveness.
- You will have examined common cultural perspectives — including personal ideas and attitudes — on those issues.
- You will have identified ways that you as an individual, your group, and your church can respond faithfully and concretely to victims of crime.

SCOPE AND FORMAT OF THE STUDY

This study guide is intended for use by an individual or by a small group, whether a Sunday school class, an evening study group, or a college or seminary class. Using the guide, the individual reader or small group will examine the spiritual and emotional issues facing crime victims.

Each study unit contains the following sections:

Objectives Targets for significant points to be learned through
the lesson
Reviewing A summary of the main ideas in the chapter
Exploring Questions and discussion points to help you examine
in depth the issues raised in the chapter
Applying Questions and discussion points to help you apply
what you have learned

SUGGESTIONS FOR INDIVIDUAL STUDY

- It is not necessary to go straight through the book. You may
want to pick the topics and writers that interest you the most
and study those chapters first.
- Use a notebook to write down your thoughts, questions, and responses as you read the chapter and think about the questions in
the study unit at the end of the chapter.

SUGGESTIONS FOR LEADERS OF GROUP STUDY

Here are a number of suggestions for structuring your group study.
As you get to know your group, you can adapt the study sessions to
fit your group style and needs.

- To get the most out of the book and the discussion times, you
and the group members, prior to each meeting, should read the
chapter to be discussed.
- With the study guide for assistance (adapted as you see fit), the
group can meet weekly, biweekly, or monthly to discuss the
chapter that has been read.
- At the beginning of each meeting, you may want to review the
"Objectives" and "Reviewing" sections as a group. The "Reviewing" section can be particularly helpful if a new person has

joined the group or if a member of the group was unable to read the chapter in the preceding week.

- Then, as leader, guide the group through discussion. You may use the questions and discussion points in the "Exploring" and "Applying" sections of the study unit, or you may raise questions and issues more directly related to your group's situation. Some weeks this may also involve having a member of the group read aloud a passage from Scripture or a small section of the chapter as background.
- The amount of time you have for each meeting depends on your situation. Here are two possible ways to structure your time — one for a longer meeting, and one for a shorter meeting. You may want to adapt these structures to fit your group's needs.

Total time — 75 minutes	*Total time — 45 minutes*
15 minutes for prayer and introduction	10 minutes for prayer and introduction
45 minutes for discussion	30 minutes for discussion
15 minutes for "housekeeping" details and closing prayer	5 minutes for "housekeeping" details and closing prayer

WHAT YOU NEED FOR THE STUDY

- A copy of *God and the Victim*
- A Bible
- Paper and pen
- An open mind and heart
- A commitment to preparation, attendance, and participation (if in a group)

SMALL GROUPS

A small group can provide a dynamic context for people to grow in knowledge and in spirit, with the whole being greater than the parts. It can also provide a positive context for forging relationships. Indeed, it can be argued that the best experiences of growth in knowledge and in spirit are most likely to occur in the context of growing relationships. What things can you, as leader, do to foster such experiences? The following ideas may help you in preparing for and leading the group study and discussion. *Your role as leader is to assist the group members in taking on the intellectual and spiritual challenges of this subject matter. This is a vital and valuable role. Enjoy it!*

Leadership Role

You do not need to be an expert in theology, criminology, or victimology. Your primary role as leader is to facilitate and coordinate the study and discussion of the group members in order to help the meetings run as smoothly and purposefully as possible.

The goal is to maximize individual involvement — allowing for personal style and expression — in the meetings. The following points about group dynamics may help your group achieve that goal.

Group Dynamics

Often every participant has different reasons for undertaking a course of study and different responses to the material, which may affect his or her participation. Each group member will be affected by, for example, what questions or issues are most important to him or her, what emotions the study evokes, and what he or she hopes to accomplish through the study.

In addition, group members will have different styles of participation. As you begin to recognize those differences, you can seek balance among them through comments, direction, and questions.

Be prepared for the possibility that the subject matter may be emotionally charged for some members of the group. They may have been crime victims or have been close to someone who was. Or the subject matter may touch on other events that are deeply emotional for them. After all, these issues go beyond particular instances of crime and apply to all of us. Allow for expression of emotions to be part of the group process.

Facilitating Group Discussion

For the participants, group discussion can often be the most significant and meaningful part of the study. For the leader, however, it can be the most challenging. Here are some ideas that may help you facilitate discussion:

- Encourage all members to take part in the discussion. You may, with discretion, ask direct questions of participants. Or sometimes you may need to carefully direct the discussion away from some group members.
- Do not be afraid of moments of silence. Sometimes people need to digest ideas before speaking. And silence can be a powerful motivator that encourages people to initiate discussion.
- Try to keep the discussion focused on the subject. People in groups have a tendency to stray from the subject and find it difficult to return to it on their own. At the same time, leave room for the Holy Spirit to guide the direction of the discussion. If the group seems to have gone off on a tangent but people are interested and engaged, you may want to stay with that line of discussion for a while.
- Welcome new ideas, questions, and perspectives.

CHAPTER ONE

Finding God in the Wake of Crime:
Answers to Hard Questions

LISA BARNES LAMPMAN AND MICHELLE D. SHATTUCK

OBJECTIVES

- To recognize the importance and nature of the spiritual needs of crime victims
- To examine the challenges and the opportunities in addressing the spiritual needs of victims
- To examine the key spiritual questions raised by crime victimization that affect all of us

REVIEWING

Using stories of contemporary crime victims and biblical stories (particularly the story of Job, the story of Tamar, and the Parable of the Good Samaritan), Ms. Lampman and Ms. Shattuck explore the needs, challenges, and opportunities that Christians encounter in responding to the spiritual issues faced by crime victims.

The authors begin this chapter by emphasizing the fact that victims have spiritual needs as well as practical and emotional needs. Through contemporary and biblical stories, they explore some of the key spiritual issues that press upon crime victims. Then they examine the reasons why we have difficulty responding to victims, especially to their spiritual needs. Yet, the authors urge, Christians must attend to victims and acknowledge and address the spiritual issues they face.

The hope is that crime victims will reach a point of restoration — physically, emotionally, and spiritually. Reaching this point will not mean that all their issues are neatly resolved, but that the larger story of God's gracious purposes in the world, seen in the sacrificial death and resurrection of Jesus, is reinforced and deepened in their minds and hearts. With this perspective they will be able to see God's essential goodness and love — greater than any evil — which can then transform their personal experiences of victimization.

EXPLORING

1. Based on your reading of this chapter and your own perspective, explain why the Church has been largely unresponsive to the needs of crime victims. Why has the Church been more active in ministering to those in prison than to the victims they left behind?

2. Ms. Lampman and Ms. Shattuck make the point that crime victims have spiritual needs as well as practical and emotional needs. What are some of these spiritual needs? (Consider the contemporary stories of crime victims in this chapter. Also consider your own experience or the experiences of people you know.)

3. Why do people, including Christians, have difficulty acknowledging and responding to crime victims, particularly in terms of their spiritual needs? (See, for example, the discussion of Job's situation, pp. 4-5.)

4. Why, according to the authors, is it important and even imperative that Christians respond to the needs of crime victims, especially to their spiritual needs?

5. How can victims of crime begin to see their traumatic experiences within the larger context of God's essential goodness and love active in the world? How can Christian caregivers assist them in this process?

APPLYING

1. Review the chapter. How can you and your church prepare to reach out to crime victims — to be a neighbor assisting with their needs?

2. What are the challenges and costs of being a neighbor to victims, especially with respect to their spiritual needs?

3. How can addressing the spiritual needs of crime victims help their recovery?

CHAPTER TWO

Original Crime, Primal Care

MIROSLAV VOLF

OBJECTIVES

- To understand more adequately evil, responsibility, and response to crime
- To explore our identification with both perpetrators and victims
- To examine the application of God's justice and grace to evil and crime

REVIEWING

For group discussion: If there is time, it will be helpful for one of the group members to read Genesis 4:1-16, the story of Cain and Abel, as well as Hebrews 11:4 and 1 John 3:11-17, before the discussion.

Commenting on the story of Cain and Abel, Volf points to two common convictions in contemporary culture: (1) Cain is not responsible for his wrongdoing; something else made him do it; and (2) God or moral codes are oppressive; thus, they are the true instigators of evil. Volf then observes that many others argue just the opposite: (1) People are free and thus wholly responsible for their actions; and (2) Only belief in God provides a true and sufficient foundation for a clear and vigorous moral code, promoting good behavior and punishing bad behavior.

In contrast to both perspectives, Volf contends that "the mystery of evil is deeper and the remedy more complex." Cain was shaped significantly by his environment, but he was not determined by it. Even granting the power of environment, Cain could have acted otherwise. He bore responsibility for his deed. Also, the story shows us that God cares for victims, and so God effects justice on behalf of victims and against perpetrators. Yet even in judgment God cares for perpetrators and extends His grace to them. Further, Volf says,

262

each of us is both Cain and Abel — at different points and different times we are perpetrator, or victim, or victim tempted to become perpetrator in response. We must care for victims and do justice, but not by "demonizing" perpetrators. In some sense, perpetrators remain among the "neighbors" for whom we must care, even as we care for victims.

EXPLORING

1. Volf discusses perspectives on evil, responsibility, and response to evil and wrongdoing. From Volf's perspective, what are the strengths and weaknesses of each of these perspectives? Why does Volf argue for a third approach?

2. What does Volf mean when he discusses the categories of "them" and "us"? What do the categories mean in relation to us today?

3. In discussing Cain, Volf describes certain characteristics or qualities of evil or wrongdoing. What are they? From your observation or experience, identify some other significant characteristics of evil and wrongdoing.

4. Why did God punish Cain? Why did God protect Cain?

5. What do you think of Volf's assertion that "each of us is both Abel and Cain"? Why?

6. What role and responsibility does God have with respect to evil and wrongdoing?

APPLYING

1. How has your understanding of evil and the response to evil changed after reading Volf's examination of the story of Cain and Abel?

2. If "each of us is both Abel and Cain," what does that mean, in practical terms, for our understanding of and response to victims and perpetrators? Further, what does that mean for our understanding of ourselves if we have been victimized?

3. How does this exploration and discussion of evil affect your perspective on crime with respect to perpetrators and victims?

4. If you are in a group, at the end of your discussion you may want to pray together the prayer, included near the end of the chapter, from the Calvinist liturgy of 1571. (See pp. 34-35.)

CHAPTER THREE

The Mark of Evil

DAN B. ALLENDER

OBJECTIVES

- To understand the fundamental characteristics and purposes of evil
- To examine the spiritual and emotional effects of evil experiences
- To explore the opportunity to grow in faith, hope, and love through a deeper understanding of evil

REVIEWING

Using real-life stories, Allender points out that encounters with evil deeds and people challenge our sense of order and meaning, including our faith in God. With this in mind, Allender explores how evil forces us to examine both God and ourselves by focusing on three issues: the heart of evil, the horror of evil, and the hope of redemption from evil. His aim is to help us understand God and ourselves better, and to love God more fully.

At the heart of evil is the evil one, Satan, maliciously against God and all of God's creation. Evil thus goes beyond mere evil deeds: evilness is actually embodied not only by fallen angels but also by human beings. Evil actually "delights" in damaging and destroying what is good in human existence — faith, hope, and love. For the victim, the horror of evil destroys hope through powerlessness, faith through betrayal, and love through ambivalence. Yet there is hope of redemption. God can transform our experiences of evil into means for growing in faith, hope, and love.

By examining evil or suffering evil ourselves, we face deep issues and doubts about ourselves and our faith. We find that we are closer to evil than we generally acknowledge. And we wrestle and argue with

265

God about His goodness and fairness and the meaningfulness of life. Yet, in the struggle between faith and doubt lies the possibility of surrendering in greater faith to God. Moreover, God can use the despair brought on by evil to drive away all false hope and to bring us to true hope in Him. Then, in faith and hope, we can act in true love. Godly love, rooted in the redemptive suffering of Jesus, lays the foundation for forgiveness and reconciliation when harm and evil have been done. In the end, evil can lead to greater faith, hope, and love — to deeper and greater participation in the redemptive purposes of God.

EXPLORING

1. What are the three internal qualities of evil detailed by Allender when he examines the heart of evil? (See pp. 39-47.) Describe each quality.

2. While examining the horror of evil, Allender points to its effects. (See p. 147.) How does evil destroy hope? How does it destroy faith? How does it destroy love?

3. Both thoughtful observers and people who have suffered the experience of evil point to the existence of evil as one of the strongest arguments against the existence of a good, all-powerful God. What do you think of this argument?

4. Allender says that there are not only evil deeds but also some people who are genuinely evil. What does he mean by "a person who is evil"? How, if at all, does that help you understand evil?

5. If Allender is correct about evil people, what are the dangers in identifying some people as evil? What hope is there for the person who is evil?

6. According to Allender, how can the experience of evil help us grow in hope, faith, and love? (See pp. 52-60.)

APPLYING

1. Identify conditions, events, or other elements in your community that seem clearly to you to be instances or structures of evil.

2. In what ways do we blind ourselves to or deny evil in our surroundings? In what ways do we blind ourselves to or deny evil in the attitudes and conduct of our own lives?

3. How do Allender's definitions and descriptions of evil relate to crime and criminal acts?

4. It can be difficult for us to "stand alongside" people who have suffered genuine evil. What inhibits us from doing so? What things can we do and what resources do we have to overcome our reluctance?

5. In what specific, concrete ways can you use your observations and experiences of evil to prevent evil in the future, both in your individual life and in your communities (church, neighborhood, and city)?

CHAPTER FOUR

Responsibility toward Victims' Rights

CARL F. H. HENRY

OBJECTIVES

- To clarify the use and misuse of the term *victim*
- To understand wrongdoing as ultimately an offense against God, and a just response to wrongdoing as an anticipation of God's ultimate victory over evil
- To explore the concept of Jesus as "victim" and "victor"
- To examine the complex nature of God's care for both victim and offender

REVIEWING

Henry notes the common definition of *victim* as one who has suffered from the aggression of another who bears responsibility for causing injury. He then points out that in some contemporary thought this definition is reversed. The offender is regarded as the victim of society's injustice. Responsibility for crime lies with society, not with the offender. Thus we appear to have an unbridgeable divide in perspectives: criminal behavior results from either individual choice or social environment.

Henry urges a third perspective. In this view, all of us, including victims, have a potential for evil and wrongdoing. Further, we must recognize that we are part of society; we bear some responsibility for deplorable social conditions that affect people adversely. None of us is completely blameless.

Moreover, crime and wrongdoing are offenses, not just against humans and human laws but against God and God's law. From this theological perspective, we understand that Jesus is both the true Victim and the true Victor.

Therefore, we must stand with the victim whose life has been injured by crime. God desires justice and healing for the victim. We must assist the victim in achieving as complete an emotional and spiritual recovery as possible. At the same time, God desires humane treatment of and spiritual repentance and redemption for the offender. Through Jesus' sacrificial death, both victim and offender may find grace and reconciliation that surpasses loss, injury, and enmity.

EXPLORING

1. Henry contends that modern society is confused over the meaning of the term *victim*. Why does he make that contention?

2. What difference does this confusion make in our understanding of personal responsibility in connection with the influences that shape social structures? How do you think personal responsibility and the influence of social environment are related? Why?

3. Compare and contrast the sense in which Jesus was a victim with the sense in which you or another person might have been a victim.

4. What does Henry mean when he says, "God stands as the unrequited victim of a criminalized society"? (See p. 64.) What do you think of this statement?

5. What relevance does the idea of Jesus as victor have for crime victims?

APPLYING

1. Henry emphasizes the concept that we all participate in a common humanity and society, including the sinfulness inherent in human existence. What difference might that make in how we view and respond to victims and offenders? And what difference might that make in how a victim perceives himself or herself, and how a victim responds to the perpetrator?

2. Henry warns the crime victim against the temptation to hold on to resentment. What are some of the spiritual, emotional, and

moral risks of holding on to resentment? What concrete steps might a crime victim take to master that temptation?

3. Henry refers to the spiritual possibility of the reconciliation of victim and offender. On what basis can we even talk about this? What issues or problems might arise in such a process? Why would it be good?

4. How could you or your church assist victims in understanding the process of repentance, forgiveness, and reconciliation in their own lives?

CHAPTER FIVE

Go and Do Likewise:
The Church's Role in Caring for Crime Victims

HAROLD DEAN TRULEAR

OBJECTIVES

- To overcome the tendency to divide Christian witness from social compassion and action
- To examine many of the basic needs that crime victims have
- To examine three core components of the Church's ministry to crime victims
- To identify various resources (i.e., organizations, programs) available to assist victims

REVIEWING

In this chapter Trulear emphasizes the Church's need to provide holistic witness amidst the realities of crime, including the needs of victims. Using the Parable of the Good Samaritan, Trulear addresses three key elements of ministry with crime victims: attitude, action, and monitoring.

In his discussion of attitude, Trulear emphasizes that love for the neighbor is an essential element of living in God's Kingdom. Yet a perfect attitude — that is, perfect love — is not a necessary precondition for action. Acts of compassion can deepen love. At the same time, Christian activists must always spend time in devotion and study so that their good deeds do not eclipse their relationship with Jesus. Further, a church's ministry to crime victims must begin in prayer if it is to be a response to Jesus' call and not merely another program of social activism.

In his discussion of action, Trulear points out that the good Samaritan's empathetic response took two forms, which model how the Church can respond to crime victims. The first involves inter-

271

vention — meeting the immediate needs of the victim. The second involves networking — coordinating resources to take care of the victim's long-term needs.

These two acts — intervention and networking, especially networking — lead naturally to the third key element, monitoring. The good Samaritan attended to the long-term needs of the victim. Following his example, churches must keep in mind the long-term needs of crime victims. Long-term assistance is often vital to victims' recovery.

The Church, like the good Samaritan, assists the victim of crime because the person is in need — and the Church does so without question, especially without trying to determine the worthiness of the person in need. Thus the Church, heeding Jesus' command to imitate the Samaritan, acts in grace-filled love and compassion — living out the Kingdom of God amid the effects of crime.

EXPLORING

1. Trulear refers to the need for the Church's "holistic witness." In the context of crime, what do you think "holistic witness" means?

2. What are the benefits and the risks of holistic witness? What are the risks when the Church's witness is not holistic?

3. Trulear focuses on three key aspects of assistance to crime victims. (See p. 73.) Review them and then describe briefly how each relates to crime victims.

4. Looking at the nine areas of potential problems that crime victims may experience (see pp. 80-82), identify the resources within your church that might be used to assist victims with particular problems. Also, identify the resources within your community.

5. The story of the good Samaritan relates that he acted because he was moved by pity. It does not describe the attitudes that allowed the priest and the Levite to neglect the victim. With them in mind, as well as your own experience and observation, what attitudes do you see in operation that permit us to neglect those in need, especially crime victims? What holds us back from assisting them?

APPLYING

1. According to Trulear, what is the first thing you or your church should do in considering ministry to crime victims? Why?

2. What needs to change in you and in your church if you are to become a neighbor, like the Samaritan, to those in need?

3. How can you and your church foster attitudes, qualities, and skills that lead to compassionate care for and effective action on behalf of crime victims?

4. What resources or groups already exist in your church and community that can provide short-term and long-term services to crime victims?

5. What can your church do to become a resource center to help victims of crime and those who serve them?

CHAPTER SIX

Victimization and Healing: The Biblical View

ELIZABETH ACHTEMEIER

OBJECTIVES

- To understand crime victimization as a result of humankind's rebellion against God, and victim assistance as part of God's renewal of the individual and the community
- To explore the desire for vengeance, the pursuit of justice, and the biblical commandment to love our enemies in the context of crime victimization
- To understand and act upon two significant forms of assistance for crime victims: offering comfort and seeking restitution

REVIEWING

Achtemeier urges us to think about crime victims and respond to their needs primarily from the perspective of God's purposes in the world rather than from contemporary cultural perspectives. Specifically, God created a world that was very good. We corrupted it by rebelling against God. As amply shown in the Bible, the results include many forms of victimization — slavery, oppressive governments, dishonest commerce, poverty, lying and slander, greed and rampant wealth, theft, murder, and even unjust treatment of offenders. Yet God desires to overcome our rebellion and the harms it causes.

With this in mind, how do we respond to victimization? While we often desire vengeance, Jesus teaches us to forgive and to love our enemies. In view of this seeming conflict, Achtemeier contends that justice was recognized in the Bible as a human activity, whereas vengeance was acknowledged as God's prerogative. Christian victims can seek justice but never vengeance. Indeed, Christian victims should seek to love and pray for those who wrong them.

What then can victims hope for in response to their needs? The Psalms describe the benefits of complete trust in and patience with God. The Bible also obligates individuals and communities to assist victims of crime. Primary assistance involves offering comfort, love, and care. Additionally, the Bible mandates another form of victim assistance — restitution.

In responding to the needs of crime victims, we should remember that God lovingly created human beings in His image, with great value and dignity. Crime assaults the value and dignity of the person. In accord with God's renewing purposes, Christian love seeks to restore the worth and wholeness of the crime victim and the community as a whole through comfort and aid.

EXPLORING

1. Achtemeier points to God's desire, in response to sin, to create a new community characterized by righteousness and justice. From a biblical perspective, how would you define righteousness and justice? How do righteousness and justice serve the well-being of a community?

2. Achtemeier points out many biblical examples of victimization. Review that section of the chapter. (See pp. 92-96.) Why does she discuss those forms of victimization?

3. What distinctions does Achtemeier make between justice, vengeance, and retribution? Why is it important for a crime victim to make these distinctions?

4. In the realities of crime and victimization, how do love and forgiveness for those who wrong us relate to the desire for vengeance and the pursuit of justice?

5. Achtemeier observes that, in Scripture, victims often can only trust in God's eventual righting of the wrong. She goes on to quote Paul's claim that "the sufferings of this present time are not worth comparing with the glory that is to be revealed to us" (Rom. 8:18, RSV). Are there appropriate ways and times to discuss these ideas with a crime victim? Explain your answer to this question.

6. Achtemeier states that the primary assistance we can offer a

crime victim is comfort. Why should we offer comfort to a crime victim, especially if the victim is not a member of our family or immediate neighborhood?

7. Using texts from Exodus 21, Leviticus 6, and Deuteronomy 22 (see pp. 103-6), Achtemeier discusses the biblical idea of restitution to address the needs of a crime victim. What is restitution, and why is it important to the crime victim?

APPLYING

1. As Achtemeier's chapter makes clear, where the Bible addresses issues of crime and victimization, it does so largely from within the belief system of the community of faith (Jewish or Christian). Would there be any differences in the way your church would respond to a crime victim who is a Christian and a crime victim who appears to have no religious faith or affiliation?

2. Achtemeier examines the harm that crime causes to both the individual victim and the community as a whole. How can you and your church assist both the individual and the community in healing from victimization?

3. If comfort is the primary assistance we can offer a crime victim, what resources or programs can the Church provide to offer comfort?

4. If restitution is important to victims and to the "righteous community" that God desires, how can your church assist victims in obtaining restitution for their losses due to crime?

5. Define the basic meanings of retribution, recompense, and forgiveness. With respect to offenders and victims, why and how should we as a society try to balance retribution, recompense, and forgiveness?

CHAPTER SEVEN

The Contours of Justice: An Ancient Call for Shalom

NICHOLAS WOLTERSTORFF

OBJECTIVES

- To examine biblical meanings of *shalom* and justice
- To explore the concept of *rights* as it pertains to justice
- To understand the relevance of justice and *shalom* today as manifested through Christ's life
- To identify concrete ways to act justly in your community, especially on behalf of crime victims

REVIEWING

Wolterstorff notes that God loves justice. In His love of justice, God cares especially for the weak, the vulnerable, and the lowly — "widows, orphans, and aliens" and "the poor." Indeed, God defines justice in terms of their well-being. The background for God's justice involves three elements: (1) God loves not just some individuals but each and every person; (2) God desires the *shalom* of each and every person — the spiritual and material flourishing of human life; (3) God's justice seeks the *shalom* of each and every person because each has a right to the basic conditions that lead to *shalom*.

We ought to love justice because we are to love what God loves and do what God desires. God's desire — and so our desire — is not only for the spiritual good of people but also for their material good. Justice intrinsically involves material welfare because *shalom* signifies the complete flourishing of human life, in this existence as well as the next.

Justice is not simply an Old Testament imperative no longer obligatory in the New Testament. In the New Testament the Greek word *dikaiosune,* translated "righteousness," can also be translated "justice." For example, according to Wolterstorff, we can translate

Jesus' words in the Beatitudes as "Blessed are those who hunger and thirst for justice." Also, Jesus spoke of the coming of the Kingdom (the realm of *shalom*, of justice) as a future reality, yet He also spoke of the Kingdom as having come in Him. Jesus desired and practiced *shalom* and justice for all. As the Church, the Body of Christ, we are to proclaim the Kingdom of God and practice the *shalom* and justice of the Kingdom, especially with the poor, the vulnerable, the outcast, the ill, and the oppressed.

EXPLORING

1. In a sentence or two, how would you define justice? What definitions of justice outside of the Bible does Wolterstorff mention? (See p. 111.) According to Wolterstorff, what is the biblical definition of justice? (See p. 118.)

2. What does "preferential option for the poor" mean? What do you think of the assertion that God has a "preferential option for the poor"? (In support of his position, Wolterstorff quotes from Psalm 146; for background, compare also Exodus 22:21-27, Deuteronomy 24:19-22, and James 1:27.)

3. Wolterstorff discusses three elements that form the background to this "preferential option for the poor." What are they? (See pp. 112-18.) In particular, what do you think of Wolterstorff's discussion of "rights"?

4. Discuss the meaning of *shalom* and its relationship to justice.

5. What do you think of Wolterstorff's claim that many Christians are tempted to think that God is only concerned about people's spiritual welfare, their "religious lostness"?

6. According to Wolterstorff, what does it mean to be holy, as an individual and as a community?

7. Discuss the issue of justice as a divine imperative for Christians today as opposed to an Old Testament concept. (See Wolterstorff's discussion of *dikaiosune*, pp. 123-24.)

APPLYING

1. Can justice be a reality in the present, or is it only a future reality, awaiting the coming of God's Kingdom?

2. How would your church put into practice a "preferential option for the poor"? Name two or three things that could be done.

3. Wolterstorff discusses Jesus' challenge to the Pharisees. (See pp. 127-29.) In general terms, who are the Pharisees of today? In your church and community, in terms of *shalom* and justice, what would it mean to be religious like the Pharisees? What would it mean to be religious like Jesus?

4. Thinking in biblical terms as described by Wolterstorff, what conditions and structures in your community show injustice or a lack of *shalom*?

5. In particular, with respect to crime victims, what conditions and structures show injustice or a lack of *shalom*?

6. Identify several ways in which *shalom* and justice can be increased for crime victims in your church and community.

CHAPTER EIGHT

Restoring Justice

HOWARD ZEHR

OBJECTIVES

- To examine the three types of justice: revenge, retribution, and restoration
- To understand better what crime victims experience and what they need
- To identify specific, restorative responses to the experiences and needs of crime victims

REVIEWING

Zehr argues that a society's response to crime can be typified as one of three R's: revenge, retributive justice, or restorative justice. Modern Western legal systems tend to be characterized by retributive justice. Crime breaks the rules, the law, which is an offense against the state, not the victim. Victims have a marginal part in the justice process. Punishment is the dominant response.

Biblical justice, however, is rooted in a vision of *shalom* — a community of right relationships. In this perspective, restorative processes become the most appropriate response, for crime harms people and relationships. A restorative approach focuses on the harm caused by crime, concern for both victim and offender, repair of the people and relationships affected, and involvement of the community in the justice process.

What needs do victims in particular have? Victims experience many reactions, often involving crises of self-image, meaning, memories, and relationships. Their assumptions about autonomy, order, and right-relatedness suffer or shatter. Angry and fearful, crime victims feel vulnerable, violated, and depersonalized. Therefore, a just, restorative response to victims provides them with a safe space and

280

helps them find restitution, vindication, answers to questions, opportunities to tell their stories, and empowerment. Various processes and programs are being developed to assist crime victims with their needs. Churches, called to be agents of reconciliation and *shalom,* have a great opportunity to become involved in ministry. Our goal should be to seek a justice that treats victims and offenders as full participants, that encourages communication and empathy, and that seeks the restoration of *shalom.*

EXPLORING

1. Describe the strengths and weaknesses of each of the three R's of justice mentioned by Zehr. (See pp. 132-33.)

2. Early in his chapter, Zehr refers to restorative justice as "the essence of biblical justice" and lists its chief principles. (See pp. 132-33.) From your understanding of the Bible, what biblical ideas and values support the principles of restorative justice? In particular, how does the biblical sense of *shalom* relate to the principles of restorative justice?

3. What does Zehr say about the role that Christianity has played in sidelining victims and their needs? (See pp. 134, 136.) How does he, by contrast, describe biblical justice? What do you think of what he says?

4. Using real examples, Zehr describes some of the ways in which victims respond to crime. Take a moment and try to imagine what those people felt. Try to explain how you might feel in the same situation. If you have been a crime victim, perhaps share from your own experience. What are some of the most difficult aspects of the experience of victimization?

5. According to Zehr, what things do crime victims need most? What can be done to assist victims with those needs? What are the aims in assisting crime victims? (See pp. 141-43.)

6. Why should individual Christians and churches get involved?

7. According to Zehr, there are both negative and positive ways that the Church and its members can support and be engaged with crime victims. What are some of the negative ways? What are some of the positive ways? (See pp. 146-53.)

APPLYING

1. Have someone read aloud the signposts of restorative justice mentioned in the chapter. (See p. 148.)

2. If you have known a person who was a crime victim, reflect on how you related to that person and his or her experience. What did you do well? What could you have done better? These questions can also be asked about your church's response to a member or members of the congregation who have been victimized by crime.

3. Identify some victim-assistance programs in your community. If you do not know of any, how could you go about identifying some? How could you or your church aid or participate in those programs?

4. What programs or services does your church offer that already assist or could assist crime victims? If there are none, what programs could your church develop to assist crime victims? What would it take to make this happen?

5. How could your church allow victims to tell their stories in ways that would be helpful and facilitate healing?

CHAPTER NINE

Behold, I Make All Things New

L. GREGORY JONES

OBJECTIVES

- To better understand the nature of forgiveness, both divine and human, and how forgiveness functions in "making all things new"
- To examine the complex relationship between forgiveness and remembering pain and sorrow, especially in relation to crime victims
- To understand the nature of remembering in healing ways — remembering well — in contrast to remembering in hurtful ways

REVIEWING

In this chapter Jones observes that crime victims often receive advice in the form of two clichés — "Forgive and forget" and "Time heals all wounds." Yet time does not heal all wounds; some fester. Can we really forgive and forget? Should we forget? How long does it take to forgive?

Jones points out that forgiveness is God's means of bringing reconciliation, healing, and restoration. As Christians, we have to learn to embody forgiveness and healing and to assist crime victims to do the same. Embodying forgiveness involves many elements, including patient truthfulness about conflicts and feelings, honesty about our own complicity in problems, openness to others, commitment to changing the root causes of the problems, and a desire for reconciliation.

Moreover, forgiveness requires that we not entirely forget. How then can victims of crime cope with their memories? How can they remember well? At the heart of remembering well — viewing the past from a place of wholeness — is learning to be forgiven by God and realizing God's engagement with our past, working to redeem it. Jones thus contends that forgiveness should be linked more closely to remembering well than to forgetting.

Still, Jones also notes that it may be necessary to experience "a little forgetfulness," especially if we are holding on to memories that prevent healing, forgiveness, and reconciliation. Jones invokes Miroslav Volf's phrase — "the grace of nonremembering" — as a better way of speaking about this, for it suggests healing and restoration more than mere forgetting. It has more to do with God's "making all things new." We recall our memories, but not in a sinful manner, because they have been healed, transformed, and incorporated into our lives through the crucified and risen Christ.

EXPLORING

1. To those in distress, why do we all too often offer advice like the clichés "Time heals all wounds" and "Forgive and forget"? What effects might those clichés have on crime victims?

2. Why does Jones suggest that the advice "Forgive and forget" tempts us to ignore or even deny Christ crucified and risen? (See pp. 161-62.)

3. Jones speaks of the process of forgiveness as a "dance" involving at least six elements or steps. Take some time to review the steps. (See pp. 167, 169-70.) Why do you think he uses the metaphor of a "dance"?

4. Implied in the steps of the "dance of forgiveness" is naming the evil; in fact, this is integral. Why is naming the evil necessary to the process of forgiveness?

5. How would you respond to an assertion that forgiveness ignores and even contradicts the requirement that justice be done?

6. Jones mentions several dynamics of traumatic memories. What are the dynamics of traumatic memories for crime victims? (See pp. 171-73.)

7. When is remembering necessary for forgiving and healing? When is forgetting necessary for forgiving and healing?

8. How does forgiveness function in God's process of "making all things new"?

APPLYING

1. What happens to a crime victim when, over time, he or she continues to remember the experience, and the community (family, friends, church members, neighbors) allows or even encourages it to fade from memory or blocks the sharing of the memory?

2. Think of the many informal and formal relationships you have — not only with your family and friends, but also through church, work, school, interest groups, and political affiliations. Do you and your church embody forgiveness within the church community and in the wider community? In what practical ways do you do this? In what ways could you and your church do better in those relationships?

3. Reflecting on your own experiences or those of others, past or present, share examples and stories of forgiveness and reconciliation that demonstrate the reality of God's "making all things new."

4. What things about forgiveness from this chapter do you think you would share with a crime victim that might help her in her recovery?

CHAPTER TEN

Every Knee Shall Bow

MARY WHITE

OBJECTIVES

- To understand the essential obligation to forgive when injured by crime or other wrongdoing
- To examine key aspects of the spiritual and emotional processes of forgiving
- To outline specific actions a church can take to assist crime victims in exercising forgiveness

REVIEWING

As a mother of a murder victim, White knows how difficult forgiveness is. Unlike other virtues God commands us to practice, forgiveness runs directly counter to our natural inclinations. Yet, she contends, the practice of forgiveness is necessary and foundational to Christian life, and to people in general. Grappling with forgiveness can be a long and arduous task. It is a process with ever-deepening levels. In the long run, however, it leads to healing and a more profound relationship with God.

The relationship between forgiveness and justice is complex as well. Forgiveness does not eliminate the need for justice to be done in response to an offender's crime. Yet human justice, administered through the legal system, cannot finally resolve the injustice and harm caused by the crime. In this respect, the administration of legal justice does not eliminate the need for the victim to strive for forgiveness.

Moreover, exercising forgiveness is not just a need; it is an obligation. The obligation to forgive stems from the truth that we all commit sin and that God offers forgiveness to all who come to Him seeking that forgiveness. On our part, forgiveness begins with an act of the will; feelings of forgiveness follow from that act. If we do not forgive, we cannot claim God's forgiveness for ourselves, because God makes forgiveness an essential aspect of His Kingdom in this world. Also, not forgiving exacts a high cost; it further devastates the spirit and well-being of the victim.

Through prayer and relational support, the Church can and ought to help crime victims face the reality of the crime, and experience and offer forgiveness. Despite the difficult nature of the task, the obligation of the Church to encourage and assist victims in restoration and forgiveness is fundamental to its very nature and witness, and essential to the needs of victims.

EXPLORING

1. In White's view, what is the purpose of forgiveness? Do you agree or disagree?

2. What do you think is the attitude of Christians in general when they think about crime, responses to crime, and the needs of crime victims? Is it one of forgiveness or retribution?

3. Are there some crimes or some persons too horrible to be forgiven?

4. Try to imagine that you have experienced what White has. Then try to imagine how you would feel when urged to forgive your child's murderer. Discuss those feelings.

5. White emphasizes the benefits of forgiveness to the forgiver. (See pp. 190-91.) Drawing on the chapter and on your own experience, describe the benefits a victim receives in the process of forgiving. Does the refusal to forgive harm the crime victim? If not, why? If so, why and how?

6. If White is correct about the benefits of forgiving and the harms of not forgiving, why is it so hard for crime victims — and us — to forgive? Why do we cling to a refusal to forgive? How does forgiveness benefit the offender?

7. White states that victims should come to forgiveness as quickly as possible. Do you agree or disagree? What are the implications of that for a victim?

8. White maintains that the idea of forgiveness can be embraced by those outside the Church. (See pp. 193-95.) What do you think of that idea? If it seems hard for Christians to exercise forgiveness, what specific issues might arise in assisting victims who are not Christians to do so?

APPLYING

1. How does the criminal justice system encourage or obstruct a victim's need to forgive the perpetrator?

2. White claims that forgiveness can present "the greatest challenge for the Church in aiding victims of crime." (See p. 193.) What spiritual and practical problems does the Church face in assisting victims with forgiveness?

3. White lists a number of specific ways a church can assist victims to forgive. (See pp. 195-97.) What steps can you or your church take, at present and over time, to provide that kind of assistance?

CHAPTER ELEVEN

"Forgive and Forget" and Other Myths of Forgiveness

DAN B. ALLENDER

OBJECTIVES

- To consider common myths of forgiveness and how they are misleading and sometimes harmful
- To examine biblical ideas about the nature and purpose of forgiveness
- To explore what genuine forgiveness is

REVIEWING

Drawing from real-life relationships, Allender seeks to describe the nature and purpose of forgiveness. To do this, in the first part of the chapter he exposes and scrutinizes several common misunderstandings we have concerning forgiveness. In the second part of the chapter he explores what true forgiveness means.

Common misunderstandings of forgiveness include the following: that forgiveness requires forgetting the harm, that forgiveness includes complete release of anger, that forgiveness involves not desiring revenge, and that forgiveness seeks relational peace at any price.

A biblical understanding of forgiveness encompasses several elements. Forgiving another involves knowing how much you have been forgiven as well as a yearning for reconciliation. Forgiveness seeks to overcome sin and move a person to repentance. Forgiveness seeks to move a person to restoration of relationship with the one who offers forgiveness and with God.

EXPLORING

1. Allender explores the myth of forgetting the harm by referring to Jeremiah 31:34 and 2 Corinthians 5:10 (see pp. 201-2). These texts seem at odds with each other. How does Dr. Allender handle this apparent contradiction? What do you think of Allender's treatment of these texts? Is forgetting sin part of God's forgiving of sin? Should we forget as part of our forgiving another?

2. God responds to human sinfulness with forgiveness. While there is ample testimony to this in Old Testament events and texts, we learn and experience this most fully in and through Jesus Christ, who died for us in our sinfulness. This is attested to in many ways in the New Testament: see, for example, Matthew 18:21-22, Matthew 26:26-28, and John 3:16. What, then, is the nature of God's forgiveness? What is the purpose of God's forgiveness (see pp. 208-9)? In considering these questions, ask also how Jesus' prayer for forgiveness for His executioners (Luke 23:34) illuminates the nature and purpose of God's forgiveness. (See p. 212.)

3. Should human forgiveness be modeled on God's forgiveness? If so, why, and in what ways? If not, why? (see pp. 208-9).

4. Allender remarks that "there is not a more important subject in the Christian life" than forgiveness. Why is forgiveness so important and necessary in human relationships?

5. Why then do we find it difficult to forgive those who have injured us? Why do we find it difficult to receive forgiveness from God and from others whom we have injured?

APPLYING

1. As we have noted, Allender contends that we have certain critical misunderstandings of the nature and purpose of forgiveness, and that there are better ways to understand it and apply it. Consider the following questions in view of Allender's arguments.

2. When is it possible and even desirable to encourage a crime victim to move toward forgiving the perpetrator?

3. In practical terms, how can you help a crime victim move from

believing some of the myths about forgiveness to gaining a better understanding of it? How can you help him or her apply those ideas in a process of genuine forgiveness?

4. When a crime victim is encouraged to forgive the perpetrator, what fears and other emotions might he or she experience?

5. What hope does forgiveness offer to victims? To offenders?

CHAPTER TWELVE

Assisting Crime Victims: A Continuum of Care

MARLENE A. YOUNG

OBJECTIVES

- To recognize and affirm the imperative to assist crime victims with great care and sensitivity
- To understand the fundamental traumatic effects experienced by crime victims
- To outline the comprehensive range of services that should be available to assist crime victims

REVIEWING

In this chapter, Young describes the traumatic effects of victimization and the kinds of services that ought to be available to respond to victims' needs. Additionally, Young makes the point that the trauma of victimization often extends to family, friends, and others who are close to the direct victim.

A victim of crime often suffers many complex and powerful reactions. These include disorientation, helplessness, fear, anger, confusion, frustration, guilt, self-blame, shame, humiliation, and grief. Many of the reactions follow immediately or very soon after the crime, yet many also persist or return long after the commission of the crime.

In view of the serious effects of crime, appropriate and skilled responses are vital in aiding victims. Toward this end, victims' assistance services, both professional and volunteer based, should include six basic components: crisis intervention, counseling, advocacy, support services during the criminal justice process, support services after the disposition of the case, and efforts to prevent victimization. Again, some services provide immediate aid to the victim, whereas some services provide long-term assistance to address continuing needs as well as new ones. The aim is to develop a "continuum of care" for victims of crime.

EXPLORING

1. What does Young mean by the phrase "victims' movement"? (See p. 218.)

2. Why did a "victims' movement" arise? What are the purposes of this movement?

3. What are the emotional reactions a crime victim commonly experiences? (See pp. 220-25.) In a sentence or two, define each one. What might happen in the life of a victim if some of these reactions lasted for months, even years? Which ones do you think are the most difficult for a victim to address on his or her own?

4. Think about what Young writes about well-meaning but negative responses to victims, or draw on actual experiences close to your life or your community. In what ways do we often respond to crime victims that only compound the effects of victimization?

5. Review the basic components of comprehensive victim-assistance services as described by Dr. Young. (See pp. 226-34.) In a sentence or two, define each one.

6. Perhaps you or someone you know has been a crime victim. Were these comprehensive services available? What is the potential impact on a crime victim if the services are not provided?

APPLYING

1. What does Young mean by a "continuum of care" as a response to victims? (See p. 226.) Why is it important to respond with a "continuum of care"?

2. Who will provide this "continuum of care"? What professionals in your community provide assistance to victims now? What volunteer-based programs now exist in your community? What services do they provide?

3. What kinds of resources does it take to develop and deliver this care? Where do the resources come from?

4. What are the obstacles to developing and delivering this kind of assistance to crime victims?

5. What role can you and your church play in this "continuum of care"? Are there any aspects of the continuum that cannot be addressed by clergy or church volunteers? If so, what are they?

6. What is your church doing now to provide assistance to victims? What might it do?

CHAPTER THIRTEEN

The Spiritual Problem of Crime: A Pastor's Call

LEE A. EARL

OBJECTIVES

- To recognize that churches must get involved in the problem of crime and in offering assistance to crime victims in their neighborhoods
- To explore the important role the clergy should play in providing leadership for a church's involvement
- To acknowledge the spiritual roots of crime while providing comprehensive ministry, spiritual and practical, to those affected by crime
- To see the essential link between love for God and love for neighbor (in this case, the crime victim)

REVIEWING

In this chapter Earl recounts the story of a homicide and his church's response to it. In this particular instance, the murder of a woman near this Detroit church becomes a test of the faith commitments of both the pastor and the people of the church. Though they have had some contact with the woman and her children, the murder victim is not a church member, and the children have only recently been involved in some church activities. How will this pastor and his church respond?

Risking his leadership position and the church's comfortable stance, Earl prods church members to reach out to the woman's family and thus to the neighborhood. They come to realize that, if they are to love God, they cannot simply retreat within the shelter of the church community and ignore the hard spiritual and practical realities of the neighborhood around the church. They must love their neighbor. They must reach out in practical love to the victims of this crime, and reach out in other ways to the people outside of the church. As a result of this realization, people's lives, including the lives of the pastor and of the church members, are spiritually changed. As it moves from responding to this crime to confronting the larger problems of the neighborhood, this church becomes a spiritual and practical catalyst for community regeneration.

EXPLORING

1. Why do you think this crime became a turning point for Twelfth Street Baptist Church? Why did this church get involved in assisting the victims of a crime?

2. When he decides to propose helping the family of the murdered woman, Earl knows that he will face some opposition in the church. (See pp. 240-41.) What do you think were the challenges and the risks for Earl and for the church in assisting the victims of this crime?

3. If you had been a member of Twelfth Street Baptist Church, how would you have felt about the church's response? What would you have done?

4. With Jesus' words in Matthew 25 and Luke 4 in mind, Earl talks about the roots of crime in spiritual terms. (See pp. 244-45.) In light of this, discuss the strengths and weaknesses of this kind of statement: "If crime is at its root a spiritual problem, the church's response should consist of spiritual witness and ministry."

5. How and why did this church become an example for the neighborhoods around it?

APPLYING

1. What do you or your church do now to address the issue of crime and assistance to crime victims in your neighborhood?

2. What challenges or risks inhibit you or your church from responding to the problem of crime and from assisting crime victims? What would it take, spiritually in particular, to overcome those inhibitions and rise to the challenges?

3. What more could you or your church do to address crime and to aid crime victims? What kinds of programs would meet the needs in your community?

4. What do you need to begin or enhance victim assistance ministry in your church and community?

Recommended Reading

Evil

Curtis, Brent, and John Eldredge. *The Sacred Romance: Drawing Closer to the Heart of God.* Nashville: Thomas Nelson Publishers, 1997.

Kaiser, Walter. *A Biblical Approach to Personal Suffering.* Chicago: Moody Press, 1982.

Kreeft, Peter. *Making Sense Out of Suffering.* Ann Arbor, Mich.: Servant Books, 1986.

Peters, Ted. *Sin: Radical Evil in Soul and Society.* Grand Rapids: William B. Eerdmans, 1994.

Plantinga, Cornelius. *Not the Way It's Supposed to Be: A Breviary of Sin.* Grand Rapids: William B. Eerdmans, 1995.

Truesdale, Al. *If God Is God, Then Why? Letters from Oklahoma City.* Kansas City: Beacon Hill Press, 1997.

Volf, Miroslav. *Exclusion and Embrace: A Theological Exploration of Identity, Otherness, and Reconciliation.* Nashville: Abingdon Press, 1996.

Yancey, Philip. *Disappointment with God.* New York: HarperCollins Publishers, 1988.

Victimization

Delaplane, David and Ann. *Victims: A Manual for Clergy and Congregations.* Denver: Spiritual Dimension in Victim Services, 1997.

Jeter, Joseph. *Crisis Preaching: Personal and Public.* Nashville: Abingdon Press, 1998.

Lampman, Lisa, ed. *Helping a Neighbor in Crisis.* Wheaton, Ill.: Tyndale House Publishers, Inc., 1997.

Leaver, Wayne. *Clergy and Victims of Violent Crime: Preparing for Crisis Counseling.* Lima, Ohio: C.S.S. Publishing Company, Inc., 1990.

Van Ness, Daniel. *Crime and Its Victims.* Downers Grove, Ill.: InterVarsity Press, 1986.

Justice

Boecker, Hans J. *Law and Administration of Justice in the Old Testament and Ancient East.* Minneapolis: Augsburg Publishing House, 1980.

Burnside, Jonathan, and Nicola Baker. *Relational Justice: Repairing the Breach.* Winchester, U.K.: Waterside Press, 1994.

Restorative Justice: Theory. Washington, D.C.: Justice Fellowship, 1989.

Van Ness, Daniel, and Karen Heetderks Strong. *Restoring Justice.* Cincinnati: Anderson Publishing Co., 1997.

Wolterstorff, Nicholas. *Until Justice and Peace Embrace.* Grand Rapids: William B. Eerdmans, 1983.

Zehr, Howard. *Changing Lenses: A New Focus for Crime and Justice.* Scottdale, Pa.: Herald Press, 1990.

Forgiveness

Allender, Dan. *The Healing Path.* Colorado Springs: Waterbrook Press, 1999.

Allender, Dan, and Tremper Longman. *Bold Love.* Colorado Springs: NavPress, 1992.

Augsburger, David. *The Freedom of Forgiveness.* Chicago: Moody Press, 1988.

Flanigan, Beverly. *Forgiving the Unforgivable: Overcoming the Bitter Legacy of Intimate Wounds.* New York: Maxwell Macmillan, 1992.

Jones, L. Gregory. *Embodying Forgiveness: A Theological Analysis.* Grand Rapids: William B. Eerdmans, 1995.

White, Mary. *Harsh Grief, Gentle Hope.* Colorado Springs: NavPress, 1995.

About Neighbors Who Care

Prison Fellowship Ministries, founded by Chuck Colson, established Neighbors Who Care (NWC) in 1993. The mission of Neighbors Who Care is to exhort, assist, and equip the Church in its ministry to crime victims and their families.

Neighbors Who Care was organized to equip and mobilize churches to reach out to crime victims. As part of its mission, NWC develops resources and materials to help you and your church serve local victims of crime. These resources include books such as this one and *Helping a Neighbor in Crisis,* a book offering practical suggestions on how you can assist a crime victim or other individuals who face a life crisis. Other resources include materials to help you and your church start crime-prevention efforts as well as support groups and prayer efforts for crime victims.

Neighbors Who Care also has established structured victim-assistance programs in different U.S. cities. With NWC's assistance, churches of various denominations have joined forces with local law-enforcement organizations, victim-assistance professionals, and community and business leaders to furnish support and resources for victims of crime. In such communities, NWC provides extensive training as well as a planning and organizational process

301

to help churches address victims' needs with compassion, sensitivity, and practicality.

If you or your church is interested in finding out more about Neighbors Who Care, starting a local NWC program, receiving a catalog of program materials, and/or receiving our newsletter, please contact us at the address below. If your church is already working with crime victims, please let us know. NWC is developing a national data bank.

P.O. Box 16079
Washington DC 20041
703-904-7311
http://www.neighborswhocare.org

Neighbors Who Care
Ministry Resources

Crisis-Response Training for Clergy and Lay Leaders

Neighbors Who Care offers regionally based training to prepare pastors and lay leaders to respond to a crisis in the community — such as a crime, a major accident, or a tragedy. This curriculum trains these leaders to intervene effectively in a crisis situation and provide appropriate assistance and support to those within their congregations and their local community.

Helping a Neighbor in Crisis Resource and Study Guide

This book and study guide are designed to assist victim service-providers, pastors, lay counselors, and others who want to help a friend, family member, or neighbor who is in crisis. It features 32 chapters — each focusing on a specific type of crisis — written by pastors, Christian trauma counselors, and crisis-response experts. It also includes material on the grief cycle and forgiveness.

Youth Cutting Crime

Through this innovative program, church youth groups are recruited and organized to spend a day "crime-proofing" the homes of the elderly, the disabled, and single mothers in their communities. Youth Cutting Crime has proven to be a successful tool in increasing community interest and involvement in preventing crime and assisting crime victims. This two-part package includes a six-week Bible study series that helps junior and senior high-school students examine a biblical response to crime and understand how this framework can be integrated into everyday life. Also included is a how-to manual for youth pastors and leaders providing step-by-step instructions and aids for planning a Youth Cutting Crime event that will be both fun and meaningful.

Bulletproof? Overcoming Evil with Good

Neighbors Who Care joins Steven Curtis Chapman to support and distribute a dramatic film and documentary package that explores the topic of student violence. The two films address possible causes of student violence. But more importantly, they examine preventive measures and alert youth and their parents to both warning signs and practical steps that can be taken to steer at-risk teens toward biblical responses and behavior. Biblically based discussion guides for youth leaders, student participants, and adults are also included.

Crime Victim Assistance: Neighbors Who Care Chapters

Your church can start an outreach ministry to crime victims in your community. The national office of Neighbors Who Care will help you assess whether your community needs a local Neighbors Who Care chapter and, if so, will help you get one started. Local chapters provide crime victims with practical, emotional, and spiritual support in the hours, days, weeks, and months after a crime. Local chapters, chartered by Neighbors Who Care, are offered a range of training and program-development services.

Acknowledgments

The authors and publisher gratefully acknowledge permission to reprint material from the following sources:

Darkness Visible: A Memoir of Madness by William Styron. Copyright © 1990 by Vintage Books, a subsidiary of Random House, Inc.

Evil and Exile by Elie Wiesel and Philippe de Saint-Cheron. Published by the University of Notre Dame Press in 1990. Reproduced by permission of Georges Borchardt, Inc., on behalf of the authors.

Exclusion and Embrace by Miroslav Volf. Copyright © 1996. Used by permission of Abingdon Press.

Genesis 1–15 by Gordon J. Wenham. Copyright © 1987 by Word Publishing, Nashville, Tennessee. All rights reserved.

Invisible Wounds: Crime Victims Speak by Shelley Niederbach. Copyright © 1986 by Howorth Press.

Justice as Sanctuary by Herman Bianchi. Copyright © 1994 by Indiana University Press, Bloomington and Indianapolis.

The Message of the Psalms by Walter Brueggemann. Copyright © 1984 by Augsburg Publishing House. Used by permission of Augsburg Fortress.

Mr. Ives' Christmas by Oscar Hijuelos. Copyright © 1995 by Oscar

Hijuelos. Reprinted by permission of HarperCollins Publishers, Inc.

"One Violent Crime" by Bruce Shapiro in *The Nation*, 3 April 1995. Cited with permission.

People of the Lie by M. Scott Peck, M.D. Copyright © 1993 by M. Scott Peck. Reprinted with the permission of Simon & Schuster, Inc.

"The Politics of Memory" by Amos Elon in *The New York Review of Books*, 7 October 1993. Reprinted with permission from *The New York Review of Books*. Copyright © 1993 by NYREV, Inc.

Power, Pathology, and Paradox by Marguerite Shuster. Copyright © 1987 by Marguerite Shuster. Used by permission of Zondervan Publishing House.

Resurrection by Rowan Williams. Copyright © 1982 by Rowan Williams. Reproduced by permission of Morehouse Publishing, Harrisburg, Pennsylvania.

The Sacred Romance by Brent Curtis and John Eldredge. Copyright © 1997 by Thomas Nelson Publishing.

Silent Scream by Martha Janssen. Copyright © 1983 by Fortress Press. Used by permission of Augsburg Fortress.

Trauma and Recovery by Judith Lewis Herman, M.D. Copyright © 1992 by BasicBooks, a division of HarperCollins Publishers, Inc.

NWC Theological Forum Participants

W. Thomas Beckner, Ph.D.
Director, Center for Justice/Urban Leadership
Taylor University
Fort Wayne, Indiana

Dale Hanson Bourke
Publisher, Religion News Service
Washington, D.C.

Rev. Reginald Broadnax
AME Zion Church
Columbia, South Carolina

Rev. Michael Bryant, Ph.D.
Staff Chaplain, District of Columbia Detention Facility
Washington, D.C.

Fred Clark
Editor, *Prism Magazine*
Philadelphia, Pennsylvania

Joan Orgon Coolidge
Ph.D. candidate
George Mason University
Washington, D.C.

Michael Cromartie
Senior Fellow, Ethics and Public Policy Center
Washington, D.C.

Rev. David W. Delaplane
Executive Director, The Spiritual Dimension in Victim Services
Denver, Colorado

A. Robert Denton, Ph.D.
Executive Director, Victim Assistance Program
Akron, Ohio

Wilma Derksen
Director, Victims' Voice
Mennonite Central Committee
Winnipeg, Canada

Dr. Bill Edgar
Professor of Apologetics
Westminster Theological Seminary
Philadelphia, Pennsylvania

Rev. Charles G. Eduardos
Pastor, Embassy of the Rock/Euclid Foursquare Church
Euclid, Ohio

Dennis R. Edwards
Pastor, Washington Community Fellowship
Washington, D.C.

David Heim
Executive Editor, *The Christian Century*
Chicago, Illinois

Lynn Herring
OMNIPLEX World Services and
Neighbors Who Care Board
Washington, D.C.

Pastor Dwayne N. Hunt
Senior Pastor, Abundant Grace Fellowship
Memphis, Tennessee

Rev. Leonard N. Jamison
Director of Graduate Admissions
Eastern College
St. Davids, Pennsylvania

Charlene Turner Johnson
Executive Director, Michigan Neighborhood Partnership
Detroit, Michigan

Richard A. Kauffman
Associate Editor, *Christianity Today*
Carol Stream, Illinois

Rev. Don R. Lewis
Regional Director, D.C. Metro Area
Neighbors Who Care
Washington, D.C.

Rev. Richard P. Lord
Minister, Rush Creek Christian Church
Arlington, Texas

Dan Misleh
Policy Advisor, U.S. Catholic Conference
Washington, D.C.

Dr. William R. O'Brien
Director, The Global Center
Beeson Divinity School, Samford University
Birmingham, Alabama

Dr. Karen Strong
Vice President, Research and Development
Prison Fellowship Ministries
Washington, D.C.

Kathryn M. Turman
Acting Director, Office for Victims of Crime
Washington, D.C.

Dan Van Ness
Senior Vice President, Prison Fellowship International
Washington, D.C.

Terry White
Vice President, Advancement Communications
Prison Fellowship Ministries
Washington, D.C.

Contributors

REV. DR. ELIZABETH ACHTEMEIER   Dr. Achtemeier recently retired after 40 years of teaching Old Testament and homiletics at five different seminaries. Dr. Achtemeier was educated at Stanford University (B.A., magna cum laude), Union Theological Seminary, New York (M.Div., summa cum laude), and Columbia University, New York (Ph.D.). She did postgraduate work at Heidelberg University, Germany, and Basel University, Switzerland. Dr. Achtemeier holds two honorary degrees. The author of 25 books, Dr. Achtemeier is known throughout the United States and Canada as a writer, preacher, and lecturer. She has been married for 47 years to Dr. Paul J. Achtemeier. She is an ordained minister of the Presbyterian Church.

DR. DAN B. ALLENDER   Dr. Allender received his M.Div. from Westminster Theological Seminary and his Ph.D. in Counseling Psychology from Michigan State University. Dr. Allender taught in the Biblical Counseling Department of Grace Theological Seminary for seven years (1983-89) and taught in the Master of Arts in Biblical Counseling Program at Colorado Christian University, Denver, Colorado, from 1989 to 1997. Currently he is a Professor of Counseling at Western Seminary Seattle. He travels and speaks extensively to present his unique perspective on recovery from sexual abuse, love and forgiveness, worship, and other related topics. He is the author of *The Wounded Heart* and *The Healing Path*, and has co-authored four books with Dr. Tremper Longman: *Intimate Allies, The Cry of the Soul, Bold Love*, and *Bold Purpose*.

MR. CHARLES W. COLSON   Mr. Colson, former special counsel to the late President Richard M. Nixon, is chairman of the board of Prison Fellowship Ministries. Mr. Colson founded Prison Fellowship Ministries in 1976, convinced that more Christians, motivated by their love for Jesus Christ and in obedience to His commands, must take the Gospel to those he encountered firsthand during the seven-month prison term he served in connection with Watergate. *Born Again,* Mr. Colson's international best-seller, dramatically details his conversion to Christianity in 1973. The author of fourteen books, Colson received the Templeton Prize for Progress in Religion in 1993. A native of Boston, Mr. Colson earned a B.A. at Brown University and finished his J.D. in 1959 at George Washington University. From 1959 to 1975 he practiced law in Virginia, Massachusetts, and the District of Columbia, and served as special counsel to Nixon from 1969 to 1973.

REV. LEE A. EARL   Rev. Earl currently serves as Pastor of the Shiloh Baptist Church of Alexandria, Virginia, and chairs the National Board of Directors of Neighbors Who Care, the crime victim ministry of Prison Fellowship. Rev. Earl has served as Director of Training for the Neighborhood Enterprise in Washington, D.C. For twelve years Rev. Earl also served as the Senior Minister of the Twelfth Street Baptist Church in Detroit, Michigan. As a pastor, he has received national recognition as an activist and church builder. In addition, Rev. Earl has chaired the Wolverine Community Development Corporation, a network of over 300 churches throughout the state of Michigan, as well as co-founded and chaired R.E.A.C.H., Inc., a community development corporation in Detroit. For over 30 years Rev. Earl has been married to the former Zandra Bowman. They have three adult daughters, who have blessed them with three energetic grandchildren.

DR. CARL F. H. HENRY   Dr. Henry has served as Visiting Professor of Biblical and Systematic Theology at Trinity Evangelical Divinity School since 1974. He began working at Trinity in 1971. Dr. Henry is a leading theologian of evangelicalism in the twentieth century. He is the founding editor of *Christianity Today*. He has written or edited over forty books, including *The Uneasy Conscience of Modern Fundamentalism* and the six-volume work entitled *God, Revelation, and Authority*. Dr. Henry has taught at the Asian Center of Theological Seminary in Korea, Fuller Theological Seminary, Northern Baptist Theological Seminary, Wheaton College, Gordon Conwell Divinity School, and the Japan School of Theology. In 1966 he was the chairman of the World Congress on Evangelism. He is a past president of the Evangelical Theological Society and of the American Theological Society.

DR. L. GREGORY JONES   Dr. Jones is Dean of the Divinity School and Professor of Theology at Duke University. He is the author of several books, including, most recently, *Embodying Forgiveness*. Dr. Jones has written widely in scholarly journals and popular publications. He is the co-editor of *Modern Theology*, an international scholarly journal published by Blackwells in Oxford, England. Dr. Jones is currently working on two books: *The Desire to Know God* and *Mending Lives: The Power of Forgiveness in Christian Life*, a book he is co-authoring with his wife, the Reverend Susan P. Jones.

LISA BARNES LAMPMAN   Mrs. Lampman serves as president of Neighbors Who Care, an affiliate of Prison Fellowship Ministries. She has served in various positions with Prison Fellowship Ministries: she has been vice president of Prison Fellowship and vice president of Justice Fellowship, a criminal justice reform organization. It was during that time that Mrs. Lampman developed the pilot program for the Neighbors Who Care initiative, a church-based victim assistance program. Mrs. Lampman is also editor of the book *Helping a Neighbor in Crisis*. Lisa Barnes Lampman served as special assistant to U.S. Secretary of Education Lamar Alexander from 1991 to 1992 and served on then-Governor Alexander's staff in Tennessee from 1979 to 1983.

MICHELLE D. SHATTUCK Mrs. Shattuck is currently working on a master's degree in counseling and serving as graduate assistant at Western Seminary in Seattle, Washington. In addition, Mrs. Shattuck provides consulting services in grant-writing and project management to Neighbors Who Care and Western Seminary Seattle. Prior to this, Mrs. Shattuck served as Resource and Research Development Manager for Neighbors Who Care from 1997 to 1999. Mrs. Shattuck also spent three years as project coordinator at World Vision Relief and Development in Washington, D.C. She has a B.A. in political science from Taylor University. She and her husband, Nathan, live in Bothell, Washington.

DR. GREGORY STRONG Dr. Strong writes in the area of theological and religious studies, and he provides consulting services for ministry nonprofits. He has most recently contributed several articles to the *Encyclopedia of Religion in American Politics,* and he provided the theological content for a new course on restorative justice for Taylor University. Dr. Strong obtained an undergraduate degree from the University of Maryland, a Master of Divinity from Trinity Episcopal School for Ministry, and Master of Philosophy and Doctor of Philosophy degrees from the Graduate School of Drew University. He resides with his wife and daughter in Sterling, Virginia, where he is on the staff of Saint Matthew's Episcopal Church.

DR. HAROLD DEAN TRULEAR Dr. Trulear is vice president and director of Church Collaborative Initiatives at Public/Private Ventures. A Phi Beta Kappa graduate of Morehouse College (B.A.) and Drew University (M.Phil., Ph.D.), he has held faculty positions at Jersey City State College, Drew University, Eastern Baptist Theological Seminary, and New York Theological Seminary. He serves on the board of trustees of InterVarsity Christian Fellowship and Messiah College. In addition to holding several academic posts, Dr. Trulear has served Baptist and Episcopal churches in New Jersey and Pennsylvania and currently serves as Associate Minister at Zion Bapist Church and St. Mary's Episcopal Church, both in Ardmore, Pennsylvania.

DR. MIROSLAV VOLF   Dr. Volf is Henry B. Wright Professor of Theology at Yale University Divinity School. He holds doctoral and postdoctoral degrees from the University of Tübingen. Dr. Volf has written or edited nine books and over 45 scholarly articles. In 1996 he was named to the list of "50 Evangelical Leaders, 40 and Under" by *Christianity Today,* and his books *Exclusion and Embrace* and *After Our Likeness* won the *Christianity Today* Book Award in 1997 and 1999 respectively.

MRS. MARY WHITE   Mrs. White serves on the board of directors of Neighbors Who Care. Mrs. White is a full-time staff member with the Navigators along with her husband, Dr. Jerry White, who serves as general director and international president. In addition to being a wife, mother, and grandmother, Mrs. White is a speaker at conferences and seminars and the author of numerous books. After her son's homicide, Mrs. White became active in the local chapter of Parents of Murdered Children.

DR. NICHOLAS WOLTERSTORFF   Dr. Wolterstorff is Noah Porter Professor of Philosophical Theology at Yale University. Before going to Yale, he taught for thirty years in the philosophy department at Calvin College. He has been president of both the American Philosophical Association and the Society of Christian Philosophers, and has given the Gifford Lectures at St. Andrews University, the Wilde Lectures at Oxford University, and the Stone Lectures at Princeton Seminary. He has also taught at Princeton University, the University of Michigan, the University of Texas, Notre Dame University, and the Free University of Amsterdam. Among his ten books is *Until Justice and Peace Embrace* (Eerdmans, 1980). He has been active in the struggle for justice in South Africa and Palestine, and was for several years head of the Palestine Human Rights Campaign.

DR. MARLENE A. YOUNG   Dr. Young serves as executive director of the National Organization for Victim Assistance (NOVA). In 1975, after earning her doctorate from Georgetown University and her law degree from Williamette University, Dr. Young became the research director in the Multnomah County Sheriff's Office in Portland, Oregon. While there, Dr. Young served on the founding board of NOVA. She served as the president of NOVA's board from 1979 to 1981 and has been its executive director since that time. Dr. Young sits on the executive committee of the World Society of Victimology, is a past treasurer of the International Society for Traumatic Stress Studies, is co-chair of the Victim Services Committee of the International Association of Chiefs of Police, and is a member of the Victims Committee of the American Bar Association. Dr. Young was also a founding board member of the American Professional Society on the Abuse of Children.

DR. HOWARD ZEHR Dr. Zehr is a writer and international consultant on criminal justice issues. Currently he is Professor of Sociology and Restorative Justice at Eastern Mennonite University. From 1979 to 1998 Dr. Zehr served as director of the Mennonite Central Committee U.S. Office on Crime and Justice. Dr. Zehr was also instrumental in developing the first Victim Offender Reconciliation Program (VORP) in the United States and has helped many other communities start similar programs. Dr. Zehr has also played a central role in the development of the "restorative justice" concept. Dr. Zehr's publications include *Crime and the Development of Modern Society* and *Changing Lenses: A New Focus for Crime and Justice.* He has also worked professionally as a photographer, and his work has appeared in many publications and exhibits.

Printed in the United States
42801LVS00006B/161

9 780802 845454